PAT WHITE OF DONABATE

Godfather of Irish Marathon Running

GERARD RONAN

Staten House

Title Spread: Pat White, Pat White's publicity photograph from the front page of the *Brooklyn Daily Eagle,* 13 February 1909, restored and colourised by Diana Tarhonii.

Also by Gerard Ronan:

The Irish Zorro
The Round Towers of Fingal
William Kelly of Portrane
Sophia Parnell Evans
Margaret Evans – Poet of Portrane
The Falsest Rogue
The Seduction of Benedict Arthur
The Killing of Thomas Towson
The Radical Reverend
Shamrock, Crown and Crescent

For the Nulty Family

CONTENTS

Will there be a real cheer
As there was for Eyrefield's Glory,
The Donabate man wins again I hear,
But who would believe the story?

Drogheda Independent,
26 May 1906.

PREFACE

FORTY-SEVEN YEARS! That was how long it took another Irish athlete to beat Pat White's best marathon time. Forty-seven years! And even then, the better time was hardly comparable, the new figure having been set in modern cushioned footwear and on straight roads. White's 2:36:45 was recorded in 1911, and run in thinly-soled leather shoes over 104 laps of a 440-yard cinder track in the middle of a Scottish winter. It was a time, furthermore, that would prove superior to the winning times in both the 1912 and 1924 Summer Olympic marathons.

Three years earlier, in 1908, White had run fourteen minutes faster than the winner of the 1908 Olympic marathon over the same course. On that occasion, he had also run quicker than the existing world record, only to be denied the new one by the Frenchman who had beaten him. He would finish that year, as he would in 1911, as the second fastest marathon runner on the world ranking lists.

On his day, and over his favourite distances, from twenty to twenty-six miles, Pat White was world-class. However, you will not find his name on the official list of Irish records because White was a professional athlete at a time when the virus of 'gentlemanly amateurism' still blighted British and Irish sport. Fostered in English public schools in the mid-nineteenth century, this odious ideology, rooted as it was in the English class system and mediaeval notions of chivalry, effectively enforced the suppression of meritocracy and the segregation of the classes in sport.[1]

> The English rules were overtly designed to keep lower and middle classes from competing with the aristocracy. The Henley Royal Regatta explicitly excluded anyone who "is or has been by trade or employment for wages a mechanic, artisan or labourer"; it barred entry, for instance, to the American Olympic champion sculler John B. Kelly, Sr., father of the actress Grace Kelly, future Princess of Monaco. (Kelly went on to win three gold medals in the 1920 and 1924 Olympics, even though he had previously played professional football.) Historians would say that this doctrine of amateurism was a case of status anxiety, a means of protecting privilege against a rising class challenge. It's significant that the one group of professionals that were allowed to compete in their Olympic sport were fencing masters, because they were by definition "gentlemen".[2]

The 1900 Olympic Games in Paris had held races for *both* amateur and professional athletes (including a six-hour professional ultra-distance race with a prize fund of F2,550). Also, in July 1902, a European Professional Championship had been held at the newly renovated Buffalo Velodrome in Paris.[3] Thereafter, however, public interest in professional running began to wane, and the Olympic movement, for all its egalitarian rhetoric, became simply an extension of societal elitism and a sporting validation of existing privileges and prejudices.

In 1908, Olympic heroes did not come from thatched mud cabins or the ranks of poorly educated agricultural labourers who worked physically demanding twelve-hour shifts in all seasons and all weather. Back then, the Olympic Games were little more than disorganised sideshows to World Fairs. Lasting months rather than weeks, they served as the exclusive playground of the landed, the leisured and the military, and were far from the celebration of our common humanity that was their supposed *raison d'être*. Only those who could travel long distances and pay their way once they got there could afford to compete. Only those who were not salary-dependent could spare the time.

Simply put, Olympic medals did not put bread on the table, and so, for the labouring classes, a full-time sporting career could only be achieved within the professional ranks. This thinly disguised segregationism, which would continue well into the 1990s, effectively branded any man who'd had even the briefest of professional careers in one sport to be, at once and for all time, a professional in all. With the possible exception of boxing, the resulting demonisation of professional athletes by an elitist amateur community has led to many of Ireland's early sporting heroes being forgotten. Such a man was Patrick Joseph White.

Idolised from the Liffey to the Boyne as 'Pat White of Donabate', though he was actually a native of nearby Richardstown, White was the archetypal local lad made good - the short and stocky farmhand who brought honour and positive attention to his country on the world stage at a time when nationalist sentiment was simmering. One of the most famous athletes in the country, he became, during the dog days of 'pedestrianism,' an inspirational figure to a class of Irish society unaccustomed to seeing one of their own admired across the social and political spectrum.

Pat White was a man who defied the limitations of his birth; a star in the firmament of hard men who were pushing the limits of human endurance to unimaginable heights; a man of endless spirit and seemingly super-human resilience; a humble farmhand who could draw tens of thousands of spectators onto the country's roads to watch him run. So eager, in fact, were his fellow Dubliners to see him in the flesh that, for one memorable week in 1908, they flocked to hear him speak over a silent film of his London race on the stage of what is now the Olympia Theatre.

Professional foot racing and gambling had always been closely linked, as the roots of pedestrianism were firmly planted in eighteenth-century Irish steeplechase contests, i.e. wagered races on horseback from one church steeple to another. The first contest took place in 1752 following a wager between two Cork gentlemen, Edmund Blake and Cornelius O'Callaghan, and it ran from the steeple of St. John's Church in Buttevant to the steeple of St. Mary's Church in Doneraile, a little over four miles apart.

That race sparked a fashion for such contests, which the landed gentry introduced to England during the early nineteenth century, eventually helping to inspire the creation of National Hunt racing. Over time, however, the idle rich, weary of racing each other, gradually began to pit their footmen against each other while they followed the contest from the comfort of their carriages.

The word 'footman' has recently come to signify male servants in general. Back in the 19th century, however, it specifically referenced those men whose job was to run in front of aristocratic carriages, open gates, and announce their arrival.[4] It was from the racing of these footmen that the professional sport of foot racing acquired the name 'pedestrianism' (from the Latin *pedester*, meaning to go on foot). This version of the sport flourished for a long time in the form of long-distance walking races.

19th-century pedestrians rarely trained for a contest; they simply showed up on race day and competed to the best of their ability. However, as interest and prizemoney began to increase, some began to intentionally prepare for these long-distance events, albeit in a vastly different manner from how we might perceive endurance training today. Back then, training consisted mainly of long-distance walking with very short intervals of running, a form of training that led to the evolution of the 'go-as-you-please' race, in which competitors could walk or run as they pleased, as distinct from pure 'pedestrianism' – the precursor of competitive race-walking – which required that they walked.

By the early 20th century, pedestrianism, or professional racewalking, had become a popular summer spectator sport and, like horse racing, a staple at local fairs and festivals. The sport, however, was largely unregulated. All manner of bets would be placed, by spectators and competitors alike, and in a manner not dissimilar to prize-fighting or horse racing. The practice was naturally frowned upon by the various churches, and, unsurprisingly, by the organising bodies of British and Irish amateur athletics. Pedestrianism, as a result, acquired a somewhat seedy reputation.

As the 'go-as-you-please' race format gained popularity, the term 'pedestrianism' gradually came to encompass all professional long-distance races conducted on foot. Then, as standards improved and fitness levels rose, these 'go-as-you-please' races slowly evolved into running races.

Pedestrianism, however, was primarily a summer sport. Winter, on the other hand, belonged to the cross-country men, enthusiastic amateurs whose sport was more team-oriented and had its origins in the mid-1870s game of Hare and Hounds. Although initially enshrined in the Victorian cult of gentlemanly amateurism, this new sport was quickly embraced by the working classes, for whom it had the attraction of being inexpensive and requiring little in the way of kit.

The egalitarian nature of the sport led to a rapid proliferation of 'harrier' clubs, which, in turn, precipitated a decline in interest in professional running. Nevertheless, the allure of prizemoney would never entirely disappear, and it would be from the sport of cross-country running, rather than track and field athletics, that working-class Irishmen would most frequently find their way into professional running.

Among the working classes, it was expected that once a talented athlete had proven himself in the amateur ranks, he would eventually try his luck as a 'ped,' for in the professional arena, the standards and, more importantly, the rewards, were significantly higher. Prior to Pat White's arrival on the scene, several Irish runners, such as George Tincler, Jack Mullen, and Mick O'Neill, had attempted to make a name for themselves in the professional arena. Only Tincler, however, had come close to matching what White would achieve in terms of celebrity, records, or world rankings.

The stigma that in the past had attached to the heresy of professionalism has ensured that the feats of the Irish 'peds' have been largely erased from the official history of Irish athletics, but their names, and most especially that of 'Pat White of Donabate', are far too important to be allowed to vanish entirely.

PAT WHITE OF DONABATE

Godfather of Irish Marathon Running

RICHARDSTOWN

ON A GRASSY hill outside the Lanarkshire village of Strathaven,[5] there sits a quiet cemetery in which a simple lichen-encrusted headstone marks the final resting place of one Patrick White. The headstone, erected in 'loving memory,' reveals little of White's colourful past and inaccurately states his age. Also absent from its roughly chiselled face are the names of the wife and children who predeceased him. It is a lonely memorial, indicative of a lonely end, and bears little witness to what, in many respects, was an extraordinary life.

For an athlete, medals, cups, and records fade to insignificance with the passing years. What remains, what potentially grows in importance, is the human story. When that, too, is carelessly thrust into the furnace of history, the athletic community becomes instantly the poorer for it. To posterity, the story matters: the journey as much as the performance, the person as much as the measure.

For 'Pat White of Donabate,' that mottled and ultimately tragic story began almost a century and a half ago, on the morning of Monday, 2 October 1876, at St Maur's Chapel in Rush. On that day, Maggie Gilshenan, then a mature woman of twenty-nine, married twenty-seven-year-old John White. Both bride and groom came

1

from farming backgrounds and were natives of Richardstown in North County Dublin. They had known each other all their lives and, by rural norms, had married late. Maggie was literate. Her husband was not. You didn't need book learning to plough a straight furrow or plant a field of wheat. He could sign his name and count money; it was all he had ever needed, until now.

A thatched cabin typical of the type the Whites lived in.

Following the wedding, John White took his new bride to live in a modest mud cabin on a lonely country lane that threaded a narrow and occasionally tree-lined path from Roscall to Wimbletown. Protective of its privacy and set self-consciously back from the lane, the cabin faced an adjoining field and from its half-door allowed only a sideways glance at passing carts or bicycles. It had three rooms, two south-facing windows, a thatched roof and a single chimney, but precious little else. Cooled by a southerly breeze in summer, it was cold and draughty in winter, warmed only by an open hearth, the lighting of which was the first task of the day, and the raking of which was the last. Adjacent stood a cow house, a calf house, a piggery, a hen house, and a shed. There was no stable, nor could they afford to keep a horse and cart.[6]

Food was grown on a small plot of land leased from the landlord, and water, fetched from the nearest pump or well, was frequently recycled, with weekly family baths taking place in the parlour and in the laundry water. In all of this, the Whites were no different from any other country peasant of their day. It wasn't a hand-to-mouth existence – they could afford to pay for schoolbooks – but it wasn't far from it. Proud nationalists, they believed the solution to their struggles lay in hard work and self-reliance at both an individual and national level. Life was harsh and simple, lived at a tranquil pace and with Catholic forbearance. They were never short of hope, or a pious platitude to make sense of the senseless.

John White was an agricultural labourer, of which there were essentially two kinds in Ireland at this time – resident and non-resident. Non-resident labourers were hired on a casual basis, responsible for their own accommodation and not tied to a single employer. They rarely put down roots and had frequently to travel long distances to find work.

Resident labourers, on the other hand, lived for the duration of their 'bargain' with the family that employed them. If unmarried, they lodged in the main house with the servants; if married, they resided in tied cottages, the possession of which bound them to their employer. They were always free to leave, but the consequences of doing so while raising a family could be devastating.

As a married residential labourer on Patrick Harford's estate at Baldurgan, the stability of John White's employment allowed him to at least dream of one day leasing a farm of his own. That dream, however, rested on the presumption of thrift, a task not easily achieved within a growing family which had, in the seven years since their marriage, expanded in number from two hungry mouths to six, Maggie having borne him, in quick succession, a son and three daughters. They were:

> Teresa, born on 20 August 1877,[7]
> Patrick/Pat, born on 18 March 1879,[8]
> Bridget, born on 26 July 1881,[9] and
> Sarah, born on 4 November 1883.[10]

And that, for several years, appeared to be their lot. Having married late in life, a small family was to be expected, and four children were about as many as they could afford, or manage. But then, as Maggie approached her fortieth birthday, she found herself, quite unexpectedly, pregnant. Baby Peter arrived on 14 April 1887.[11] The dream of financial independence was put on hold.

Suddenly, eight-year-old Pat had a brother, a rival for his parents' affection and attention, and an interloper for whom, as the years progressed, he would be expected to provide a begrudging example. Competing for parental approval with his sisters had been one thing – a baby brother was another matter entirely. The baby held all the cards, or so it seemed at the time.

From the start, Peter was the surprise child, and Maggie would have known he would be her last. A baby to his mother and a living doll to his sisters, he was, to all intents and purposes, born into a different generation. Spending little time during his formative years with his older siblings, who, with the exception of Sarah, were already attending the national school, Peter enjoyed a largely cosseted existence. Of all his siblings, only Teresa had understood what that was like, but hers would have been a very different experience, an unspent childhood marked by an obligation to help in the raising of the others. Dragged along in his siblings' wake, Peter was forever playing catch-up: the last to comprehend the privy looks and coded conversations, the tail-ender forever alert for nuggets of forbidden knowledge, yearning for something that was his, and his alone.

With seven mouths to feed and seven bodies to wash, a kettle or pot was forever on the crook. And with more than enough domestic chores to go around, the children were expected to shoulder their fair share. The work never stopped. There was always wood to be chopped, water to be fetched, hens to be fed and closed in for the night, lamps to be lit, a fire to be started or raked, a tub to be filled, potatoes to be washed, walls to be whitewashed and flags to be scrubbed – physical tasks that have largely been banished from our collective memory but which were once a staple of family life beyond the big houses.

The girls shadowed their mother, cooking and cleaning, kneading and churning, wringing and plucking, sowing and foddering, and, more importantly, helping to care for the babies. The boys shadowed their father in the fields, learning

5

to reap and sow, to thresh and winnow, to handle horses and ploughs, perhaps even to shear. They grew strong at the business end of a spade.

For children born to a threadbare existence, hard physical work was neither a punishment nor a chore; it was simply a fact of life. Childhood was not a time of innocent joy, but a long and unyielding apprenticeship for adulthood, for a working life that would begin at fourteen, either out in the fields or in the domestic service of some landed family, more often than not, the father's employer.

And perhaps it was harder on the boys, for each in their own way would be marked by it, and by their hurried attempts to escape it. It was a hard life, and it built hard men and hard women. Endurance, resilience, and thrift came naturally. Athletic ambition did not. Life was demanding enough as it was.

INTO THE WEST

IN THE LATE 19th century, book learning, like childhood, generally ended at fourteen for working-class children. Secondary education was not yet the norm for the labouring classes in Fingal – the Christian Brothers had yet to arrive in Swords – and as soon as it was legally permitted to do so, children were expected to work, most commonly by entering domestic service or being hired away on a six or nine-month contract as a farmhand.

The latter was almost certainly Pat White's fate. Holding nothing more than a parcel of spare clothes and a pair of boots, he would have been taken to some hiring fair or other, told to draw himself up tall and strong so as not to appear weak or lazy, and wait to be inspected and questioned by a prospective employer. Looking helplessly on as his father made his bargain with some gentleman, he would have held his tongue until the bargaining talk was done. Tucking his bundle under his arm, he would have left with his new master without so much as a hug from his father, proud to be taking his first tentative steps into manhood.[12]

The life of a nineteenth-century farm boy was harsh and occasionally brutal. He would get paid on his term day and not a minute before. In the meantime, he would take whatever punishment was meted out to him as the master got his money's worth. Only when he grew big enough to defend himself would that particular burden ease. There were good masters and bad masters, but it wasn't always easy to tell them apart at a hiring fair, for a man would take to one boy and against another, and a bad reputation in one quarter would be countered by a good one in the next.

Farmboy at market in 1903.

Almost nothing is known about Pat's life as a farm boy, or even at what age he was sent away from home. Even less is known about the man, or men, who hired him. We know only that, by his mid-teens, he was to be found living and working out in East Galway as an agricultural labourer. Beyond that, we have only race reports to identify his whereabouts.

There is no record of Pat White being involved

in any form of competitive sport prior to his move out west, although that would not have been unusual at the time. Sporting activities were frequently discouraged in poor families. Clothing, especially footwear, was expensive and expected to be cared for; coats and trousers were patched and darned rather than discarded, and little shame was attached to the sight of a visible mend. The wear and tear of sport was an extravagance the poor could rarely afford.

In Galway, however, having toughened up and come of age, Pat White now had an income of his own. Unconstrained by family responsibilities, he was soon embracing the rough and tumble of the handball alley. By 1898, he had been introduced to cross-country running by Ballinrobe-born William Lally, with whose encouragement he joined a local club, Ballinasloe Harriers.[13]

Accustomed to long days on his feet and working outdoors in hail, rain, or snow, he took to the sport like the proverbial duck to water. Running long distances was no heavier a task to him than a day of digging ditches or ploughing a grassy acre. He had, in a way, been bred for it. Cross-country racing in those days was not unlike the steeplechase races of old, in that competitors had to leap ditches and hurdle fences during the race. Despite his size, White, by all accounts, an outstanding hurdler.

Track and field athletics was very much in its infancy at this time. The Irish Amateur Athletics Association's first national championships, for example, had only been held in 1873. Cross-country running was at an even earlier stage of gestation, the Cross-Country Championship Association of Ireland having only been formed in

1881, two years after Pat's birth. Considered, at the time, to be entirely separate sports, each had its own rules and organising body.

Neither sport, however, attracted large crowds. Polite society had long since deemed the sight of athletic young men cavorting in outfits resembling contemporary underwear to be unsuitable for the female gaze. Indeed, in announcing the Irish National Athletics Championships of 1879, the *Irish Sportsman* had felt compelled to reassure potential spectators that 'nothing to offend the eye' would come within reach of even the most fastidious female.

Little had changed a quarter of a century later, when Pat made his competitive debut. Knee-length shorts had replaced drawers, but singlets and bare arms were still considered so risqué that, when American athletes first appeared in sleeveless tops in the U.K., they were warned by the British Amateur Athletic Association of the consequences of wearing 'inappropriate kit'.[14]

By 1899, long cotton shirts and long knee-length shorts were still the standard kit in Ireland, though even these had not been entirely accepted as proper attire by the 'quality'. Attitudes, however, were changing across the water, and the sight of a well-toned masculine physique was slowly becoming something for all to admire and celebrate, irrespective of class or gender.

Increasing respectability inevitably led to increasing popularity, a trend the professional game was far quicker to exploit than the amateur. The sporting public, as a result, began to lose interest in the amateurs, and the best of the Irish professionals would soon find themselves standing on the threshold of celebrity. None more so than Patrick Joseph White.

INTERNATIONAL ATHLETE

HEARING THE OLD folk speak of him, I had imagined him differently. In my mind's eye, he was a Lasse Viren-type character, a loping, deer-like creature with scarcely a pick of body fat on him, a tall and blonde descendant of the Norsemen from whom the local area takes its name – a true Fingallian. But of course, he was nothing like that. The illusion lasted only as long as it took to discover a photograph.

He cut a brawny and diminutive figure, did White. Five feet eight and ten stone in weight, he stood as solid and as foursquare as a lightweight boxer. If you didn't know him, you would never have guessed that he was a runner. As tough as old boots and accustomed to distributing his effort throughout the working week, he knew the value of the unhurried day and possessed from the start the kind of metronomic pace judgment that was to become his sporting trademark.

Pat White's fitness came neither from the gym nor the track, but from the barn and the field. You could tell that much at first glance. Indeed, the most disappointing year of his sporting life would be the one in which he laboured in neither. Life had dealt him a tough hand, but it was in playing that hand that he discovered who and what he truly was. Had his youth been easy, would he have been as successful?

It was all part of the same puzzle: the hard

work and the talent, the deprivation and unquenchable thirst for success. There was not a farmer in Ireland who didn't get his money's worth from a purchase, be it a suckling calf or a young farm boy. Running away from hardship or trouble was not an option. There was shame attached to that. No matter how tough the conditions, the hireling was expected to endure them. Until he came of age, his family would depend on him to complete his term and honour his father's bargain. And so, one way or another, he was obligated to survive until his term day, when he would get paid. He would not dare to return home empty-handed. When it came to suffering and fatigue, however, Pat White could outlast just about everyone.

White's first championship race took place on 28 January 1899, on a cold and frosty afternoon in Glasnevin, on the outskirts of Dublin. Running more on natural talent than on a solid base of training, he finished as one of the also-rans, a non-scoring member of the Ballinasloe Harriers team that won that year's National Junior Cross-Country Championships.

Back then, the term 'Junior' referred not to an athlete under twenty years of age, but to an athlete who had yet to finish in the top twenty-five in the National Senior Championships.[15] The modern equivalent, in Ireland at least, would be 'novice.' Untamed and untrained, he struggled home in thirty-first place.[16] Commendable, but hardly noteworthy. Then again, he was just nineteen, competing against grown men, working for cash, and running for fun.

Two months after his championship debut, White formed part of the Ballinasloe Senior team that competed for the rival Gaelic Athletic Association's national championship, this time over a ten-mile course at Dolphin's Barn in Dublin. Once again, he finished a non-scoring member of the winning team,[17] and once again showed little to suggest that he might one day become one of Ireland's greatest athletes.

His time with Ballinasloe Harriers, however, was to prove short-lived. In the Spring of 1900, he returned to Dublin, where he and his younger brother, Peter, the jocular problem child of the family, had been offered live-in employment on the Harford farm at Baldurgan.

Links between the Whites and the Harfords were cordial and long-standing. Even the midwife who had delivered Pat and his sister Bridget had been a Harford.[18] They had been good to the Whites, and the Whites were beholden. It was a dependency John White would never willingly have imperilled.

Peter, at this time, was in his last term at the village school – a term he would never actually complete. At thirteen, the parental tap of unconditional affection and protection was slowly being turned off. It was time for him to fly the nest. He would be the last to leave, as he had been the last to everything else; every milestone in his life diminished for having already been passed by four siblings.[19]

With the benefit of hindsight, it is tempting to view Pat's return as more of a summons than a homecoming, that the family were uneasy about letting Peter go to the Harfords and had asked the responsible middle child to come home and be both a mentor and an example to his troublesome younger brother. This would be Peter's first time

14

living away from home, his first time answering to anyone more demanding than his parents. Time was to justify their concerns.

The Harfords were the mainstay of Fingal Rovers, a cycling and athletics club based in nearby Oldtown.[20] They had been involved in the club since its foundation in 1890,[21] and Richard Harford was one of the club's best runners.[22] But cycling and track athletics were summer sports, and Pat was a dyed-in-the-wool cross-country man. Athletes could, and did, compete in both, but spring and summer were the busiest periods on farms, and it was always easier to get time off in winter.

In Ballinasloe, Pat's running had been dictated by the need for companionship. Returning to his childhood haunts, however, he was no longer short of friends and, for a full year after his return, he neither raced nor joined another club. But then, at the turn of the new century, his outlook began to shift. He began to miss the thrill of competition.

There had not been much to celebrate in the early months of 1900, least of all for nationalists like the Whites. Home Rule seemed as far away as ever, and popular support for the Boers in their resistance to the British Empire had led only to the disappointment of Mafeking. Some light relief from the gloom, however, was still to be hoped for in the Paris Olympics.

No Irish sporting medals would be won at these games – Jack Yeats would be awarded a silver for painting and Oliver St. Gogarty a bronze for literature – but the simple fact that they were taking place was enough to quicken public interest, and, hitching that enthusiasm to a worthy cause, Fingal Rovers hosted a sports day to raise funds for the repair of St. Maur's church. It took place in Lusk on the first Sunday in July, just before the start of the haymaking.

With little or no training behind him, Pat won the senior half mile in 2:02.50. The following year, he won the open mile. Towards the end of August 1901, he would try his hand at various handicap sprints from 100 to 400 yards at the Malahide Sports, without success. And that, for now, was about as far as it went – country fairs and sports days. Racing was simply a bit of fun, a means of making friends and passing the time.

Then suddenly, as the swallows departed for warmer climes and the first of the autumnal frosts began to glisten in the fields, Pat suddenly, and unexpectedly, joined a Dublin club.[23] Oddly enough, that club was not Fingal Rovers, but City and Suburban Harriers, one of the oldest cross-country clubs in the country.

The City and Suburban Harriers' base at Jones' Road, Glasnevin (later renamed Croke Park) lay a good ten miles south of Richardstown.[24] It is unlikely White trained there very often, if at all, and most of his training appears to have taken place in a local field. To this day, that field, about a mile in circumference, is known locally as 'Paddy White's Field.' It forms part of Liam Cooney's farm in Ballyboughal. Back then, it was part of Patrick Merrick's farm, where Pat occasionally worked.[25]

On 31 December 1901, John White finally reached an agreement with Patrick Harford to lease the five acres of prime farmland that lay across the lane from his cabin, with the rent, set at £5 4s 4d, to be paid twice yearly on the first

16

days of May and November. It was hardly a bargain. The lease was heavily in favour of the landlord and left room for only a small profit. What it did offer, was independence.

And so, at 10.15 a.m. on New Year's Day 1902, when the deed was officially registered, John White forsook the security of tied employment to begin life anew, not as an agricultural labourer but as a small farmer.[26] He would have to crop every square inch of his holding to survive, but he was confident he could do it. In time, he would add another couple of acres to the total.

The father's ambition was quickly reflected in that of the eldest son. On 10 May 1902, at a sports day in Newbridge, Co. Kildare, Pat raced unsuccessfully in a one-mile handicap.[27] Two weeks later, however, he ran in an 800m steeplechase handicap at the Gigas Bazaar at Ballsbridge, a charity event in aid of the Royal City of Dublin Hospital.

Crowds back then were a novelty to country folk, exciting in a manner that city dwellers could never fully understand. Following his first experience of racing in front of a truly large one, Pat found that he rather enjoyed the attention. Described in the handicap lists as 'P. Whyte, Oldtown,' he started off an allowance of 40 yards and finished first in a time of 2:05.40.[28] Until that win, serious training had seemed hardly worth the effort on top of a physically demanding job. His victory at Ballsbridge, however, stirred a fresh ambition within him.

There were no paved roads in North County Dublin back then, nor was there much in the way of public lighting beyond the streets of the larger towns. Running at night, even under a moonlit sky, was asking for trouble. Buffeted by a scything southerly, a man could so easily sprain an ankle or lose an eye to a straggling bramble.

Pat White at twenty-three.

From Monday to Saturday, then, Pat could only walk, and though he could run on Sundays, even that required a hard neck, as the sight of someone running on country roads or round a local field was still very much a novelty. But, steeled by hardship and adversity, he persevered, training so hard and so consistently that, on 7 February 1903, when he lined up at the start of the National Junior Championships at Elm Park, he did so as a leaner, fitter, and more resilient athlete.[29]

18

The weather that afternoon was wild and wet and played to Pat's strengths. P.J. McCafferty of Clonliffe Harriers romped home ten seconds clear of Hugh Muldoon of Haddington Harriers, but Pat managed to come in third, just twenty seconds behind the winner. It was, by a fair step, his best-ever placing in a championship race, and it was about to get even better.

Following the race, Cork City Harriers lodged a protest, claiming that the winner, McCafferty, who had for several years resided in Edinburgh, was not in compliance with the residency rule, which required him to have lived for the preceding six months in the administrative region of the club for which he competed. McCafferty, as a result, was disqualified. Pat was promoted to runner-up.[30]

Four weeks later, on a bitterly cold day at Clonskeagh, Co. Dublin, Pat finished fourth in the National Senior Cross-Country Championships behind established stars like John J. Daly, Tom Hynes and Frank Curtis, but a full nine seconds ahead of Muldoon, who had beaten him in February. It was enough to earn him a place on the Irish team for the cross-country international in Glasgow on 28 March.[31]

This was an enormous deal in North County Dublin and, indeed, for many miles beyond. Pat White was no longer a common labourer, no longer protected by the anonymity of mediocrity. He was somebody now. His name was in the papers.

The Glasgow race was won by Alfie Shrubb, who would go on to become the greatest middle-distance runner of his generation. Tom Edwards of Manchester took second, and John J. Daly of

Galway Harriers third. Pat finished sixteenth, third Irishman home and a scoring member of an Irish team that finished second in the team race.

Pat White (between numbers 16 & 27), taken with the Irish Cross Country Team at Hamilton Palace in March 1903 (digitally enhanced).

Describing the first International cross-country championship, decided at Hamilton Park on Saturday, is an easy task indeed. It was simply a case of Alfred Shrubb, the Londoner and national champion of England for the last three seasons, being first and the rest nowhere.

Equally so might the quest for country championship honours be described, for England furnished six men in the first seven home, and the "predominant partner" finished many points ahead of Ireland, who provided the second-best team; while Scotland came third and Wales were the whippers in.

But regarding the race, run, by the way, in the most miserable weather (heavy rain), it was as good as over after the first two miles had been run... But it was Shrubb's race, and his alone. The present was his first visit to Scotland as a harrier – a competitor over the country. He has been seen here in flat-racing events, but on Saturday he showed us his wonderful pace at cross-country work. He is not the best of fencers, indeed, compared to John Daly (Ireland, who finished third), he was a poor hurdler; but he is a marvellous stayer. This has been a wonderful season for him.[32]

A stellar career in cross-country running now beckoned for White, but amateur athletics in Ireland was already in decline and about to face one of its most significant challenges.

In 1903, the *Evening Herald* decided to sponsor a 'go-as-you-please' race from the canal bridge at Inchicore to the courthouse at Naas, an eighteen-mile road race that would leave an indelible mark on the Irish sporting landscape. As there would be significant cash prizes, any amateur who competed would automatically surrender his amateur status, or so the Irish Amateur Athletic Association would have had them believe.

The "Herald" contest was thought of at a time when the public mind was exercised by consideration of the feats of pedestrianism in England and elsewhere. The public appetite was whetted by reading of these feats, and the question arose: "Why can't we have something like this in Ireland?" We were to have a King's visit, a great motor contest, an International Regatta, and all the attendant excitement, but for this feast of sensation to be properly relished required a savoury "first course".

The "Evening Herald" initiated a great pedestrian competition, open to all. The manner in which the promoters went to work left no room for doubt as to the ultimate success of the great sporting contest. A committee was formed to consider the conditions under which the race should take place. This body, including many experienced sportsmen, after due deliberation, came to the conclusion that to make the contest a walking one, pure and simple, would, owing to the difficulties in the way of judging, be altogether unsatisfactory.

The number of entrants promised to be very large, so the committee decided to make the contest a "go as you please" (walk and run) and to award the prizes to those competitors who reached Naas in the fastest time. From the day the conditions were published entries poured in by the dozen, and when the last day for entering names of intending competitors arrived, the number of entries had reached the flattering total of 225.[33]

The *Herald* race promised to generate considerable public interest in athletics and promote the sport as a whole. However, it was still a professional event, and the I.A.A.A. remained resolute in its refusal to promote it or to sanction the participation of its members. Nevertheless, the allure of decent prizemoney, examples of which had been few and far between over the previous decade, saw Tom Hynes of Galway Harriers, perhaps the biggest star of the amateur code, announce his intention to compete. A barrage of criticism was consequently unleashed upon the organisers by the I.A.A.A., compelling them to respond. On the eve of the race, the editor of the *Herald's* sister paper, the *Irish Independent*, had this to say:

> Now that the race promoted by the "Herald" is on the eve of its accomplishment, we desire to refer to the proclamation issued by the Irish Amateur Athletic Association. While at all times willing to admit the wisdom and justice of the action of the ruling bodies of amateur sport in this country in the furtherance and encouragement of all kindred pastimes, we fail to see by what right this body aggregate to themselves the authority to declare it was against the standing rules of the I.A.A.A. to promote or assist in the promotion of a professional contest, and, in addition, we challenge the Hon. Secretary, or any other official, licensed or otherwise, to point to a single rule or bye-law, in the constitution of the I.A.A.A. to hall-mark the attempt to interfere with the right of an individual in taking part in the promotion of this event...
>
> As a matter of fact, we can call to mind several professional athletic contests held in this country in which well-known members of the ruling body of the I.A.A.A. officiated without interference. Why, may we ask? Because the committee then in power knew the rules of the Association and did not wish to make themselves ridiculous in the eyes of the general public. We now leave the matter, feeling we have done our duty in pointing out to the wiseacres of the I.A.A.A. who act first and think afterwards, the folly of their actions.[34]

The publicity surrounding the spat did little to deter public interest in the event, and when the race took place as planned, on Saturday, 23 May 1903, it drew enormous crowds onto the course and made a desert of the city centre.[35] Of the fifty-one competitors who started, just twenty-three managed to finish. To the further delight of the sponsors, the winner, Hynes, would go on to generate even more publicity after the race when it became known that he had no sooner crossed the finish line, than he was calling for an Apollinaria to celebrate the news that, while he'd been running, his wife had given birth to a son.[36]

The winner that day took home £14. Second place received £4, and third place got £2. There was no prizemoney beyond that, and Christopher Farrell, who finished sixth, was later arrested in Naas, cap in hand, begging for money to pay for his fare home. Charged with vagrancy at Naas Petty Sessions on the following Monday, he was sentenced to fourteen days' hard labour.[37]

But the winner's prize! Fourteen pounds! That was enough in 1903 to purchase an acre of land. To a common hireling like White, that was a small fortune. The average wage of agricultural labourers at the time was just twelve shillings a week.[38]

He resisted the temptation to chase the cash. Cross-country running had made him a minor celebrity in North County Dublin. To risk all that in a professional race he could not be confident of winning, would have been madness. He had yet to race over such long distances and had yet to beat Hynes over *any* distance. But it was always there, dangling before him, and did set him thinking.

1903 was also the year of the Wyndham Act, a piece of legislation that enabled many Irish tenants to purchase their holdings from their landlords, courtesy of British government loans. As a result of this legislation, John White should have been able to purchase his smallholding outright. Why he did not is unclear.

Pat, by this time, had left Baldurgan to work on John Dempsey's farm at nearby Grace Dieu. He would work there during the day and spend his nights sleeping on the settle in his parents' parlour. For the next two years, his training would continue to consist of long walks in the countryside after work and the occasional ten-mile run on his days off.[39]

It was common practice at the time for marathon runners to train by walking rather than running. Contemporary footwear lacked shock absorbency, and walking carried a lower risk of injury and attracted less attention. His training, such as it was, paled in comparison to that of full-time professionals like Len Hurst, who trained three times a day.

Pat did not run any championship races in 1904. He had left John Dempsey's employment by then and, like every other non-resident farmhand in the country, had taken to travelling the high roads and by-roads of rural Ireland, scratching for a living in whatever seasonal employment he could lay his hands on.

Early in the year, while working in County Antrim, he appeared at several low-key handicap races, running for the Belfast club, Hibernian Harriers, including the annual sports day at Ballynafeigh, Belfast, held on 4 April 1904, where he finished third in a one-mile steeplechase handicap.[40] By November, however, he had returned to Dublin and joined Santry Harriers, a cross-country club based at what was then a tiny village on the Dublin to Drogheda road. Running in the Santry colours, he took fourth place that autumn at the Donore Harriers' Five Mile Invitational Cross-Country at Dolphin's Barn.[41]

The only other occasion on which Pat's name appeared in a cross-country race report during the 1904/5 season was when he returned to his old stomping ground to act as the official starter during a triangular match between Ballinasloe Harriers, Galway City Harriers, and Tuam Harriers. That race took place in Athenry on St. Stephen's Day.

The following year, still running for Santry, Pat finished fifth in the Cross-Country Association of Ireland's National Senior Championships at Elm Park.[42] One week later, he placed third in the GAA National Senior Championships at Jones' Road.[43] Based on these results, he was selected to compete in a trial race at Jones' Road to select a team to represent Ireland at that year's cross-country international, scheduled to take place at Baldoyle. The trial took place on 5 March.

> Doyle burst away at the pistol, but on settling down, White went into front place, and was leading passing the judges for the first time, with Muldoon, Finnegan, Harris, O'Hara, L. Kelly, Mernagh, Doyle, McCluskey, and Curtis in close order. At two laps to go, Muldoon was in command, three yards in front of Harris, who was leading White by five yards... Entering the last lap, White was leading ten yards in front of Harris, Muldoon was third ten yards away... After passing the judges White put on a tremendous spurt, and, getting gradually away from his field, he finished 120 yards in front of L. Kelly (Donore) who was twenty yards ahead of Harris.[44]

The emphatic nature of Pat's win guaranteed his selection for the Irish team, which also included Tom Hynes, who had been preselected. Despite having threatened Hynes with the loss of his amateur status for running in the 1903 *Herald* race, Hynes was back running cross-country as an amateur, and had been doing so since at least December of 1904.[45]

The international race took place at Baldoyle on 26 March, on ground so glutinous that John J. Daly dropped out early. The race was won by Albert Aldridge of England, with Hynes in second place and Joe Deakin of England in third. Pat, the third Irishman home, finished eighteenth, a full two minutes behind the winner and eighteen seconds behind his old adversary, Muldoon. In the team competition, Ireland finished third.[46] Reflecting on the disappointment of a mediocre winter season, Pat came to a momentous decision. Come the summer, he would try his hand at the longer distances.

Training for the longer distances was no easy task on top of a full working day. The longer walks and runs meant spending even more time alone, absorbed in a silent, physical, and meditative activity that strengthened the mind and body, but left little time for developing friendships or pursuing romance. The more he trained, however, the more he improved, and the more comfortable he became in his own company. That was the price of glory. T'was ever thus.

As the year drew to a close, life threw another curve at the Whites. On 5 December, young Peter ran away from home, lied about his age, and enlisted in the British Army. With scarcely a second thought as to the consequences, he signed on for nine years with the colours and three with the reserve.

Three days later, having passed his medical, Peter was posted to the East Lancashire regiment and sent to Preston to join them. On 25 February of the following year, he was transferred to the Connaught Rangers only to be listed as having deserted two weeks later. Quickly caught, he was returned to his regiment and sentenced to twenty-eight days in prison.[47] His absence was felt on the family farm. It may even have hurt John White's pocket if he had to hire an extra hand during the planting season.

THE 1905 'HERALD' RACE

SINCE THE ADVENT of the modern Olympics, presentation ceremonies had become the norm, and, at least in the public imagination, the status of the *Herald* event had quickly assumed such importance that it almost demanded a trophy. For the 1905 race, therefore, the organisers decided to reduce the prizemoney for the winner from £14 to £10 and to use the remainder to purchase a silver cup.[48]

THE "HERALD" RACE, 1905.

In just two short years, the race had become one of the most important sporting events in Ireland, prefiguring the worldwide marathon mania that would follow the London Olympics of 1908. Free to watch on account of being a road race, it attracted crowds as large, if not larger, than the classics of the horse racing season or the funerals of nationalist heroes. It truly was that big.

The prizes for the 1905 race were listed as follows: first man home would receive £10, a handsome cup, a thousand Juvarna Cigarettes, and a second-class return ticket to Wicklow, with a week's free accommodation thrown in. Second place would receive £5 and five hundred K Brand Cigarettes. Third place would receive £3 and a hundred Doctor's Mixture cigarettes.[49] They were different times.

The race took place on Sunday, 25 June 1905, following a spell of dry weather and the start of the haymaking season. Had it been held on a Saturday, Pat might not have been able to compete. As it was, he was likely to have been working the day before, if not on one of the local farms, then on his father's. But he was accustomed to making such accommodations. It was part and parcel, not just of farming life, but of amateur sport in general.

This was one of those occasions that could never be taken back, at least not by those who were seen as dispensable. By competing in a professional race, Pat White was effectively surrendering his amateur status. But he was already twenty-six. How long had he got left in the sport? Five years, maybe: eight if he was lucky. If he was to make the leap, it had to be now.

Come race day, twenty to thirty thousand spectators lined a course that stretched from Tolka Bridge in Glasnevin to the coastal town of Balbriggan, a distance of eighteen and a half miles. They came prepared, and they came early, to check out the runners, place their bets and enjoy the festival atmosphere. Gambling was very much part of the appeal of such events in those days, as indeed was the spectacle, and the *Evening Herald* race had by now surpassed even the attractions of Fairyhouse on Grand National day.

> As early as nine o'clock in the morning ice-cream cars, cider butts, and rickety-looking, springless caravansaries laden with sweets, sugarsticks, oranges. and buns and cakes of all sorts and doubtful substance were moving out of Drumcondra way to await the crowds promised by previous races on the Dublin to Naas Road.
>
> At eleven o'clock there must have been ten thousand people occupying the road between Tolka Bridge and The Thatch, and at noon this congestion was added to by ever-increasing thousands coming by crowded trams and vehicles of every description. Hundreds were on cycles; thousands were on foot...
>
> There was plenty of bustle and crushing and excitement, but nothing approaching disorderliness. At one o'clock there was such a mighty concourse of people along this road by Whitehall that, without exaggeration, if they were placed in single file, a long line of humanity would stretch halfway to Balbriggan.[50]

The festive atmosphere was no less apparent at the finish line:

> Large numbers patronised Balbriggan on Sunday last owing to the fact that the "Herald" "Go-as-you-please Race" was to finish there. Great

enthusiasm was present all day in the town, and towards evening the crowd present was of large dimensions. The day was uncomfortably hot, but the breeze on that pretty seaside resort greatly moderated the oppressive heat. Owing to the watering of the town not being quite good enough, some discomfort was felt from the clouds of dust raised by the many cycles, motors and hackney cars passing through the streets...[51]

Back at Tolka Bridge, forty-seven competitors prepared to start, including some of Ireland's most famous distance runners. The majority appeared lean and well-trained, but among the scrawny and sturdy, there were not a few oddities:

> ... for while most looked grim and stern, and determined to do or die, not a few looked comical. To shelter his closely-cropped head from the fierce rays of a sweltering sun, one competitor had a wreath of cabbage leaves, giving him the appearance of a Greek slave in the play. Another carried his wardrobe on his back, his limbs being protected by an athlete's outfit that must have seen service in many fields, and one man ... carried a stick in his right hand and a fierce look in his eye.[52]

As punters debated form and weighed the chances of the favourites, the one name that never crossed their lips, not even among the 'dark horses', was that of Pat White, who on his entry form had given his address as 'Richardstown, Donabate'.[53] Odds were offered, and bets were placed, but as the start drew ever closer, White still failed to feature in the betting. Hynes was not present that year, having travelled to New York to compete in a number of amateur races under the auspices of the Galway Men's Athletic Association.[54] His absence is likely to have been a contributory factor in Pat's decision to compete.

The competitors came from all parts of the country. Jim Steele, of (Moate, Westmeath), the winner of the " Herald" Race last year, was here again in all his glory. And Mick Dalton, an admirer of the Marquis of Queensberry, was here, too, in his war paint. He hails from Denmark Street, Dublin, and he was fifth two years ago and second last year. He looked in the pink of condition on Sunday.

There were many "dark horses." F. Harvey, who ran from Clonmel to Cashel, paced by a motor, in record time, was considered an absolute certainty by his many friends from Tipperary, who were present in force. Conspicuous also amongst the starters, were the finely-trained Jim C. Smith, of Monasterevin, who was third last year; William Cusack, of Dublin, who was fifth last year; and Dan O'Brien, of Drumcondra, who was sixth last year.

The Curragh Camp, and military circles generally, were very liberally, and very ably, represented amongst the competitors. J. Ward, R.H.A. Newbridge,[55] fourth man last year, looked well and for this journey; but in better fettle by far were W. Worsfield, of the 11th Hussars; Gunner Packer, of the R.H.A.; and Pat Conway, of the Military Barracks in Waterford. Of the military lot, Conway and Worsfield were unquestionably the best groomed. They looked fined down to the last ounce.[56]

At precisely ten minutes past one, the whistle

blew and the soldiers dashed straight to the front, moving almost as a team. Three miles later, they reached Santry, where Horsfield was the first to crest the hill, closely followed by Ward and Thompson. White, at this point, had settled in the group behind, which included Flynn, Tindall, Dolan, and the previous year's winner, Steele.

Early in the race, the gaps were not significant, and no one appeared to be unduly worried about the military men's lead. By the time the leaders reached Cloghran, however, Worsfield and Ward had opened a two-minute gap on the chasing pack. Steele now panicked, putting in such a surge that, by the time he reached the village of Swords, he had, in the space of just two and a half miles, completely reeled in the leaders and pulled the chasing pack with him. Ward, by this time, had shot his bolt and had been swallowed by the chasing pack.

Finding himself with fresh company, Worsfield began to push the pace and quickly opened a gap of a couple of yards on Steele. But then, as he approached Ballough, a townland on the outskirts of Lusk, he got a splinter in his foot. Stopping to remove it, he was passed by Steele, who by that point had just a few yards' lead over Conway, Tindall, and White.

By the time the leaders reached Balrothery, Steele had dropped out of contention, and White, looking fresh and buoyed by local support, decided to make a run for home. It was a brave move, but not a decisive one, for he was closely followed by Conway, who refused to give him an inch. The pair ran side by side to the outskirts of Balbriggan, where White, summoning what remained of his reserves, conjured up a sprint that took him away from Conway and to a famous victory. Richard Tisdall, another 'outsider,' finished third.

White had covered the eighteen and a half miles on dusty dirt roads and under a scorching sun in precisely two hours.[57] Once again, his name was in the papers, but this time as a headliner. Every child in Fingal walked a little taller following the news of his great success.

In just one race, White had earned almost four times the monthly wage of the average agricultural labourer. His amateur days were over. It is hard, in this respect, not to contrast White's experiences in this regard with those of Ireland's top cross-country runner, Tom Hynes. Following his win in the 1903 *Herald* race, Hynes had been permitted to return to the amateur ranks. And yet, despite this, he had chosen to go to the U.S., where he was currently causing a stir on the amateur circuit and making a mockery of the selective leniency of I.A.A.A.

> Thomas Hynes, of Galway, and John Joyce, the Irish-American long distance champion in the States, are in hot water. The Registration Committee of the Metropolitan Association of the American Athletic Union has suspended both athletes, pending an examination of their amateur standing.
>
> One of the charges is that a manager of one of them applied to men handling a set of athletic games for a sum of money in case they competed. Another charge is that they agreed to appear at Celtic Park last Tuesday week, permitted it to be announced, and then competed in Boston instead.
>
> There are, in the opinion of the committee,

suspicious circumstances which the athletes must explain, or be suspended for all time.[58]

It might seem somewhat incongruous to modern eyes to see the word 'manager' mentioned in connection with two amateur athletes of that time, but under the rules as they then existed, it was permitted in limited circumstances. An amateur athlete could not accept payment as a prize or accept appearance money, but he could accept minimal expenses and training costs. It was recognised, nevertheless, that there were exceptional demands on elite athletes, and a manager was therefore permitted to remove the administrative burden on the athlete by helping to arrange and administer his expenses, control his race calendar, and book transportation and accommodation. An amateur athlete's manager was not, however, prohibited from earning a share of the gate money at challenge events or from betting on the outcome of races. Big wins from the bookies might even be shared, as long as the athlete could be trusted to keep his mouth shut.

It would be incorrect, therefore, to assume that amateur athletes did not make money from the sport at the time. The rules were frequently bent, and under-the-counter payments were far from unknown. Prior to losing his amateur status, for example, the great Alfie Shrubb had managed to accumulate enough through inflated expenses to give up carpentry and labouring on building sites and purchase a tobacconist's shop in Horsham.[59] But Hynes and Shrubb were considered indispensable to their associations at the time; Patrick White was not.

Hynes was eventually stripped of his amateur status by the American Athletics Union, primarily as a result of two races at Celtic Park, where the performances of both he and Joyce were considered to be so 'open to suspicion' that they warranted the cancellation of his permit.[60] There was to be no such leniency shown to Pat White, nor any suggestion that he sought it. He had gone into that race with his eyes wide open and had accepted the likely consequences.

Various professional challenge matches would take place in the weeks following the *Herald* race. For instance, a two-hundred-yard sprint for a purse of £10 was held at Phoenix Park on 24 September; a walking race from Donnybrook to Bray was held on 7 October, and a challenge race with a £25 side bet was arranged between Tom Hynes and J.P. O'Flynn of Waterford.[61] No challenges, however, were received by Pat White, nor did he go out of his way to make any. He had learned two valuable lessons from his first experience in professional sport. Firstly, the longer the distance, the better he fared; and secondly, to make money, you needed money.

Professional running was a business, and Pat White knew little about that world. To secure a profitable match, he needed a manager or, at the very least, the financial backing necessary to guarantee an attractive purse. He had neither. He would not race again that summer.

Peter, meanwhile, having been released from prison on 7 June and returned to barracks, couldn't manage to keep himself out of trouble and, following two weeks of garrison duty, he deserted again. After almost two months on the run, he rejoined his regiment on 8 October.

Arrested on the spot, he was placed in detention awaiting trial.[62]

Just one week later, on Sunday, 15 October, Pat White made an appearance at Richard Ball's estate in Reynoldstown for the annual Naul Gymkhana and Sports Day. The morning began misty and cold, but by midday the sky had cleared and the crowds had begun to gather. A small and largely local affair, the event featured a mix of athletic and equestrian events, several of which were reserved exclusively for members of the band.

The highlight of the day was to be a four-mile open handicap featuring local hero Pat White. For many, it would be their first opportunity to see him run. Scheduled to start towards the end of the day, between the donkey race and the obstacle race for ponies, the announcement of his planned participation still failed to attract opponents from outside the Fingal region. Starting off scratch, he won by a yard from Paddy McGuinness of Oldtown, who had started off twenty yards, and Joe Connell of the Naul, who had started off a hundred. It was, in everything but name, an exhibition run.

It is not known who first approached whom regarding Pat's appearance at the gymkhana, but it is perhaps worth noting that the Clerk of the Course that day was thirty-two-year-old Bernard Colgan,[63] a well-dressed, well-fed, and well-spoken scion of a respectable commercial family. Pillars of the local community, the Colgans were well-known in the Naul, where they ran a village shop, a post office, and a saddlers.[64] Their post office, which coincidentally lay adjacent to one of the village's two pumps, was a constant hive of activity. Everyone knew, and had at one time or another, depended on the Colgans.

Sociable, shrewd, and popular, Bernard Colgan was the Honorary Secretary of both the Naul Branch of the United Irish League and the Naul Sports Organising Committee.[65] Practised in the arts of promotion and public speaking, he was the kind of man to whom even gentlemen tipped their hats. Whether he and Pat had already come to an arrangement that October is unclear, but by the start of the new year, Bernard Colgan would be Pat White's manager.

One curious aspect of the *Drogheda Independent* report of the gymkhana was the manner in which it referred to White. The reporter was clearly familiar with the Naul and its surrounding townlands, correctly identifying competitors as natives or residents of such remote townlands as Oldtown and Naptown. And yet, though Richardstown was no more distant to the Naul, Pat was still referred to as 'P. White, Donabate.'

Back on 1 July, while reporting on the *Herald* race, the same paper had referred to White as 'Pat White, Richardstown', so it was known within the office where White was from.[66] It is possible, given the time of year, that Pat was labouring in Donabate at the time. He had worked on so many farms in the district that it would not have been unusual for him to have been engaged by one of the major landowners on the Portrane peninsula.

Donabate, however, appears to have had very fluid borders at the time. As late as 1916, for example, Baldurgan would still be considered a part of greater Donabate.[67] It is possible, therefore, that Richardstown was too. Whatever the reason, from this point forward, and for the rest of his life, White would become popularly known throughout Ireland, and beyond, as 'Pat White of Donabate'.

Two days after the Naul Gymkhana and Sports Day, at the Connaught Rangers' garrison in Galway, Peter White was sentenced to a further twelve weeks in prison. Released a week early for good behaviour, he would rejoin his regiment on 3 January 1906.[68] Unrepentant and unashamed, it was only a matter of time before he would see the inside of another cell.

A MARKED MAN

THINGS HADN'T QUITE worked out as planned following White's audacious victory in the 1905 *Herald* race. Lucrative head-to-head challenges never materialised, his victory written off as a fluke, attributed to Hynes' absence and Worsfield's splinter. There was nothing to be done now but prove everyone wrong. Alas, that was easier said than done. Pat White was now a marked man, a known quantity. The bookies' odds and his rivals' tactics would reflect that. The element of surprise was gone.

A degree of anxiety was only to be expected as the days crept slowly towards the 1906 race. Interest in athletics had been heightened weeks earlier by Peter O'Connor's gold and silver medals in the Triple Jump and Long Jump at the Intercalated Olympic Games in Athens. This series of International 'Olympic' Games was initially intended to be held halfway between what is now known as the Games of the Modern Olympiad and to be forever held in Athens. At the time, they were considered to be an Olympic Games and endorsed by the International Olympic Committee. After 1906, however, they ceased to be held.

O'Connor's fame had resulted, not just from his medal-winning performances, but from his subsequent scaling of the presentation ceremony flagpole to remove the Union Jack and replace it with an *Erin go Bragh* flag, in protest at having been forced to compete on a British Team. And so, as sport became the latest vehicle for expressing nationalist sentiment and national pride, O'Connor's actions left Ireland hungry for even more sporting heroes and, despite the absence of foreign competitors, fed into the extraordinary sense of occasion that marked the build-up to that year's *Herald* race.

PAT WHITE

Lying awake at night, his heartbeat quickening in mental rehearsals, Pat would have quickly realised that starting a race as the favourite posed a vastly different challenge to starting as an unknown quantity. Nothing had hung on the result of the previous *Herald* race, but this time he would carry the hopes and expectations of his supporters, friends, and family. For perhaps the first time in Pat White's life, there was pressure to perform. Gambling, after all, was part of the attraction of events like these. On the positive side, Hynes, who was even now still battling to hang on to his amateur status, would not be competing.

The 1906 *Herald* race took place on Sunday, 20 May. From the start at Inchicore Bridge to the finish at Naas Courthouse, it measured sixteen and three-quarter miles. On this occasion, despite the fine weather, only half of the hundred entries turned up to face the starter.

> They ranged in appearance from youth to old age. A slip of a boy of 20 from Ship Street, Dublin, took his place near an old veteran, who looked every day of fifty, hailing from Francis Street, and this old man, with grey locks and original style outfit, had one inseparable association – a smile of rugged consciousness that spread over his ragged features.[69]

At precisely six minutes past one, the starting whistle was blown, and down the hill from Inchicore Bridge, the gallant half-hundred and their cycling attendants swarmed. For two miles into the countryside, they found the road lined with an irregular and broken line of spectators, cheering and jeering by turns, excited by the spectacle.

> In high spirits, the competitors trotted gaily along for the first couple of miles. Then the pace gradually began to tell, and even then, when the exercise had not yet developed into hard labour,

they were heard to crack jokes among themselves, and to respond in merry spirit to good-humoured comments from lookers-on.

"You'll lose the race if you keep looking at the ladies," called out one of them to a colleague with whom he was racing neck to neck. And here let it be stated that a considerable number of Dublin's daughters cycled to Naas, keenly following the fortunes of the day from start to finish.

As for wheels, there were wheels around wheels, in and out and roundabout. The marvel was that ambulance wheels had not to play a part in the procession. For the roads were slippery, rather heavy, but always slippery, and did not lend themselves to the experiment of close formation on the part of wheelmen.

But on the travelling masses progressed. The road seemed alive with people, men, women children, traps, cars, and vehicles by the hundred, bicycles unlimited, motor cars few, but observant and observable. And in the midst of all this, the racing men found their elbow room.

That was the surprising part of it. For five miles they coursed their way through vendors of oranges, cakes, and light refreshments, unheeding of the warning calls of car drivers or the insinuations of enterprising bookmakers, or even the boisterous "toot, toot" of the motor horn.

Through all the din the sporting following played fair by the principals, who at first ran well in a cluster, and then spread-eagled. The best forged well ahead. The non-stayers dropped to the background.[70]

As the leaders entered the third mile, Pat Fagan began to draw away from the pack. White let him go, confident in his pace judgement. By the time Fagan reached Tallaght Crossroads, he had eked out a lead of about half a mile and was running so freely he could take the time to wave to the crowds.

Running in second place at this point was Cusack, accompanied and paced by two friends on bicycles. Behind him came Borley of the Curragh and then Conway of the Royal Field Artillery, runner-up the previous year. Trailing in twelfth place, White was still running steadily, accompanied by Murphy of Dundalk and McArdle of Dunleer, the latter of whom had finished fourth in 1905. The trio appeared to be already out of contention.

From Tallaght, the macadamed road became 'slushy' and energy-sapping, and while the inexperienced runners continued to plough the hungry ground in the middle, the smarter runners headed for the pavements in search of traction. With so many bicycles following the race, the athletes were by now cloaked from head to toe in dust.

> The roads improved as Rathcoole was approached. Fagan entered the village alone – that is, so far as competitors were concerned. Looking back over the country, there was no sign of the others in the race. Here was the chance for the local humorist.
>
> "Yerra, is it a walkover?" asked one in quite a serious and disappointed vein.
>
> "Yes," responded a wag from a car; "the rest is all gone back." [71]

With Fagan almost a mile in front, it was vital to White's chances that the gap did not widen further. For White, whose approach to racing closely mirrored that of the great Len Hurst, i.e.

'to let them go and let them come back', a mile was just a little too much, and, informed of the gap as he exited Rathcoole, he decided to make his move.

At Kill, thirteen miles from the start, the official record was as follows:—Fagan, White, Cusack, Conway, Malone, Corrigan. O'Byrne, Thompson, Murphy, Harney, Dunne, Steele. A dozen others were struggling behind, and were perforce content to share the honours of the 'also-rans.'

Along to Johnstown the positions underwent no material change, but White was plainly overhauling the leader, and now the crowded cars and jostling cyclists began for the first time to contemplate the possibility of a close finish. Fagan was blowing hard. Buoyantly he had dashed off at Inchicore and gallantly he had led throughout, and now the splendid effort was telling on the wiry athlete. Coming onto the railway bridge that bent into the town of Naas, Fagan's name was shouted by hundreds and hundreds.

The poor fellow appeared to be breaking up. Encouraging shouts rent the air, and it was then that White came charging along like a thoroughbred. He caught his man, challenged him into the street, and in sight of the crowd that densely packed the pavements, the Donabate hero raced into Naas and to the courthouse with a final sprint worthy of a hundred yards champion.

It was decidedly a marvellous feat after such a journey. He stood up to the tape proud and fresh. He had run 16¾ miles in 1:40 – a feat of athleticism and a test of stamina. Amongst the many who cheered and marvelled at this remarkable finish was J.J. Daly, Ireland's representative in the great Marathon race at Athens, and he did not conceal his surprise at, and admiration of, the abilities of the men who bore the principal honours in this sporting trial of endurance.[72]

John Joseph Daly, the 'Ballyglunin Boy,' was one of Ireland's leading amateur athletes. At the 1904 Olympic Games in Missouri he had won the One Mile Handicap race. He had just returned from the Intercalated Games in Athens, where, along with Con Leahy and Peter O'Connor, he had been entered for the games by the IAAA and GAA. All three athletes had been given green blazers and caps embroidered with a gold shamrock and an 'Erin Go Bragh' flag. Shortly before the games, however, the rules had been changed so that only athletes nominated by their national Olympic Committees were eligible to compete. As Ireland did not have an Olympic Committee, the British Olympic Council claimed the three athletes as their own, and they were registered as competing for Britain.

Daly had finished third in the five-mile competition only to be subsequently disqualified for having obstructed Edward Dahl of Sweden. He had also been forced to abandon the marathon after eighteen miles due to blisters and an ankle injury that cost him three days in hospital. Before the advent of modern running shoes, marathon runners typically ran in leather shoes and often without socks. Daly's lasting claim to fame, however, had come from what would long be remembered as the first political protest in modern Olympic history.

When O'Connor won the silver medal in the long jump, he was so enraged to see the Union Jack raised for his medal ceremony that he shimmied up the flagpole, took down the Union Jack, and replaced it with the Irish flag while Daly stood guard at the bottom, preventing officials from reaching him. Since that day, Daly and O'Connor had become national heroes and Daly's presence at the finish line of the *Herald* race, though reflective of popular support for the race, proved acutely embarrassing to the Irish Amateur Athletic Association and gained much-needed publicity for White.[73] Daly would soon after take himself off to New York, where he would spend the remainder of his days.

> Pat White of Donabate, the hero of last year's Herald race from Dublin to Balbriggan, has once again brought honour to himself and the barony he hails from. Last year, he finished first in the race from Dublin to Balbriggan. Yesterday he won the great running race from Inchicore to Naas in a truly sensational manner.
>
> The distance from start to finish is 16¾ miles, and the winner covered this in 1 hour 40 mins and 50 secs, beating the record made by James Steele in 1904 by 13 minutes and 40 secs. It should, however, be borne in mind that in 1904 the event was brought off on a broiling summer's day, and the competitors had to pick their way through clouds of dust and clusters of cars and cycles. Yesterday, despite the rain, the roads were in perfect condition, and competitors were given a comparatively clear passage.[74]

The *Drogheda Independent* – a paper that catered to a significant portion of White's fan base – went even further, prefacing a report of the race with a short poem in Pat's honour and comparing his popularity to that of a famous racehorse:

Will there be a real cheer,
As there was for Eyrefield's Glory,
The Donabate man wins again I hear,
But who would believe the story?

Yet it is true that the Great Irish Marathon from Inchicore to Naas was won on Sunday last by Mr Pat White, Donabate – that redoubtable racer who last year won the same race from the Tolka to Balbriggan. Had he lived in ancient Greece in the days when Olympia was in high renown his fame would have been sung by a sacred poet, but in this era, men are too prosaic for that and forget a champion's deeds when he lays down the gauntlet. However, Pat White is the man of the hour and we wish him a rattling good, jolly, hearty time of it during his week's stay in Wicklow and at Wicklow's leading hotel whither he has been invited by the proprietor.[75]

MAKING HAY

THIS TIME IT *was* different. The manner of his victory, or, more accurately, the manner of Fagan's loss, had created an instant demand for a rematch. White now possessed what he had lacked the previous year – an entertaining rivalry, a reason for people to come out, to cheer, and to stake their hard-earned cash. It was Dublin vs Fingal, City vs Country, and people were hungry to see them race again, at any time, and over any distance. It mattered little if White were to lose. A defeat would only whet the public's appetite for more.

Bernard Colgan set the ball rolling on Sunday, 10 June 1906, at the Naul Sports. Lying on the main road from Dublin to Balbriggan, the village of Naul was easily reached. It was where the mail coach stopped to change horses and just a smidgeon over five miles from the train station at Balbriggan. People flocked from all over Dublin and its neighbouring counties, not just to watch White and Fagan race from Balbriggan to the Naul, but to enjoy the brass bands and pony races that were to provide the bulk of the day's entertainment.

Towards Balbriggan on Sunday last, the crowd wended its way from the surrounding and outlying districts, and the trains arriving at that seaside station brought a large concourse of sporting men and women. But though Balbriggan might be the venue for a brief space, soon was it deserted, and on the road leading to Naul was a perpetual cloud of dust during the afternoon, indicative of congestion in traffic.

The nearer one came to the crossroads where a neat card was marked "This way to the course," the more congested was the way and the more pedestrians, cycles, and hackneys were huddled together as in one combined mass...

The panorama was exquisite, bedecked as it was with the beauty, the manhood, the gay and the busy, of all classes and conditions of people, both near and far. On the course could be seen as large a crowd as ever patronised a sports meeting. But those who came erred not, neither were they mistaken in the slightest degree for the amusement afforded was quite enough to satiate the sporting appetite, even of one fresh from the Olympian Games in Athenian climes.

A conspicuous feature of the day was the enormous number of vehicles present, and each of which had a goodly number of visitors. But those who came in the family private carriages were wise in their generation for nothing could surpass the exquisiteness of being seated behind four chargers while the Balbriggan Brass and Reed Band, or mayhap the Swords Fife and Drum Band, rendered classical selections of Irish and popular airs most melodiously, and whose sweet sounds were wafted on the prevailing gentle zephyr to the farthest end of the field...

The Go-as-You-Please Race was the event of the evening, and throughout the length of the journey, viz, from Balbriggan to Naul, the route was lined with sightseers eager to see Pat White and Fagan tie for the championship...

White and Fagan kept together all the way from Balbriggan with Joey Connell in close

51

attendance. Coming by the Churchyard at Naul, White and Fagan came with a terrific burst, Fagan just winning by about 2 yards, midst great excitement, with Joey Connell close up third. Winner's time, 24 min; Connell's, 29 mins.[76]

That the shorter distance did not suit White was almost universally understood, and the loss did little to dampen interest in seeing him race again. In fact, from a betting point of view, his defeat would considerably lengthen his odds in any rematch. Four days after the race, therefore, Colgan contacted the *Irish Independent* seeking to organise another race, this time over twice the distance.

Pat White, of Richardstown, Donabate, the hero of two of the long-distance races promoted by our enterprising contemporary, the "Evening Herald", is anxious to meet P. Fagan of Dublin, in a race of ten miles or upwards for £10 a-side. Fagan, it will be remembered, finished second in the recent run to Naas, after leading nearly all the way. The match, if arranged, should certainly be interesting.[77]

It took three weeks to raise the purse and to secure an enclosed venue, but, on 2 July 1906, a date for a ten-mile head-to-head between the pair was announced in the pages of the *Drogheda Independent*.

On Sunday, July 15th, a Go-as-you-Please Race for £10 aside, will be held over the Ashtown Course, commencing at 3.30 pm. The competitors are Pat White, Donabate, and P. Fagan, Dublin. Both candidates have been so successful on all previous occasions in long-distance races that speculation is rife as to which will win the

Challenge. A visit to the Ashtown Course, on the 15th inst., will certainly be something to be remembered.[78]

The 'Ashtown Course' was a half-mile harness racing circuit close to Dublin's Phoenix Park. At ten miles, the planned race lay midway between each man's specialist distance. More importantly, the enclosed venue meant there would be substantial takings at the gate. And so it was to prove.

Yesterday's great trial of athletic stamina drew a huge crowd to the well-known Ashtown Trotting Enclosure. The race was over a distance of 10 miles, and the competitors were Pat White of Donabate – the winner of the "Herald" race from Dublin to Balbriggan in 1905, and again from Dublin to Naas last May – and "P. Fagan", a well-known ex-amateur harrier.

Both men had a large following, White's supporters hailing from Drogheda, Balbriggan, Navan and Skerries, while Fagan's effort was watched by a numerous gathering from the city. From the time the gates were thrown open at Ashtown, a continuous flow of anxious spectators assembled, and at the time of the start the muster totalled in or about 3,000.

There was a considerable amount of speculation, but it was only to be expected that White would be the favourite, and in the wagering that took place odds from 5/4 to 6/4 were freely laid on him. At no point was more than even money tendered against "Fagan," but both men had plenty of supporters.

A finer afternoon could not have been wished for, and, despite the strong sun, a cooling breeze rendered matters for the competitors really pleasant. The track, however, was a heavy one, and in the circumstances, the time for the journey – 57 minutes and 15 seconds – cannot be regarded as other than very creditable.

"Fagan" was first to appear on track and indulged in a preliminary canter. He looked trained to the ounce, and his backers appeared to have great confidence in him. A few moments later Pat White emerged from the enclosure clad in a green vest and white knickers. He, too, looked in splendid condition for the long journey, and received a great ovation on toeing the mark...

The start was timed for 3.30 and shortly after that hour Mr. Rynd took the men in hand.[79] Fagan at once took a slight lead, but before half a lap had been covered White headed him, and showed the way until three miles had been got over, when Fagan yet again went to the front.

The first half-mile had been covered in 2 mins 21 seconds, but they occupied 2 mins 37 seconds on the second lap so that the time for the first mile was 4 mins 58 seconds. They had kept very close company so far, and when they finished on the sixth lap Fagan was only a foot ahead.

From this, until the fifth mile had been left behind, the phases of the race were very varied, as may be gathered from the fact that the men led alternately, still running closely together. At the half distance Fagan settled down in front, but was never allowed to get far away from the Swords man, until a quarter of a mile from home, when he sprinted, and just before turning into the straight for home held a twenty yards advantage.

Then White seriously set to, and, rapidly catching his man, won a great race in what, considering the heavy state of the track, was a really good time. Fagan did not actually finish,

he being picked up by some of his admirers, a
yard or so from the tape. Needless to say, White
was accorded a great reception, while Fagan was
also well cheered, and indeed the race from start
to finish was of a stirring nature.[80]

On the afternoon following the race, when Pat
and his manager attended the offices of the
Evening Herald to collect their winnings, they
were informed of a challenge from J.J. Mullen, a
Wexford runner who had competed professionally
over distances from two to five miles in the late
1890s.[81] They accepted the challenge, but
Mullen, who had not raced for several years,
never followed up. White, however, was not short
of alternatives and, on 7 August, he won a 'go-as-
you-please' from Tullamore to Kilbeggan and back
– a distance of fifteen miles – against a field of
seventeen in a time of 1:29:30.[82]

One week after the Kilbeggan race, Pat's
brother, Peter, was dishonourably discharged
from the army for being both 'incorrigible and
worthless.' He had recently received two further
periods of detention of ten and fourteen days, for
bad behaviour. And that was just in July alone,
the second offence occurring just four days after
his release from detention for the first. Despite
his nine-year contract, the army had had enough.
Peter White was more trouble than he was
worth.[83]

Subsequent reports would claim that Peter's
dishonourable discharge came as the result of his
mother having bought him out of the remainder
of his contract.[84] There is no reference to this on
the surviving documents, which only refer to his
service and pension entitlements, but, if true, this

would have cost the White family a considerable sum. At the time, a 'discharge by purchase' could cost anything from £10 to £12. There would have been severe financial consequences for the entire family, Pat included. Equivalent to the annual cost of the lease, it would have wiped out the profits, threatened the farm, and most likely placed them in debt.

As for Pat, it wasn't all about racing. Mostly, people wanted to see him run, but occasionally, event organisers were happy to have him put in an appearance. On 26 August, for instance, though originally due to race Fagan again, Pat was instead invited to serve as a guest starter and handicapper for a four-and-a-half-mile road race from The Ward to Garristown as part of the Garristown Bazaar.[85] At the revival of the Naul 'pattern' in September 1906,[86] he was again engaged as the official handicapper and starter for another four-and-a-half-mile 'go as you please' from Ballyboughal to the Naul.[87]

White and Fagan would not race each other again that year until 14 October, when they would run from Donnycarney to Malahide in a six-mile road race promoted as part of the Malahide Sports. The resumption of their rivalry generated such interest that they were followed by 'a vast concourse' from start to finish. In a race of just four competitors, Pat emerged a clear winner over Fagan in second.[88]

Pat White was now enjoying such celebrity that a coursing greyhound was even named after him.[89] But although the prizemoney, appearance fees, and gambling winnings he had accumulated during the summer weekends were substantial, they were never enough to warrant him throwing in his job, and he continued to labour at Grace Dieu, a few hundred yards across the fields from his parents' cabin in Richardstown. In the person of John Dempsey, he had found not just a sympathetic employer, but a fan.

Pat was now twenty-seven, still single, and still living from time to time with his parents. He was earning a respectable income and making life a little easier for his family. His brother, Peter, on the other hand, was travelling in an entirely different direction.

On Sunday, 2 December 1906, Peter was arrested in Baldurgan while coursing in the company of about twenty young men on the lands of Michael Dodd, a local justice of the peace.[90] That he failed to escape with the others suggests that at least one of the dogs was his. Undeterred by his arrest, he was apprehended for a second time the following Sunday while coursing on the lands of Joseph Byrne at Cookstown.

Convicted, later that month, of 'trespass in pursuit of game', Peter was fined a guinea.[91] This time, none of his family were willing or able to bail him out and, unable to pay the fines, he returned to court on 9 January 1907 to be sentenced to a month in Kilmainham Gaol.[92] Following his release from this, his fifth term of imprisonment or detention in two years, Peter failed to turn his life around and continued to add to his reputation as a wastrel who had never done a hand's turn in his life:

> [Peter] White, when a young lad, was very wild. When quite a boy he ran away from home and joined the army from which he was subsequently "bought out" by his mother. He never is known

to have done an honest day's work: but kept himself alive by sponging from his parents and picking pockets at race meetings.[93]

That report was neither entirely fair nor accurate, for Peter was known to have helped his father around the farm and to have worked occasionally as a labourer in Ballyboughal. But a reputation for criminality had stuck to him and, inclined to bouts of prolonged revelry, he had similarly gained a reputation as a prankster. Local tradition has it that he would steal women's knickers off their washing lines and hang them as bunting around the locality for a laugh.[94] Despite multiple arrests and imprisonment, he would continue to keep a greyhound until at least 1916, when his paramilitary activities began to take precedence.[95]

THREE IN A ROW?

ON 8 FEBRUARY 1907, Bernard Colgan placed the following advertisement in the pages of the *Evening Herald*.

PAT WHITE TO ALL IRELAND

Pat White, of Donabate, is willing to run any man in Ireland from 5 miles to 10 miles for £10 a-side.[96]

There were, alas, no takers and, as May approached, Pat gave up seeking head-to-head matches to prepare for that year's *Herald* race, which was to be run over the same course as the previous year. The talk of the betting ring this time centred on who, if anyone, could stop White from completing the hat trick.[97] Would Fagan, having learnt a painful lesson about pace judgement in the previous year's race, be able to make the necessary adjustment? Had any of the others improved significantly over the winter? Were any of the dark horses worth a flutter?

In the absence of a clear challenger, it became nearly impossible to get decent odds against White, who had every reason to feel confident. But then disaster struck. White fell victim to Achilles tendonitis. The pain was at its worst first thing in the morning, but as it tended to decrease with activity, he decided not to withdraw.

Winning three successive *Herald* races would confirm him as the best Irish distance runner of his generation, but, even if he were to lose, the prizes for the minor placings were still of such magnitude that he could ill afford to scorn them.

> From a comparatively early hour ... the streets on the South side of the city leading to Inchicore were black with people making their way towards the starting point. The grey promise of the earlier hours was falsified towards midday by a brilliant burst of sunshine... A strong south-easterly breeze was blowing, but it did not materially discomfort the spectators, though the thirty competitors probably had cause for complaint.[98]

White was joined on the starting line by Pat Fagan, the runner-up from the previous year, and Pat Conway of Waterford, the runner-up in 1905. These three were considered the favourites, though most of the 'smart' money appeared to be on White.

> The scenes on the way to Inchicore were suggestive of the Epsom Road on Derby day, when London goes down to watch the race for the Blue Ribbon of the turf. Tramcar conductors barricaded their cars – crowded ere they left College Green – and spent strenuous time in vigorous expostulation with the persistent pedestrians who, nothing daunted by the interposing chain, sought to board each vehicle as it passed.
> Cyclists innumerable incurred the anathemas of those who were using 'Shank's mare', and the clangour of their bells intermingled with the coarse cries of motor cars and the objurgations

of irate jarveys, who found their driving skill put
severely to the test in the hurrying crowd.[99]

Herald Race Cup 1907.

The *Herald* race had by now transcended class
and prejudice, and, unlike many other sporting
events of the day, there was no entrance fee.
Attracting spectators from all walks of life, it had
become a family day out, a festive 'occasion' that
was not to be missed. And like most festive
'occasions', people came as much to witness the
crowds as the race.

Nearing the starting point the crush became
greater. One wondered if all the population of the
Irish metropolis was concentrating itself upon
Inchicore Bridge and speculated as to the empty
appearance of the other parts of the city if that
was the case. All sorts and conditions of men,
women, and even children were hurrying along
towards the country.

Here, Paterfamilias and Materfamilias, eminently
respectable, and acutely conscious of the fact, were

dragging along a reluctant offspring, whose footsteps were delayed rather than hastened by the bribe of an orange. There a group of young men were glowing with the stress of unwonted exercise after indoor work.

The aroma of a prosperous city merchant's cigars mingled with the petrol perfume of his motor as he whirled past in a cloud of dust; a carload of sporting gents shouted "sporting offers" to friends in the crowd, secure in the consciousness that the speed of their hack saved them from acceptance of the bets; a barefooted youth on an antique "crock" rang his bell as imperiously as any of his fellow-cyclists on twentieth-century machines; orange girls shrieked their "two a penny" from the kerbstone in sturdy contest with the lusty voices of boys selling "Herald Race Cards", – babel indescribable, dust and hurry everywhere, good humour abounding...

The competitors divested themselves of their ordinary clothes and fought their way to the line where the starter, Mr. Kenneth A. Rynd, stood, whistle in hand. Their discarded garments were placed in the "Herald" vans, which were in readiness for the purpose and all present were breathlessly waiting on the word to go.[100]

At the finish line in Naas, the scene was just as chaotic. Despite competition from the Irish International Exhibition in Dublin and a major Gaelic football match in Kildare, numbers were even larger than the previous year.[101] The bridge that spanned the canal was so congested that not all of the competitors were able to push through the crowds to reach the start in time. The starter, however, observing that all of the favourites were present, decided not to wait.

At one o'clock to the minute the whistle sounded, and, amid the cheers of the spectators, the athletes started on their long journey. P Fagan, of Dublin, who came second in last year's race over the same course, led by a few yards, and received many shouts of encouragement, as also did Pat White (who secured first prize in 1906 and 1905) and C. Thompson, Dublin, all of whom were strong favourites.

Almost ten minutes after the start C. O'Brien, Dublin, arrived, and quickly stripping to racing costume started out undauntedly in the wake of the other competitors, who had up to that time vanished in the distance, followed and surrounded by cycles, motors and hackney cars...

Bright as was the sunlight, it was difficult to see more than a hundred yards one way or the other, and the difficulty of following the race in all its details was enhanced by the throngs of cars and the cohorts of cyclists who were making the journey. Here and there, one could discern a competitor threading his way through the dense procession. But the number was the surest guide to his identity, for after a time layers of dust so obscured everyone's features that one's most intimate relatives might be pardoned for passing without a nod of recognition.

Last year's runner-up, P Fagan, led the way. Flanked by cyclists and attended by a friend on a car, who now and then flicked the dust off his face, he travelled at a clinking rate. After about two miles he held a lead of nearly 600 yards and maintained it almost to Kill. He has a fine style of running – perhaps the most attractive of any in the struggle.[102]

At every roadside cottage for at least three miles beyond Inchicore, people gathered to watch, with chairs arranged in front gardens to accommodate family and friends. Old women and little girls noted the competitors' race numbers as they passed and then looked up their names on the race card to see if it was someone famous. From the start, Pat was quickly surrounded by cyclists.

> The winner of the race for the last two years, Pat White, Donabate, escorted by a phalanx of enthusiastic admirers, covered the distance to Red Cow in 13 minutes. He was going in great form at a strong, steady pace, and his performance was particularly fine in view of the fact that he was suffering from a strained sinew, for which he had to wear an electric stocking.
>
> For a considerable part of the distance Lance Corporal Hill ran almost abreast with him, but the pace was too hot for the corporal, and he had fallen out before Blackchurch was reached. Going in easy style, Fagan passed through Blackchurch 57 minutes after the start, followed a minute later by Thompson and Conway. All three looked fresh...
>
> Conway, who gamely contested two previous "Herald" races, being placed second in 1905 and fourth in 1906, was travelling splendidly. Two minutes afterwards White arrived, and three minutes subsequently Cusack and Lynch. The others were tailed off and were passing this point up to 2.20 p.m.[103]

Fagan, who seemed to have learnt little from his experience of the previous year, set off again at a fast pace, reaching Kill in just over an hour and eighteen minutes, a full minute ahead of White and Thompson, who appeared to be running comfortably within themselves at this stage.

Approaching Kill, Thompson overhauled and
passed Fagan, with Conway close up. The next
feature of the race was Conway taking the lead
amidst the cheers of a number of soldier
friends who had cycled from the Curragh to
meet him, and, as was subsequently learned,
with confident anticipation of his victory.[104]

Racing conditions were about as difficult as they
could be, and fifty-seven minutes into the race,
while Fagan was passing through Blackchurch, no
fewer than seven competitors abandoned the race.

The dust was blinding. It filled the nose, mouth
and ears of all. Enough road material was
carried to Naas on the clothes and features of the
occupants of jaunting cars, of cyclists, and
competitors, to wring the heart of a road
contractor. Hooting motors spurned it around in
clouds; it eddied off circling wheels, settled here
there and everywhere. The route lay through
some of the finest pastoral scenery in Leinster,
but it could not be seen except in spots, and few
had any eyes for it.
    Almost everyone was a partisan of one
competitor or other. "Go on, Fagan," "Good old
White," "Let them have it, Conway," and such
like encouraging cries echoed along the way from
throats hoarse with dust.[105]

At approximately 2 p.m., the newspaper vans
began to arrive in Naas, followed two minutes
later by a convoy of cars carrying staff reporters
from various newspapers, as well as several
dignitaries and officials. Their arrival ignited an
eruption of cheers from the crowd, heightening

65

the anticipation that the leaders would arrive shortly thereafter.

> At Johnstown, Conway was two minutes ahead of White, who had passed the others, and whose nearest competitor behind was Thompson. From this on to Naas Bridge, Conway kept his lead, and at the bridge was three minutes ahead of White and five ahead of Lynagh. His reception by the great gathering on the bridge was most enthusiastic, and the rest of his progress to the tape – and to victory – was made amidst continuous cheers.[106]

Forty minutes after the race cars entered Naas, Fagan entered the town, four minutes and forty-two seconds ahead of White, who in turn led Lynagh by two minutes and fifteen seconds. Pat had lost the race, but his runner-up position had preserved his reputation as a top contender and kept his name prominent among those to whom a lucrative head-to-head challenge might subsequently be made.

THE DROGHEDA DEBACLE

THERE IS NO record of Pat and Peter White having ever raced against each other in the same race. Peter may have joined Pat on the occasional training walk or run, but the only record of the two even competing at the same event was at the Swords Sports on 25 August 1907.[107] Here, despite his ongoing Achilles issue, Pat participated in a four-mile race in which he set the early pace for Tom McCann of Balbriggan until, at the two-mile mark, injury forced him to withdraw. Peter, for his part, ran in the mile, where he finished third.[108]

One week later, on September 1, Pat renewed his rivalry with Fagan in a nine-mile race between Ballough and Gormanstown. He finished fourth, some forty yards behind the winner, Frank Curtis.[109] Disregarding the injury had clearly aggravated the problem, but the racing season was short, and he was reluctant to surrender the opportunity to make money while it lasted.

Six days after the Gomanston race, Peter White decided to try his hand at the longer distances favoured by his brother and entered a six-mile road race from Man O'War to the Naul, held as part of the recently revived Naul Patron celebrations. He finished third, in a time of 40:30, ninety seconds behind the winner. Here, once again, despite this being a local event, where everyone, including reporters, would have been

67

more than familiar with the names of the various local townlands, Peter was listed in the race results as 'Peter White, Donabate'. Richardstown, it seemed, was just too small to be recognised outside of its immediate hinterland.

Between the signing of race contracts and their attendance at various political meetings, Pat White and Bernard Colgan had seen a lot of each other in the early months of 1907. As might be expected from an agricultural labourer, Pat was particularly exercised on the subject of land rights and regularly attended Naul branch meetings of the United Irish League, as well as Sinn Féin meetings on labourers' employment rights.[110] They should have been meeting more often to arrange races than at political meetings, but Pat's injury proved annoyingly persistent.

It took months rather than weeks for Pat's injury to clear up, and by the time it had, the summer racing season was almost over. In search of opportunities to capitalise on his client's fame before winter set in and the crowds stopped venturing out to watch foot races, Colgan placed the following notice in the *Evening Herald* of 26 September 1907:

PAT WHITE TO ALL IRELAND

Pat White, of Donabate, will run any man in Ireland for £10 a-side. An early reply to Mr. B. Colgan, The Naul, Balbriggan, will lead to business.[111]

There was that word again. Business! Nothing is known for certain about Colgan's financial relationship with White, but there must have been something in it for him, or he would scarcely have continued to 'handle' White for so long. Whatever it was, Pat almost certainly never got to keep 100% of his winnings and could not afford to give up the day job, though how much of that had to do with an unequal split, and how much to do with Peter's allged buy out from the army, is anyone's guess.

Colgan's latest newspaper challenge managed to hook Tom Hynes, who had finally given up on trying to rescue his amateur status. A race was scheduled for the Boys' Brigade Grounds in Drogheda on Sunday, 20 October, yet another enclosed venue at which an entrance fee could be charged. Upon reading of the proposed event, the professional runner, George Blennerhassett Tincler, a.k.a. 'The Gander', promptly announced that he would challenge the winner.

A former Clonliffe Harrier, Tincler had turned professional in 1894. Three years later, he travelled to the USA to race the Irish American Tommy Conneff at the Massachusetts Oval. Before a crowd of 10,000, which included Theodore Roosevelt, Tincler won easily in 4:15.2. All told, he won all but one of the thirty-six races on his American tour, including the American 2-Mile Championship.

The year after his return from America, Tincler defeated Fred Bacon in a highly anticipated clash for the Professional World Mile Championship at Rochdale, winning in 4:16.4. As one of the world's great milers, he had been entered in the 400m and 1500m professional races at the 1900 Paris Olympics but failed to appear for either. He would also fail to secure a match with White or Hynes, presumably because neither was willing to drop down to the shorter distances.

To ensure a large turnout for the Drogheda event, two additional races were added to the race card: a one-mile race between Thompson and Fagan, and a four-mile race between the same pair, both with a £5 purse.[112]

> The tussle for the Irish Championship will be a determined one, and should easily prove the most interesting event of its kind held in Ireland for some time. White, of Donabate, will work like a Trojan to win the coveted title of Champion. To offer any opinion as to the result would be unsafe, as in the present Champion [Hynes] he has a foeman worthy of his steel.[113]

This was Bernard Colgan's first attempt to promote a race at a closed venue since the race between White and Fagan at Ashtown the previous July.[114] The timing and location could hardly have been better.

> Great interest is being taken in the contests in Drogheda, and owing to the "slump" in amateur athletics at present prevailing, it is not unlikely that a few more of the "good uns" will don the garb of professionalism in the near future.[115]

Having confirmed four of the top names in Irish professional racing for a three-race card, the Drogheda event promised to attract a far greater crowd than the three thousand that attended the Ashtown event the previous year. Indeed, such was the interest surrounding the event that a special train was even arranged from Amiens Street to ferry intending spectators from Dublin.[116]

PAT WHITE (DONABATE) v. T. HYNES (GALWAY).

The match over five miles has now been arranged between the above well-known runners, and we understand the money, £10 a-side, has been deposited. The race will take place probably on tomorrow (Sunday) fortnight at either Drogheda or Dundalk and, at either of those venues, there should be a good crowd to witness the contest, for White is an idol with the folk in and around the historic Boyne.[117]

The Boys' Brigade ground, a five-acre site off Drogheda's Windmill Lane, was just a thirty-minute walk from the train station and a fifteen-minute walk from the town centre. No admission price was stated on the poster for the event, but there almost certainly was one, because turnstiles were in operation on the day. A shortage of manpower, however, saw them quickly overwhelmed.[118]

On Sunday last the five-mile professional go-as-you-please race between Pat White, Donabate, and Tom Hynes, Galway, came to a speedy termination. Both men turned up and there were large crowds in attendance also. It would appear that when about two hundred people had passed through the turnstile a man under the influence of drink thought to enter, but was refused admission.

The crowd by this time, eager to hasten in, passed on and the result was that the gate was swept clear in. Owing to that fact, the committee in charge refused to run the race at all. This was certainly hard lines on the many who had come long distances to see the event which promised very much, and its putting off went to show the credentials of professional racing.

No price for admission was stated on the poster, but even so, the people would gladly have paid to see the match. Drogheda was stated to be a suitable venue for such a contest, but after last Sunday's display one is inclined to think that "tin," not venue, is the basis on which professionalism is going.[119]

Having witnessed the interest shown in Drogheda and gained extra, albeit unwanted, publicity from the cancellation, neither Hynes' nor White's backers were willing to forego a bumper payday, and so the match was hastily rearranged for 10 November at the Show Grounds in Navan. On this occasion, the race went off without a hitch.

The afternoon held up gloriously fine, and the track was in admirable order. There was quite a large crowd of spectators present when the men lined up at the starting point, Hynes looking exceedingly fit.

The Galway man took a slight lead at the start, being closely followed by the Donabate pro. The latter had not gone far when one of his pumps loosened and this fact alone practically put an end to his chances of winning. Hynes, striding in beautiful fashion, forged ahead, and quickly had gained a winning lead, which he maintained to the finish, clocking 25 mins 30 secs for the full distance. White continued to run gamely, and completed the course somewhat exhausted.

By his taking part in yesterday's race Hynes has once more forfeited his status as an amateur, and he is now anxious to meet any of the "stars" in England, Scotland, or Wales.

Certainly, he stripped in the pink of condition, and had he been fully extended his time would have been much faster.[120]

On 19 November, Colgan posted another challenge to Hynes, which Hynes promptly accepted on the condition that the race would take place on the grounds of Galway Grammar School. He had accommodated White on two occasions by leaving his native county. It was time for White to face him on his own turf.[121] Pat accepted, and a five-mile race was scheduled for St. Stephen's Day.[122]

Things did not go any better for Pat in Galway than they had at Navan, as he and Hynes had to race in the teeth of a storm. Hynes won again, in a time of 25:30, a full minute ahead of Pat. Both were reported to have looked surprisingly fresh at the finish.

As Pat was preparing for his race with Hynes, his brother Peter, who may well have been joining him on his long runs at this stage, finally decided to try his hand at cross-country and joined Pat's old club, Santry Harriers. Peter would run for them during the 1908 season,[123] but after that he would give up on the longer distances altogether. He would enter the occasional open mile at summer fetes and sports days for several years afterwards, but without noteworthy success.[124]

1907 had been a mixed year for White, but it was already clear that if he were to have a future in professional sport, it would be at the marathon.[125] He was fast enough to be competitive at the shorter distances but, more workhorse than a racehorse, he was nowhere near fast enough to win against the specialists. It was apparent to everyone by now that he was, in equestrian parlance, quite simply 'a stayer.'

TROUBLE ON THE HILLS

ON 5 APRIL 1906, the Neapolitan volcano, Mount Vesuvius, erupted, killing more than two hundred people. The cost of repairing the damage and caring for the thousands made homeless by the eruption had fallen unexpectedly on the Italian government. Forced to redirect funds to rebuild Naples, they abandoned their plans to host the 1908 Olympic Games.

Photo of Vesuvius Eruption, 6 April 1906.

The Olympics were subsequently awarded to London and scheduled to take place between 27 April and 31 October 1908. A new stadium was hastily built at the White City in Shepherd's Bush to provide the centrepiece of an Olympics that would prove to be the longest on record.

This would be a summer of sport like no other, generating such public interest that it would not only establish the Olympic gold medal as the epitome of sporting achievement, but also see the implementation of standardised rules for several sports and the tradition of walking behind national flags. Throughout Europe, this blend of international attention and national self-interest would mark the beginning of the end for professional athletics. And yet, for all that, over in Ireland, the sporting conversation was still very much centred on that year's *Herald* race.

White City Stadium in 1908.

1907 had ended for Pat with a persistent Achilles tendon injury and a poor run of results. But for every defeat, there had been a plausible excuse, and he saw no reason to alter a training regime that had proved so successful for him in the past. There was, however, to be an additional challenge in 1908. The new course would be exceptionally hilly.

Pat White did not like hills. There were few enough around Fingal, and he was not accustomed or indeed partial to training or running on them. In this, he was not alone. Many prospective competitors, Fagan included, had been quick to recognise the extra challenge that the hills would pose and had been training regularly on the course. The first cut of silage, however, was already underway, and Pat was limited in the lead-up to the race to a solitary inspection of the course, made on Sunday, 22 June.

> Judging by the number of men training daily over the course, and the fast times reported to have been done by several local runners, it won't be "go as you please" for the winner, but go as fast as you can. Fagan, who has run so prominently in previous "Herald" Races, has been putting in good work over the course, as have Thompson, who was fourth, and Atkinson, who finished sixth last year. Hynes is a certain starter if his leg is well, and White, who has won the event twice, had a trial spin over the journey yesterday.[126]

Once again, the race proved to be the premier sporting event in Ireland, attracting over thirty thousand people to the course. Along with Hynes and Fagan, Pat was again regarded as one of the bookies' favourites.[127]

> There was considerable animation around the betting stands, where odds were being given against all but the three just mentioned. They were the "favourites" as our horsey friends would say, and the bookmakers, knowing them all by experience, took no risks.[128]

The runners were sent off at precisely 2:10 p.m. on Sunday, June 21, under clear skies and oppressive heat. After a fast first mile, the pace eventually settled down, and White, Hynes, Fagan, Curtis, and Timmins formed a breakaway group at the front, with Murphy and McArdle of Dunleer trailing about two hundred yards behind.

The leaders continued to run together as they passed through the five-mile point at Stackallen Cross, but by mile seven, Fagan and Hynes had begun to pull ahead. Defying the gradient on the steep climb to Slane, the pair dug deep, and by the time they exited the town, they held a two-minute lead over White and Curtis, with Timmins and Thompson a further three minutes adrift.

> Near where the little river Mettock cuts through the road in Rossin, a point that is reached by Fagan and Hynes in exactly one hour from the time of starting, both men look very dust beaten, and their condition was hardly bettered by the dozens of cyclists that surrounded them. Dozens, too, accompanied Curtis, who was leading White, both looking comparatively fresh...[129]

By the time Pat reached Slane, he was running alone in third place. He'd lost a lot of time on the hill, but was far from alone in his suffering. Many of the competitors behind him had also been forced to stop at the top and catch their breath before continuing.

Fagan, by now, was flying, and by the time the leader, Hynes, reached Slane Castle, a mile further down the road, he held only a slight lead over the Dubliner. Exhausted on the hill, White by that time had slipped back through the field.

> Up Fernhill was another very stiff climb, and it proved too much for Hynes, who dropped back. Fagan ploughed along through clouds of dust

with a considerable lead over Curtis, a lead that increased yard by yard. The Obelisk was now in view and Fagan was able to take things easily. He looked back again and again, but at this stage he had completely "streeted" his opponents. Indeed, away in the distance, one could see nothing but banks of dust, and hear nothing but the roars of thousands...

It was now a run-in to the finish, and the lane of people that stretched away into the town soon spread the news along. The first man was in sight. Who was it? What was his number? The number was 18; the name was Fagan. The cry arose – Fagan! Fagan! FAGAN!

Into the town he dashed, limbs painted and hair matted with dust and perspiration. For years he had been striving for this honour, and now it was his. When he had breasted the tape, his friends crowded around him to "fan" him and refresh him, but he waved them aside and looked game enough to go on some miles more.[130]

Fagan's winning time was 1:37:00. White, who had rallied on the flatter roads approaching Drogheda, could manage no better than seventh, for which he received a handsome pipe, presented to him by the well-known grocer, J.J. Callan of West Street, Drogheda. Of the thirty-four who started, only fifteen would finish. Indeed, it would be 6 p.m. before the last of the tail-enders limped into town, by which time Fagan was well on his way to Dublin, where his jubilant supporters would carry him shoulder-high from the train.

White, who knew himself to be in far better shape than the *Herald* result suggested, was eager for a rematch. It was the hills that had done for him, he was convinced, and not the distance. The first opportunity to redeem himself, however,

would not arrive until August – an open race from Newry to Rostrevor and back, a trip of twenty-one and three-quarter miles.

> The "Go-as-you-please" Race, promoted by the "Newry Reporter" was about the last thing in novelty in regard to competitions of this class. The race was open to all Ireland. It started at Trevor Hill, Newry, and the competitors ran to Rostrevor, and back to Newry.
>
> Thousands of people witnessed the contest on Saturday. There were prizes galore. Several traders offered prizes to the first man to call at their houses after completing the race. There were pounds of tea and pounds of soap, and prizes for youngest married men and oldest married men and bachelors, and lightest men and heaviest men.[131]

The Newry race attracted a stellar field, including the *Herald* winner, Fagan. But on the flat course, White decimated the field, winning in 1:53, a good six and a half minutes ahead of Fagan. A world-class performance by the standards of the day, it passed largely unnoticed and unremarked in the outside world.

White and Fagan would meet again in September, at the annual Naul Sports at Reynoldstown, their presence facilitated once again by Bernard Colgan, who once again acted as Honorary Secretary and Clerk of the course. The highlight of the day was a professional race from Skerries to the Naul.

> The committee left nothing undone to make things pleasant for all. The 'bookies' from Dublin were present in large numbers, and of the 11 items on the programme the first was a 'go as you please' race from Skerries to the Naul, a distance of nine miles.[132]

In glorious summer weather, the crowds thronged the streets of the towns along the route to watch White defeat Fagan by almost two minutes. The winning time was 51:30. Frank Curtis was third.

THOMAS ASHE AND THE BLACK RAVENS

A MUSICAL ASIDE. Between 1905 and 1908, Pat White won numerous prizes for which he had little or no immediate use. Most of these related to the consumption of tobacco, from which he steadfastly abstained. Perhaps the most significant of these unwanted prizes, however, was a set of bagpipes.

The race for which White received the pipes has been lost to history, but his subsequent disposal of the instrument proved more than a little noteworthy. That casual act of generosity, in fact, would play a significant role in the musical history of Fingal.

The pipes had lain unused in the cabin at Richardstown until 1908, when a twenty-four-year-old country schoolmaster from Kerry, Thomas Patrick Ashe, arrived in Lusk. Ashe had come to take up the role of principal at Corduff National School.

A native Irish speaker and the son of a Gaelic scholar, Ashe quickly made his mark in the locality and became heavily involved in nationalist politics. Immediately upon his arrival, according to his sister, Nora, he began to publicly declare his nationalist credentials by having the children march over a Union Jack at each morning's assembly.[133] Ashe would later become a founding member of the Lusk Branch of the Irish Volunteers.

Given his political affiliations, it is more than

Thomas Ashe

likely that Ashe would have come into contact with Pat's brother, Peter, who was similarly active in republican circles. But whether through mutual republican connections or because of their respective sporting activities, Pat White and

83

Thomas Ashe came into contact sometime in 1908 and, upon discovering Ashe's interest in music (he was reputedly a fine singer), Pat gifted him the unused and unwanted set of bagpipes. Ashe immediately set about teaching himself to play.

Sometime about 1910, Ashe would join forces with John Rooney of Raheny House, Lusk, a local farmer. With financial help from the Naomh MacCullen Hurling Club, of which Ashe was a founding member and team goalkeeper, and Rooney an outfield player who could reputedly hit the sliotar from one goalmouth to the other,[134] they would start a club for bagpipers that would become famous throughout Ireland as the Black Raven Pipe Band.

It was not uncommon, prior to 1916, for piping clubs to be established as a cover for I.R.B. activity. Indeed, Pat White's great rival, Thomas Hynes, would join one such club, Cumann Píobairí na Gaillimhe, sometime about 1912, and through it find his way into the Irish Republican Brotherhood. As a leading member of the I.R.B., Ashe would later count amongst those under his command the revolutionary leader and hero of the Irish struggle for independence, Michael Collins.

That close link between republican paramilitaries and pipe bands would be further underscored at the 1914 Oireachtas in Killarney, when the Black Raven Pipe band would lead a march of two and a half thousand Irish Volunteers through the town armed with rifles and in full military regalia. Three years later, the Black and Tans would raid the Black Ravens' band room, seizing many instruments and the by now famous Black Raven Flag.

Had Pat White not gifted Thomas Ashe his unwanted set of bagpipes, Ashe might never have taken up the instrument, and the Black Raven Pipe Band, which would win the 2024 World Pipe Band Championships in Glasgow, might never have been formed. From little acorns!

THE 1908 OLYMPIC
MARATHON

PROFESSIONAL FOOT RACES over distances up to and including twenty-five miles had regularly been held throughout Europe during the 19th century. The first to be actually called a 'marathon,' however, did not take place until 1896, when the first Games of the Modern Olympiad were held in Athens. The race had been named to commemorate a legendary twenty-five-mile run by a Greek messenger boy, Pheidippides, from the town of Marathon to the city of Athens, to bring news of the Greek victory over the Spartans in 490 BCE.

According to legend, having uttered the immortal *Nenikekamen!* (We won!), Pheidippides collapsed and died. Whether there ever was a Pheidippides, or even a Eucles (the name by which Plutarch identified the runner), or even a single messenger who had run the entire distance, mattered little to an Olympic organising committee determined to celebrate a classical feat of endurance. As a result, the first 'marathon' was born.[135]

That 1896 race, just short of twenty-five miles and won by Spyridon Louis, a twenty-four-year-old Greek goatherd, established a trend for naming any race longer than ten miles a 'marathon.' Beyond that, it failed to spark much interest in endurance running, a cause that was hardly helped by the fact that subsequent 'marathon' races had all too often proved to be highly unregulated affairs mired in allegations of cheating.

At the 1900 Olympic marathon in Paris, for example, the American delegation accused the winner, Michael Theato, of having taken shortcuts. They claimed that, as a French baker, he was intimately familiar with every backstreet in the city. It later transpired that Theato was neither a baker nor a native of Paris, having been raised in Luxembourg. Nevertheless, the legitimacy of his victory remains clouded in controversy to this day.

A similar scandal befell the 1904 Olympic marathon in St. Louis, Missouri, when the first man over the finish line, an American named Fred Lorz, later admitted to having hitched a ride in a car between miles nine and twenty, and to having resumed running only when the car broke down. The man subsequently declared the winner would also admit to having fuelled his run with a cocktail of brandy, egg whites, and rat poison (an early form of doping).

At the time, alcohol was the order of the day and commonly believed to be healthier than unchlorinated tap water. Rat poison, on the other hand, was known to be dangerous because it contained strychnine, a colourless, odourless drug which, when taken in minute doses of 5 mg or less, was believed to act as a stimulant. The abuse of the drug, however, was so widespread during the early days of the modern Olympics that athletes frequently became habituated to it and could tolerate doses that would kill an ordinary person.

By 1908, the public perception of marathon

running was far from the heroic ideal envisaged by the organisers of the first games in 1896, and the wisdom of including the event in future games was being widely questioned. All of that, however, was about to change, and change heroically.

The 1908 London Olympic marathon took place on the hot and humid afternoon of Friday, 24 July. The distance, initially intended to be 'about 26 miles' plus a lap of the track, had been extended at the last minute when it was decided to push back the start to the lawns of Windsor Castle in order that the Princess of Wales could start the race in the presence of the royal grandchildren.[136]

Another change to the original course was subsequently required when the planned entrance to the stadium was found to be unsuitable, necessitating the use of an alternative entrance, which meant that finishers would now run less than the scheduled full lap of the track if they were to finish, as planned, in front of the royal box. And so, between the jigs and the reels, the final distance of the course was extended to 42.195km. This 'London distance' would slowly become accepted as the standard distance for all championship 'marathons' and remains so to this day.[137]

Fifty-five competitors from sixteen nations lined up at the start of the Olympic marathon in 1908, but, as the field was restricted to amateur runners only, none of Ireland's top long-distance athletes could participate. The race, nevertheless, was not entirely devoid of Irish interest.

The pre-race favourite, the cigar-smoking Canadian, Tom Longboat of the Onondaga Nation, was managed by Pat Flanagan of Kilmallock, Co.

Limerick, a Toronto hotel owner, gambler, and sports entrepreneur. In the lead-up to the games, Longboat had spent considerable time in County Limerick, where large crowds had gathered to watch him train. That he was there at all, however, was almost as controversial as Thomas Hynes' return to the amateur ranks in 1903.

As an openly professional athlete, Pat White was barred from competing in the 1908 Olympics. Tom Longboat, on the other hand, was still allowed to compete, despite, like Thomas Hynes, having lost his amateur standing with the American Amateur Athletic Union, which felt that his avaricious Irish manager had been playing too fast and loose with the rules of amateurism.[138] The Canadians, however, reluctant to lose the gold medal favourite, refused to accept the American ban, and Longboat was cleared to race.

Also of Irish interest was the irrepressible Johnny Hayes. Born and raised in a New York tenement (apart from a short spell in Canada), Hayes was the eldest son of Michael and Ellen Hayes of Silver Street, Nenagh, who had left Ireland in 1880.[139] Hayes would represent the United States.

And finally, there was Charles Archer Hefferon, the English-born son of an Irish father and English mother. He would be representing South Africa, the newest addition to the British Empire. The British press viewed thirty-year-old Hefferon as *their* best chance of denying the Americans yet another gold medal in a Games the latter had thus far dominated.

Anti-American hostility was rife at the 1908 games, and one of the largely unacknowledged reasons for this had its roots in the anti-Irish sentiment that was widespread in Britain at the time. This sentiment was partly due to racial prejudice and partly to the political activities of the Home Rule movement. The boycott of the Games by many Irish athletes, on account of the British Olympic Committee's refusal to allow them to compete under their own flag when other parts of the Empire had been permitted to do so, had also garnered much sympathy within the American team, a significant number of whom were Irish-born or of Irish descent.

> Only a few Irish Athletes participated for "Great Britain and Ireland," but many Irish American athletes competed very effectively for the United States. The problem of Irish nationalism and home rule colored these athletes' reactions to the British and may also have affected the British officials' responses to contested results.[140]

During the Games, such bias would never have been hinted at, let alone openly admitted. Later that year, however, in the 19 November edition of the *Times,* it would be openly acknowledged by at least one correspondent that one of the unspoken reasons for the open hostility between British and American athletes during the Games was the number of Irish-Americans who competed. 'It might almost be said,' the writer complained, 'that the British athletes at the Stadium competed with Irishmen, not with Americans.' [141]

Come the start of the marathon, the over-excited British runners went out much too fast and, having led the race for the first ten miles, then faded badly. At seventeen miles, the lead was held by the South African, Hefferon, who was closely followed by the Italian, Pietri, and the Canadian, Longboat. Following an unsuccessful surge at sixteen miles, Longboat began to flag, and Hayes, who had run conservatively for the first half of the race, started to close in on him. By the time Longboat collapsed at mile twenty, the original field of seventy-five athletes had dwindled to just twenty-seven.

Close to Shepherd's Bush, twenty-two-year-old Dorando Pietri took the lead. The little Italian baker, in his white shirt, baggy red shorts and a head covered by a knotted red handkerchief, staggered into a stadium packed with 70,000 spectators. At that stage, he held a substantial lead on Hayes, who was running strongly in second.

Pietri, however, was running on fumes. He had hit the proverbial 'wall' and was rapidly losing control of his legs. Barely conscious of his surroundings or capable of walking without assistance, he had been undone by the heat, the extended length of the course, and, it was widely rumoured at the time, by an overdose of strychnine, though the latter was never confirmed as fact.[142]

In the final stages of the race, Longboat had experienced a collapse similar to that of his Italian counterpart. This led to allegations from Canadian team manager J. Howard Crocker, who suggested that Longboat had been unknowingly doped by his Irish manager, Tom Flanagan, who was rumoured to have bet heavily on the race outcome.[143]

As for Pietri, five times he staggered or collapsed inside the stadium, and five times he was helped to his feet by British Officials determined to deny the Americans another victory. Anxious to ensure he did not die in front of the Queen, the Chief Medical Officer, Dr Michael Bulger, a Dubliner, even stepped in to render medical assistance. Massaging Pietri's legs, he helped him to rise.

Pietri Falls on the Stadium Track, 1 Aug 1908.

With Hayes rapidly closing, Pietri, surrounded by helpers, managed to summon enough strength for a short spurt. Caught as he collapsed over the finish line, the barely conscious Italian was quickly stretchered away. Thirty seconds later, Hayes crossed the line under his own steam. Hefferon came in third. Both were of Irish extraction.

As the Italians celebrated, the Americans protested, and, after several hours of deliberation, Pietri was disqualified for having received illegal assistance. Hayes was now declared the winner, and the American, Joe Forshaw, promoted to third.

Pietri (left) and Hayes (right) cross the finish line.

The sympathy of the British press lay not with Hayes but with the plucky Italian, whose much-vaunted heroism had better caught the public imagination than the achievements of the actual medalists. Queen Alexandra would later present him with a special gold trophy, Irving Berlin would compose a comic song in praise of him,[144] and the King would name a horse in his honour. A craze for marathon running had been born.

In the wake of the dramatic conclusion to the Olympic marathon, Hayes' triumph was hailed by Irish nationalists and their American cousins with equal fervour and delight. His victory, fraught with symbolism, earned him an invitation to the House of Commons, where he was received by several Irish Members of Parliament and photographed in their company. The political motives underpinning such photographs and public celebrations would be no less potent two months hence, when Pat White would find himself at the centre of a similar, if not greater, media frenzy.

There were no less than thirty-three Irish-born medallists at the 1908 Olympic Games,[145] and, back in Ireland, their success on the international stage gave an enormous boost to national self-esteem and morale, even if the celebration of those medals was necessarily diluted by the fact that their recipients had all been competing in the colours of a foreign country.

Irish nationalism was on the rise. The G.A.A. had been in existence for twenty-four years, and the influence of the Gaelic League was growing steadily. No less than 600 branches of the latter were currently providing Irish language classes, organising Irish-speaking social gatherings, publishing a newspaper and leading campaigns to have the Irish language integrated into the national educational system.

Culturally, the Irish identity was being asserted with increasing confidence, but in the sporting arena, it was being stifled by the requirement to compete under a foreign flag. Politically, I.R.B. activity was similarly on the rise. The country was less than eight years from the Easter Rising and hungry for opportunities to wave the green flag.

Had the Irish-born medallists been able to compete under their own flag, Ireland would have finished fourth on the medal table, behind Great Britain and the United States, but ahead of France, Canada, Germany, and Hungary, and with more medals in total than third-placed Sweden. How much greater would the joy have been, had even one of those medallists been competing solely as an Irishman?

THE £100 MARATHON

Following his visit to the House of Commons, the by now world-famous Hayes left London to pay one last visit to his grandparents in Ireland, where it had not gone unnoticed or unremarked that both he and the silver medallist, Hefferon, had Irish parents. Some weeks later, word began to filter across the Atlantic that not only had Hayes turned professional, but he had also begun to exploit his fame on the vaudeville stage, where he was reportedly making phenomenal sums per appearance.

The dramatic finish to the Olympic Marathon, or rather the melodramatic press coverage of it, helped to popularise the event worldwide and left a disappointed British public hungry for redemption. The race had been a dramatic watch, not just for the closeness of the finish, but for the battle between one man's indomitable will and a body that simply refused to go on. Although he had lost the race, Pietri's efforts were popularly considered the more heroic, and the manner in which newspaper reporters had gleefully gilded the Olympic lily had helped to create a craze for tests of stamina and to make endurance the latest benchmark of masculine strength and virility. All manner of opportunists descended on the sport like gulls on a freshly ploughed field. If Joe Public was entertained, he would pay to watch.

On 17 August 1908, less than a month after the Olympic race, the London *Evening News*, responding to the massive public interest, announced its intention to sponsor a second marathon over the same course. Unlike the Olympic marathon, this race would be open to all comers, especially professionals. The first prize would be £100; ten times the amount offered to the winner of the latest *Evening Herald* event. That, in and of itself, raised the status of the event. The other factor driving public interest was the expectation that, in the cooler weather, the British athletes would give a better account of themselves.

The great success of the Marathon Race at the Olympic Games was marred somewhat by two disappointments – the bad times made and the complete failure of the English runners. No one believes that we have not in this country long-distance runners able to best the performances of July 24, and in order to put the matter to the test *The Evening News* has determined to offer substantial prizes in order to bring out the latent talent which it is certain this country possesses...

The date of the race has been fixed for the second Saturday in October, and the arrangements will follow as closely as possible on those of the Marathon race. It will be impossible, of course, to follow exactly the precedents as to starting-place, etc., but an equivalent distance from Windsor to the Stadium, will be adhered to.

Arrangements have been made with Mr. Imre Kiralfy for the use of the Stadium at the finish, and full details as to the regulations will be made shortly. The first prize will be ONE HUNDRED POUNDS and other prizes will be awarded to the second, third etc., These details will be announced later. Meanwhile, entries may be sent in. The race is not confined to the United Kingdom, but open to the world...[146]

One of the first changes the organisers settled upon was to ensure that, unlike in the Olympic event, the finishers would complete one and a half laps of the stadium, thereby ensuring that *all* of the paying spectators would get to see the runners up close. Tickets were priced between sixpence and five shillings, depending on whether you stood or sat.

The dog days of August brought confirmation of the details. The prizes would be £100 for first place, £15 for second place, £10 for third place, and £5 for fourth place. An athletics meeting featuring sprint and middle-distance races would take place simultaneously within the stadium. The date was confirmed for 10 October.[147]

Entries quickly poured in from all over Europe from professional runners of equal and, in many cases, superior talent to those who had contested the Olympic event. With their names being announced as quickly as their entries were accepted, the sporting public was quickly assured that this race would be a *true* World Championship, and a far sterner test than the Olympic marathon.

ANOTHER IRISH PHEIDIPPIDES

Patrick White, who describes himself as the champion distance runner of Ireland, has entered for the Marathon Race, which is being organised by the London "Evening News." [148]

Arriving in London during the build-up to the race, White found himself exposed to what 'professional' running in the rest of the world truly entailed. Mixing with the Americans and continental Europeans, he not only learnt about the size of the purses available elsewhere – purses that far exceeded anything on offer in Ireland – but also about the nature of professional preparation. Many of the athletes had brought personal managers, masseuses, and even doctors with them. During the race itself, the true professionals would also have manned feeding stations to supply them with drinks, supplements, and chemical stimulants.

Victorian athletes were perfectly free to take stimulants, or "tonics" as they were then called, and pharmaceuticals during sports events. Injections of strychnine, tinctures of cocaine and sips of alcohol were all used in normal medical practice to treat aches, pains and fatigue, so the idea was that if an athlete experienced these symptoms during their sport, they were allowed to take medicine to cure them just like anyone else.

The realisation that some drugs don't just cure sick or weak bodies but actually push us beyond our natural physical limits (and are therefore unfair) did not take hold in sports until well into the 20th century. Even in the 21st century we still sometimes struggle to tell the difference between legitimate, curative drug use, and unhealthy or unfair doping.

It was the Edwardians who brought in the first doping ban in competitive sports, at the first London Olympic marathon in 1908, but this was probably due to fears about the athletes' health in this particularly stressful event and not because it was "cheating" or "unfair" (the rules only applied to the marathon, after all).[149]

Back in February 1876, the famous American pedestrian, Edward Payson Weston, had set off to walk a hundred and fifteen miles in twenty-four hours. His only challenger, a British walker, 'Mr Perkins,' dropped out after fourteen and a half hours. Weston would complete the whole twenty-four, but would fall five and a half miles short of his goal. According to an indignant protest later published in the British Medical Journal, Weston had been chewing on coca leaves throughout the race.[150]

Weston (centre) setting out on a long-distance walk in 1913.

Nor was cocaine all that Weston was reported to have been taking. In the 1840s, the German chemist Justus von Liebig developed a food supplement based on his theory that protein was the body's primary energy source. He had called it *Liebig's Extract of Meat*. Weston was known to be fond of this extract, which he believed was even more effective than the coca leaves. By 1908, that same extract was being sold commercially under the brand name 'Oxo', and the company had become the official caterer to the 1908 Olympic Marathon. Some runners had even been provided with free samples to take as a supplement during the race, while others had received samples from the rival brand, 'Bovril.' It was the early 1900s' equivalent of Coke vs Pepsi, and the best athletes were paid to endorse one brand or the other.

Commercial sponsorship was a new concept to White and Colgan, and Colgan was not slow in exploiting it. On race day, Pat would wear a printed tee shirt featuring the name, in large capitals, of Gamage's Department Store in Holborn, famous at the time for its sporting goods. Opportunities for commercial sponsorship like that simply did not exist in Ireland.

Compared to the seasoned professional teams where every advantage, no matter how small, was zealously sought, Pat's support team, which consisted only of his manager, was still an amateurish operation, professional in name only. But their eyes had been opened, and whatever the result of the race, for which Pat was never at any time considered by the British press to be among the favourites, there could be no going back to the old ways.

At 2:35 p.m. on the afternoon of Saturday, 10 October 1908, in 'beautifully fine' weather, Princess Victoria of Schleswig-Holstein, granddaughter of Queen Victoria, sent eighty-nine competitors

Princess Victoria with the starting pistol.

representing America, Belgium, Germany, Italy, France, England, and Ireland on their way. Some had lined up with serious hopes of victory; others had more eclectic motivations, such as fifty-one-year-old Walter G. George, a former world record holder for the mile and now a renowned athletics coach.[151] George had announced his intention to run the race with the assistance of oxygen supplementation.[152] The overwhelming favourite, however, was the French athlete Henri Siret, a three-time winner of the twenty-four-mile Tour de

101

Paris.[153]

As in the Olympic Marathon, the English runners were first to show, with Cook, Hill, and Hopkins racing to the front, accompanied by the Belgian, Jenssens.[154] After about two miles, Young took the lead from Hopkins, who was thereafter joined by the French athlete, Bagre. They held this position for the next three miles.

Siret (bottom left), passing through Ruislip.

By Langley Marsh, five miles into the race, Henry Farrow, the flying fish porter, had taken over the lead. By the time he reached mile eight, he had opened a 400-yard gap on White and Abe Crudgington of Bethnal Green, who were now running second and third. The two French men at this stage appeared to be running well within themselves, with Edouard Cibot holding seventh place and Henri Siret, who had run a marathon in Milan just two weeks prior, back in tenth.

Between Uxbridge and Walworth, the lead

102

changed hands again as the Englishman Thomas surged to the front. By the time they reached Ruislip, however, less than a mile from the halfway point, Thomas had faded significantly, and Farrow, White, and the veteran, Crudgington, were sharing the lead.

White (118), Farrow (41) and Crudgington (56).

Farrow now began to force the pace, and at twenty miles, he paid the price and was forced to stop and walk. For the Billingsgate fish porter, it was to be his last shot at fame, at least while he was alive. Five years later, he would be stabbed to death in Southwark by the landlord and landlady with whom he had lodged for almost twenty years. His death would consume far more column

103

P. White.

Le champion d'Ir... lande, P. White,
a terminé 2ᵉ à 3 m. ... du vainqueur.

inches than his running ever did.[155]

As the race passed through Harrow, White, more by default than design, found himself in the lead. He was closely followed by Crudgington, with the Frenchman Sirct closing fast in third. Approaching Willesden Junction, Siret surged past the leading two, and though White managed to hang on to him as far as mile twenty-three, the gap to the Frenchman gradually widened.[156]

Siret enters the stadium.

There were close on fifty thousand spectators gathered around the arena as the time drew nigh upon which the Marathon runners might be expected to appear. Presently a wild yell told of the approach of the first man, and shortly after the lithe form of Siret appeared in the entrance. Running steadily with any amount of spare strength in hand, he circled the track and finished with a fine burst of speed. Just as he entered the final straight, White appeared, with Keywood two hundred yards behind; Crudgington was the next man to appear, and then Aldridge. Keywood walked off the track and seemed a little upset by his long journey.[157]

Siret (2:37:03) and White (2:40:15) had beaten Pietri's Olympic time by seventeen and fourteen minutes respectively, a feat that was rendered all the more impressive by the fact that the course had been lengthened by a further two hundred yards on account of the refusal of the Crown to allow the race to start from the lawn of Windsor Castle.[158] Nevertheless, despite the extra two hundred yards, which would have added another thirty to forty seconds to their times, the first seven finishers ran faster than the new Olympic record,[159] spectacular performances by the standards of the day.

This was a watershed moment for White. The most challenging part of any marathon is the final four to six miles. It is here, even among professional runners, that the distance begins to take its toll, where the body starts to deplete its glycogen and dig into its fat reserves. It is also during this stretch that the pain peaks, where even the slightest misjudgement can send a runner crashing into the proverbial "wall. " Yet, it was in the final six miles that White truly excelled, not by outpacing all but one of his rivals, but by outlasting them.

LOCAL HERO

THERE HAD BEEN no national flags for the professional marathon, and no team singlets. The competitors ran as individuals, referred to only by their country or city of residence. Nevertheless, following the race, White found himself being chased by reporters from the British press anxious to celebrate him as the best of the 'British' finishers. Subjected to a glaring cascade of praise and attention beyond anything he had experienced before, he handled himself well and was most frequently described, to the delight of his fellow countrymen, as an Irishman.

This, in the public eye, had been a true world championship, not just because of the size of the prize, but because it was open to all-comers. In many ways, it had a value higher than the Olympic Games, which had yet to reach the status they enjoy today. And in this true world championship, Pat White had not run in a British singlet, nor had he marched behind a British flag. Here, at last, was a performance the Irish public could properly claim as their own, a hero that could be authentically celebrated as home-grown, even if some of the British press were inclined to do the same.

Patrick White eschews both tobacco and alcoholic refreshment. He is a typical Irishman. Aged 26, he stands 5ft 8in, and weighs about

10st stripped. Unlike some of the competitors, he declares that he had no special preparation for Saturday's race. He trained, he says, exactly as for the Irish Marathons, by working daily in the harvest fields and having occasionally during the week a spin of some ten miles.[160]

Oddly enough, for a man who had just leapt to international recognition, there was no sense of disbelief or what today we might call 'impostor syndrome,' and neither was there any attempt at false modesty. If anything, White felt cheated, not by another athlete, official or organisation, but by his circumstances. When interviewed about his performance, he was quick to highlight the amateurish nature of his preparation:

I felt confident of being well up at the finish, and until Siret overtook me near Harlesden, I feared no one, despite the fact that Crudgington stuck to me. Siret is a clinker, and today the best man won. Had I received the preparation that some of the other runners have had, I'm sure I should have done better.[161]

White was supported in his assertions by the third-place finisher, Jack Keywood, a builder from Bromley in Kent. Keywood also expressed his frustration at having had to fit in his training after a full day's work, unlike those professionals who had been able to undertake specialised training for the event and had team members stationed at key points of the race providing them with nutrition and rendering medical assistance where necessary, in the form of chemical stimulants.

The observations of White and Keywood were

108

neither unreasonable nor unjustified. The winner, Siret, for instance, was later reported to have been running fifteen to twenty miles a day in preparation for the race, mileage that far exceeded anything either White or Keywood were capable of achieving while holding down a full-time job. A day or so later, still feeling his oats, White vented his frustrations on the London correspondent of the *Irish Independent*.

Mr. White said Saturday's event was a great race. It broke the world's record. His own time in the race was the best he had ever accomplished. Asked as to his previous achievements, Mr. White recalled the fact that four years ago he won the 'Evening Herald Race from the Tolka Bridge, Drumcondra, to Balbriggan.' He had, he added, won the "Herald" race two years in succession, and took second place in the third year. Questioned as to his impressions of the form shown by the other competitors in Saturday's race, Mr. White replied. – "I had practically no opportunity of watching them, seeing that I made the pace for them all for 23½ miles."

Asked what was the principal difference he noticed between the race from Windsor to the Stadium and the Irish races, he replied that on Saturday the running was much faster than it was in Ireland. The course for the Marathon, he observed, was far better than the Irish course. There were a great many hills on the Irish course, which was a much heavier one than the English one. Such hills were not encountered on the English track which proved a much faster one. "I attribute my defeat, he stated, to the fact that I had not enough training."

"I understand," adds our London correspondent, "that White has been approached with an offer of an engagement to appear at music halls in Dublin, Belfast and Cork, one week in each city. The salary mentioned is £40 a week for the three weeks' engagement. The offer is under consideration and probably the engagement will be agreed upon. It is proposed that a cinematograph representation of the race shall be shown, and Mr. White shall appear on the stage and tell the audience his impressions of the race.[162]

Pat's run in London had placed him firmly amongst the best in the world, and his profile, both at home and abroad, rocketed. Though debarred from amateur competition, he was no longer beneath notice, having become, in just one race, a tonic to national self-esteem and a newly woven thread in the tapestry of national identity. He may not have been running in an Irish singlet, but his Irishness could not have been more celebrated had he raced in a crown of shamrocks. There was, as a result, no shortage of Irish people waiting to exploit his celebrity.

Ballymaclinton, 1908. Courtesy of Charlie Verrall Collection.

Immediately after the race, Pat and his manager were gifted free passes to Ballymaclinton by Mr H. B. Amos, press secretary of the replica Irish village erected by McClinton's Soap for the 1908 Franco-British exhibition at the White City. Here, for an entry fee of sixpence, paying visitors could explore several dozen full-sized 'Irish' buildings, from thatched cottages to round towers and even a replica of Blarney Castle, complete with Blarney Stone. The village, populated by 250 Irish 'colleens', even had its own fully operating Post Office, which sold souvenir postcards extolling the complexion-whitening virtues of McClinton's soap.[163]

Just two months earlier, Johnny Hayes, following his Olympic victory, had been invited to the House of Commons to meet several Irish MPs. And so, with White having just demolished Hayes' world and Olympic record over the same course, it seemed only fair that he, too, should be invited, as an opportunity to rub English noses in yet another sporting embarrassment if nothing else. That White had been beaten by a Frenchman was not half as important as the fact that he had finished ahead of the English. And so, following their visit to Ballymaclinton, White and Colgan were invited to visit the House of Commons by the Irish MP, John Pius Boland.

Just two years previously, Boland had become the first Irishman to win an Olympic gold medal by claiming the tennis singles and doubles titles at the Intercalated Games in Athens. At Westminster, he introduced White and Colgan to the Land League agitator Willie Redmond, to the anti-Parnellite journalist William O'Malley, and to Cecil Harmsworth, the celebrated author, director of Amalgamated Press and chairman of Associated Newspapers. If photographs were taken on this occasion, they have not survived.

One week later, seeking to cash in on the public interest, Thomas Hynes challenged both Siret and White, offering to race either or both of them over any distance from five to fifteen miles, distances over which, Hynes claimed, he had 'little fear for the result'.[164] Neither man responded.

Press reports of White's claim to have had the potential to do a lot better had he not had to work in the run-up to the London race prompted some of his admirers to organise a subscription fund to reward him for having done his country proud on the international stage, and to help him better prepare for future races.

> Mr. Peter Murtagh, Ballough, Lusk, Balrothery, informs us that he will receive subscriptions from any of the ARGUS readers who wish to show their practical appreciation of the great feat of Pat White, Donabate, who was second to the Frenchman, Siret, over the 26 miles course in the great Marathon Race, on Saturday, beating competitors from America, Belgium, Germany, Italy and England.[165]

Another admirer keen to collect a cash payment for White was his proud-as-punch employer, John Dempsey:

> The admirers of Pat White's prowess as an athlete have resolved to make him a presentation of a purse of sovereigns. When it is remembered that Pat carried out his training for last Saturday's London Marathon Race under the

most difficult circumstances, it will be conceded that his remarkable success is all the more deserved.

Mr. J. Dempsey, Grace Dieu, Donabate, his employer, states that White begins his day's work on the farm at 6 a.m. and continues steadily, with a short interval for dinner, until 6 p.m. Then, after tea at his parent's home, he starts for a 15 miles run on the heavy roads in the neighbourhood. Given proper training, White's admirers are convinced that he would have won the Marathon Race.[166]

Today, when marathon running has become what Chris Brasher loved to describe as the 'Great Suburban Everest,' it is difficult to imagine the degree of admiration and public acclaim once heaped upon those who competed successfully over what was then considered a trial of will on the fringes of human endurance. Indeed, so many Irish people wanted to share in celebrating White's success that the various subscription funds quickly exceeded all expectations. The people of Rush alone would donate more than £12, more than Pat had received for winning either of his *Evening Herald* races.[167] He was neither embarrassed nor ashamed to accept it.

TREADING THE BOARDS

FOLLOWING THE OLYMPIC marathon of 1908, such was the explosion of interest in marathon running and marathon runners generally that the Olympic champion, Johnny Hayes, found himself in high demand as a vaudeville act.[168] In Ireland, a similar interest was now being shown in Pat White.

There was just one problem. Hayes was an energetic and talkative extrovert who would go on to have a successful career in business. White, on the other hand, was a quiet man with a rudimentary education, unaccustomed to public speaking. Persuaded to give it a go, White signed a contract committing him to a week-long engagement at the Empire Palace Theatre on Dublin's Dame Street (renamed in 1920 as 'The Olympia'). The contract, reportedly worth £40 a week, was lucrative, even allowing for his manager's cut. Professional athletics had entered the world of show business.

> The new series of Empire pictures include a very fine film of the recent professional Marathon Race, in which Pat White of Donabate won second place, over the same course to the Stadium which made Dorando and Hayes famous. They have actually engaged White, who beat Dorando's and Hayes' time by the handsome margin of fifteen minutes.[169]

114

EMPIRE PALACE THEATRE

To-Night, 7.30......Early Doors 6.45......Mat. Sat., 3.

MENDEL,

THE MARVELLOUS BLIND PIANIST.

Tennyson and Wallis. Will Jones. Daisy Martell,
And the Great, Grand, Versatile Comedian,

GUS GARRICK.

Annie Laurie..................................Mario Goodwin

First Time of the Unparalleled Eccentricity,

HUMPSTY BUMPSTI.

The Most Laughable Act in the World.
ANOTHER SENSATION! A GREAT ATTRACTION
THE GREAT MARATHON RACE
(Shown by the Empire Pictures).
Depicting Every Stage of the Big Contest and the
Triumphant Finish by

PAT WHITE, DONABATE,

Who will appear personally each Night.
TO-NIGHT.   TO-NIGHT.

GREAT BOXING CONTEST.

Frank Curry v. Jack Coughlan.
Bookings 11 to 5.   'Phone 824.   Bikes Free.

Pat's stage debut took place on Monday, 19 October 1908. Limelit and lionised, he was stripped to his vest and shorts to show off his trim and muscular physique and paraded in front of the audience like a circus pony. A rough diamond in need of polishing, his natural shyness came quickly to the fore and rendered him temporarily mute.

Pat White, of Donabate, the winner of two "Herald" races and who, running second, beat Hayes' and Dorando's time by 15 minutes in the great professional Marathon race in the Stadium,

115

London, recently, appeared on the stage at the Empire last night, when a splendid series of cinematograph pictures of the event were displayed. Pat came forward at very short notice to describe the race, but an attack of "nerves" proved too much for him and he retired amid sympathetic applause, with an assurance to the audience that he would be better prepared tonight. He was dressed in racing costume, which displayed his magnificent physique to advantage.[170]

Regarding his subsequent appearances, the Dublin audiences were both forgiving and supportive. He was an authentic pocket-sized Irish hero: young, ripped, and handsome – almost like a movie star in the public eye, despite his diminutive stature. The welcome he received was nothing short of tumultuous.

Pat White's appearance on the stage was the signal for a great outburst of cheering from the audience. He describes incidents in the race, and it is only natural, considering the abundant enthusiasm aroused by the performance of the Irish-American Athletes, especially the genial Hayes of Marathon fame, that sportsmen will welcome the appearance of one who, although less proclaimed, has yet eclipsed the performance of those whose praises have been so bountifully sung throughout all the three Kingdoms.

He explained that, in all probability, had he been able to secure the necessary training, and necessary stimulants on the long journey, he would have been able to render a much better account of himself than he did. He appeared in the costume he ran in, in the Marathon race...[171]

White's success was doing wonders for national pride and morale; his humble background regarded not so much as a handicap as a badge of honour. Despite having come second in London, he was well on his way to accumulating more than the £100 in prizemoney that he would have received had he actually won the race. In the eyes of his fellow countrymen, Patrick Joseph White was nothing less than a national hero.

> Sir –
>
> Would you please allow me to draw attention through your columns to the great feat accomplished by Ireland's representative (Mr. P. White) in the above race. He had proved himself on this occasion to be the second-best long-distance runner in the world. He had placed Ireland in the front rank. He laid low the pick of England, America, South Africa, etc., together with the much-admired Mr. Hayes, who won over the same course quite recently, but took fifteen minutes longer to do it. Whatever training he did was in his native place, unassisted by experienced foreign trainers, and not without considerable expense to himself.
>
> Many would have liked to have assisted him in his preparation, but did not get the opportunity, owing to want of publicity. But now there is an opportunity for all true athletes and sportsmen of Ireland to make some presentation to Mr. White for his great achievement, and not let such a glorious feat by an Irishman pass unnoticed by his fellow countrymen.
>
> J. COLLINS.[172]

Letters to the editors of popular newspapers, like the one above, were common and indicative of the pride that was being taken in White's achievement. This was especially true of Irish emigrants living in the U.K.

> Sir –
>
> Knowing how much Irishmen like to see their countrymen victorious at home and abroad, I write to suggest that a subscription be opened for Patrick White (who was second in the Marathon race), with a view of bringing him forward in the "Marathon Circle." Such suggestion, I know, will be appreciated by every true-hearted Irishman.
>
> I may remark that if Patrick White received the same training and feeding as those Marathon champions on Saturday, he could bear comparison with the best in the world.
>
> AN IRISHMAN,
> Uxbridge, London, W., Oct. 12, '08.[173]

Pat was now in high demand, but the stress of public speaking proved too much for him, and the planned engagements in Cork and Belfast never took place. Challenges to let his legs do the talking, however, were more kindly received. Tom Hynes offered to meet him over any distance from five to fifteen miles,[174] while Frank Curtis offered to meet him over twenty.

The proposed distance being closer to a full marathon, White accepted Curtis' challenge, but, secure in the knowledge that he was the bigger draw, he demanded that the purse should reflect that, and that the purse should be at least equal to that which had been offered to the winner of the London race. Having proven himself world-class, he expected to be paid accordingly.

Pat White, of Donabate, who came second in the latest Marathon Race at the Stadium, in reply to Curtis, states he is ready to meet him at 20 miles over any course for £100.[175]

The demand, a common negotiating tactic in professional boxing, was not well received in an athletic community unaccustomed to what was seen in many circles as vulgar and unapologetic professionalism. Curtis, bridling at White's impertinence, attempted to put manners on him. His reply was cutting.

TO THE EDITOR OF THE FREEMAN'S JOURNAL
Baltrasna, Ashbourne, Co. Meath, October 19, 1908.

Dear Sir,

Pat White says in your issue of today that he will be glad to run me twenty miles over any course for £100 a-side. I have no hundred pounds, being only a labouring man's son, and P. White is, I am sure, well aware of this. Therefore a match under these conditions is impossible. But, to be practical, I will be happy to run him anywhere for any distance for half the gate money.

Yours faithfully,
FRANK CURTIS.[176]

That was never going to happen, at least not in the short term, for it was not Frank Curtis that people would be coming to see, but Pat White, the London runner-up. Had he not earned the right to capitalise on his recent success? In the USA, that would have been understood. In professional boxing, that would have been understood. But this was Ireland, where professional running was still a part-time activity, and that was not how everyone saw it.

THE POWDERHALL
MARATHON

THE QUESTION HAD remained unresolved since the conclusion of the Olympic marathon. Who was truly the better athlete? Had Hayes deserved his title, or had Pietri been unfairly treated? Nowhere were these questions more hotly contested than on the streets of New York, where Irish and Italian interests would fiercely debate and defend the reputation of their respective champions.

Quickest to spot the commercial potential of this simmering stew of public interest and national pride was Irish American baseball supremo and former manager of the New York Giants, Patrick T. Powers, who also dabbled in sports promotion. Powers had impressive form. A skilled orator and shrewd businessman, he currently managed several professional athletes, boxers and cyclists and, back in 1902, had successfully organised an international six-day running race for teams of two at Madison Square Garden, which he had promoted as the 'Six Days Championship of the World'.

Shortly after the Olympic Games, it was Powers who had convinced Pietri and Hayes to turn professional and to race each other again in the United States for a share of the gate. In that match, which had taken place at Madison Square Garden on 29 November 1908, ten thousand highly excited, partisan and paying spectators witnessed Pietri defeat Hayes by sixty yards.

Pietri's winning time of 2:55:18 was fifteen minutes slower than Pat White's time over the same distance in October, and put to bed once and for all the excuse that the July heat had been responsible for the discrepancy in times between the Olympic Marathon and the subsequent professional race over the same course.[177] Irish newspapers naturally seized on the revelation and began to stoke public interest in seeing White race the world's best once more.[178]

> The management of the Madison Square Gardens is arranging another Marathon Race between Longboat and Alfred Shrubb for January 9th. After that there will be a free for all between Longboat, Shrubb, Dorando, and Hayes. Alfred Shrubb cabled to England, his wife stating that he will be able to arrange terms with Longboat and Dorando for races at three distances.
>
> The ex-amateur champion, who has decided upon taking up his residence in America, will pay a short visit to England in February or March, when he will issue challenges to all comers. Then perhaps Pat White, of Donabate, and Hynes, of Galway, and other Irish Marathon runners, may have something to say to Shrubb.[179]

Before any of that could happen, however, there was the small matter of the inaugural Powderhall Marathon to be taken care of. Scheduled to take place on New Year's Day 1909, it was to be the feature event of the Powderhall Festival of professional athletics. The race would start in Falkirk and finish at the Powderhall Stadium in

Edinburgh.[180]

Powderhall is an area located to the north of Edinburgh, situated between Broughton Road and Warriston Road. The name originates from a gunpowder factory and its associated buildings, which were located on the edge of the Water of Leith in the early 18th century. Back in 1869, a stadium had been built here to host cycling and athletics events, and it was here, in 1870, that the first Powderhall Sprint, a professional handicap footrace over 150 yards, had taken place.[181] The Powderhall festival of professional athletics soon became a fixture of the city's New Year celebrations and has remained so to this day.

The explosion of public interest in marathon running that followed the drama of the 1908 Olympics had forced the addition of a marathon to the Powderhall program, and entries had flooded in from France, England, Ireland, Scotland, and Wales. The Irish contingent was particularly strong and included such stalwarts of the *Evening Herald* race as Pat White, Tom Hynes, and Pat Conway. White, the betting favourite, was offered at odds of four to one against.[182]

The first prize for the inaugural Powderhall marathon would be £80, less than had been on offer in London in October, but still a substantial amount by British standards. However, during the build-up to the race, on 15 December 1908, reports began to emerge that no less than fourteen thousand people had crammed into Madison Square Garden to watch Tom Longboat defeat Dorando Pietri over the London distance in a time of 2:45:05. Longboat's reward for that victory was $3,750, or £770 sterling.[183] That would be the equivalent of £119,449 today. Pat White would not have been alone in Edinburgh that year in wondering whether he was racing on the wrong continent.

After the call to the start, despite each entrant having already furnished a medical certificate prior to the race, the competitors were asked to line up before Dr Russell Cargill, a well-known Scottish rugby player, for a cursory last-minute medical. Only one athlete was found to be in less than perfect health, but even he was allowed to compete, his condition being deemed too mild to preclude his participation.[184]

Owing to the recent inclement weather, with snowfall followed by rain, the roads around Falkirk had been left in a muddy and slushy state. An inspection of the route earlier that morning had revealed some sections to be more like a cross-country course than a road race.[185] Some of the downhill sections, in fact, were judged to be so perilous that, of the fifty-four competitors who faced the starter, several were observed to be wearing spikes![186] At least the weather on the day was kind: dry, balmy, and windless.

At the drop of the starter's flag, the competitors set off together for a lap of the cinder track before heading out onto the roads, accompanied by the customary caravan of motor cars carrying journalists, sponsors, and race officials. The Irish contingent, with the exception of P.J. McCafferty, who went off with the leaders, departed at a steady pace, running almost as a pack and allowing others to set the early pace.

Having passed down Thornhill Road, the

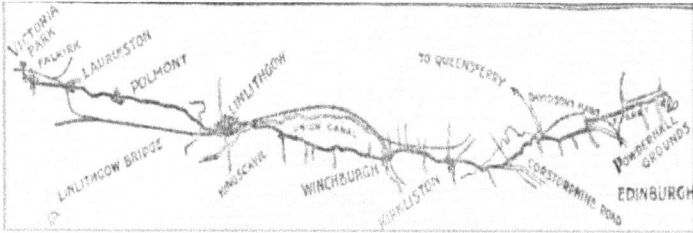

The 1909 Powder Hall Marathon Route.

runners made their way to the Edinburgh Road via Kerse Road and Callender Riggs. Here, the road was so soft in places that, by the time they reached Laurieston, almost everyone was covered in mud. McCafferty, at this point, was running strongly in a leading group of five, which included Henri St. Yves, an unknown Frenchman said to be participating in his first marathon. By the head of Laurieston Brae, however, the English runners Haddow, Dinning and Farrow had moved into the lead. They were running three hundred yards clear of McCafferty and St. Yves, who in turn were followed by a small group that included the Irishmen, White, Fagan and Curtis.

Coming into Linlithgow, some of the runners found themselves joined by attendants on bicycles who rode briefly alongside their respective clients, providing them with a 'pass or two of a sponge moistened with eau de Cologne' and a 'taste of Oxo meat extract' to renew their energy stores. By the time they exited Linlithgow, Farrow had been dropped from the leading group, and the bookies' favourite, White, was so far back that he had dropped to even money in the betting.[187] Nobody, at this early stage, was giving the twenty-year-old Frenchman a chance.

Fagan, at this point, decided to leave his fellow

countrymen and chase down the Englishman, Cook. As he disappeared up the road, White continued to run conservatively in a group that also contained McCafferty, Hynes, and Curtis, all of whom seemed to be focused on each other, confident that the leaders, or at the very least Fagan, would eventually return to them. Fagan, after all, had a habit of blowing up towards the end of races.

However, as the field passed through Kirkliston, punters and competitors alike were forced to re-evaluate their opinion of the Frenchman. Haddow was currently leading Dinning by a hundred and fifty yards. Still, it was the diminutive Frenchman, St. Yves, a French waiter living and working in London, who appeared to be running the most comfortably of all. He was currently running third.

Half a mile beyond Kirkliston, Haddow dropped out, complaining of sore ankles and thighs, and George Dinning assumed the lead, with St. Yves running just a yard or two behind him. As they turned the corner towards Cramond, however, the Frenchman found a higher gear and broke clear. On the long hill, surrounded by half a dozen panting cyclists, he stretched his lead to a couple of minutes.[188]

By the time St. Yves reached the Queensferry Road, he was well clear of the chasing pack, which by now was composed exclusively of Irishmen, with White, Curtis and Hynes running stride for stride and a fading McCafferty following a short distance behind. The Irish pack now found themselves on the horns of an unexpected dilemma. Had they underestimated the French novice? Should they attempt to chase him down or wait for him to hit the wall? To chase after him would be to risk blowing up and allowing oneself to be beaten by a fellow Irishman. To let him go could mean surrendering any chance they might still have of winning the race.

> ...coming near the end, White admonished his fellow Irishmen to precipitate their steps, which they did, but unfortunately were found slowing up again. White, on noticing this, left his comrades and went off, increasing his speed, endeavouring to reach the Frenchman.[189]

At twenty-two miles, Hynes' legs began to cramp, forcing him to stop and walk. He would have retired there and then but for one of his attendants, who rushed to give him some fruit and a hot drink. Having fed himself, he was able to resume.[190]

Pat's belated surge, while distancing him from his compatriots, made little impression on the leader, St. Yves, who, although failing to increase his four-minute advantage, was now too far ahead and running far too steadily to be caught. White had left it too late.

> Ferry Road, Edinburgh, was crowded with enthusiastic spectators, and they heartily cheered Yves, now a certain winner. His entry into the city was like that of an important personage, hats and handkerchiefs being waved as he passed...
>
> Several hundred spectators utilised the wall of Warriston Cemetery as a point of vantage, and they were among the first to observe the leading runner as he crossed the bridge which spans the

Waters of Leith. Some time prior to this, however, his approach was heralded by the arrival of one of the official motor cars, the occupants of which vouchsafed the information that "67" was leading at a mile from home.

A glance at the race card showed the number to be that of H. Saint Yves, London, and just before 2.40 the Londoner plodded across the bridge, down the road, and through the entrance gate in great style... He appeared comparatively fresh in spite of the fact that the weight of the mud attaching to his person must have been considerable...

The Frenchman was meantime finishing amid great cheering, which was renewed as he was assisted off the track, and continued for the benefit of White. Then came T. Hynes, Ireland, who ran fresher and in better style than any of the other two, and following was Curtis, County Meath, another strong finisher.[191]

Having taken the lead about three miles from home,[192] Henri St. Ives had raced to a comfortable victory in 2:44:41, finishing two and a half minutes ahead of White, who clocked 2:47:15.[193] Both times were world-class by the standards of the day. The course, however, was measured at twenty-six and a half miles (a quarter of a mile longer than the 'London' distance), and the race had been run in mud, slush, and snow, which would suggest that the performances were considerably better than the times had indicated.[194]

The Irish competitors didn't hang around after the race. They left Edinburgh for Liverpool together and arrived at Dublin's North Wall in the early hours of the following morning after a pleasant overnight sailing.[195] Pat's £20 runner-up prize was far short of the £80 he had expected to be returning with, or the £100 he had previously sought to race Curtis. Still, there was a pleasurable sense of self-justification to be harvested from having finished ahead of the other Irish competitors. He was not, however, without regrets.[196]

> It was a mistake on the part of White that he didn't come out sooner, but Pat wasn't selfish; it was his sole delight to see his chums figuring well. The finish was a splendid one, the Frenchman winning by about 600 yards.[197]

The *Irish Independent* version probably raised a few hackles with a turn of phrase that appeared to lay the blame for White's defeat at the hands of his 'chums.'

> Pat White might have won well had he gone away by himself. It was waiting for his Irish chums and pacing with them that killed his chances.[198]

It is doubtful that Pat White's delight in seeing his 'chums' finishing well would have been so readily apparent to a press reporter had any one of them managed to finish in front of him. It is also doubtful that press reports blaming his defeat on his 'chums' had won him many friends at home. Nevertheless, the Irish papers remained solidly behind him. The Irish public needed sporting heroes, and White's story was simply too good to debunk.

As for the winner, St. Yves, it was only after the race that concrete information about the twenty-year-old's background began to emerge. He was not, after all, an untrained runner, though he *was*, allegedly, a novice at the marathon. He had come to London in 1908 intending to run in the professional marathon, only to find that his late entry had not been accepted.

Since then, St. Yves had been working as a waiter in London and, while training on the Windsor course, had allegedly run faster than Siret's winning time in October.[199] That he had so cleverly concealed that information from bookies would suggest that he had also backed himself to win, and at longer odds than might have been the case had his form been known.

Like Hayes and White before him, St. Ives was quickly offered a week's engagement on the stage, in this case at the Edinburgh Empire Palace. Here, accompanied by a silent movie of the Powderhall event, he, too, gave a brief narrative of the race and showed off the trophy.[200] The Frenchman then took off for Paris to run a challenge race against Siret, before heading to the U.S. to pursue a professional career.

The organisers of the Powderhall Marathon, unfortunately, appear to have been either lax in their explanations or weak in their translation of 'challenge trophy.' The charitable assumption was that St Ives had simply failed to understand that the cup was not the winner's property to keep but rather a token of victory to be held for a year and then returned to be presented to the subsequent year's winner.[201] Neither St Ives nor the trophy were ever seen in Edinburgh again.

THE MAURETANIA

SEEKING TO STRIKE while the iron was hot, American sports promoter Patrick T. Powers sent Brighton-born journalist and boxing promoter, Ernest H. Crowhurst, to London in January 1909 to recruit athletes from a variety of European countries to compete in an international six-day go-as-you-please relay marathon in New York.

The race, which was scheduled to take place on March 7 at Madison Square Garden, would consist of two-member teams from each country. Each team would start and finish each day at a specified hour, with each member running twelve hours per day, and teams credited with the cumulative distance covered each day. The team with the largest total at the end of the six days would be declared the winner. The race had a prize fund of $5,000 (£1,026).

Sometime over the course of the fortnight that followed the 1909 Powderhall Marathon, perhaps even while he was in Edinburgh, White had decided to accept an offer from a 'syndicate' to ply his trade in America, where his backers hoped to make a killing by matching him against the best in the world.[202] The members of this syndicate were never revealed, but given the timing, one particular group comes immediately to mind.

A syndicate comprising of Patrick T. Powers, 'Big Jim' Kennedy and Amos G. Batchelder,

131

known to New Yorkers as the 'Holy Trinity', had for years run six-day cycle races at Madison Square Garden. Kennedy had died in 1904, but the other two were still active. As it had been Powers who had despatched Crowhurst to Europe to recruit for their latest six-day extravaganza, Powers would seem to be the most likely source of White's invitation.

Crowhurst had initially selected Pat White to represent Ireland in the six-day race, subject to him finding a suitable partner. Those wishing to be considered for the role were asked to write to Crowhurst care of *The Sporting Life*.[203] By the time Crowhurst's invitation hit the Irish papers, however, Pat was already on his way to America,[204] where a craze for all manner of endurance trials from running to roller skating was in full swing, and serious money was being offered to successful competitors.

Something appears to have changed soon after Crowhurst announced White's selection, and White was asked instead to make haste to New York, with or without a partner. The reason for this is unclear, but it may have had something to do with Johnny Hayes leaving Powers' stable and striking out on his own. Powers had always preferred to have an 'Irish' competitor in his stable to exploit the loyalties of the large Irish community.

Offered the chance to become one of a handful of athletes worldwide engaged full-time in professional athletics, and confident he could make a decent fist of it, Pat didn't hesitate to accept the offer. And why would he? In America, after all, he could earn in a single race more than he might win in a lifetime of prizemoney in

Ireland. The decision to head to New York, however, brought an end to his relationship with Bernard Colgan, who soon after left his family home in the Naul and moved to Balbriggan to start his own business as a saddler.

> Pat White, the well-known long-distance runner, of Donabate, County Dublin, who ran second to the Frenchman, H. St. Yves, at Powderhall, and had long been a prominent long-distance runner, has left Liverpool on the Mauretania for New York. He has gone out at the request of a syndicate, who propose to arrange matches for him with Longboat and Dorando, the terms, we understand, being very favourable to White.
>
> It has not yet been definitely settled which man he will meet first; but, win or lose, it is almost certain that he will be given an opportunity of running against the Italian and Indian.[205] As to the six-day race in New York, the entries for which close at the end of the present week, it is doubtful if he will take part in that, and, at all events, up to the time of his departure from Dublin, White had made no arrangements as to competing in it.[206]

On the ship's manifest, drawn up before she sailed, Pat White was listed as a twenty-seven-year-old steerage passenger who had paid for his own ticket, and his occupation recorded simply as 'labourer.' By the time the ship set sail, however, he had been upgraded to second cabin (2nd class), the upgrade recorded as having been paid for by a 'friend'. On the upgraded booking, Pat's occupation was listed as 'gentleman,' and his age as thirty.[207]

On both of the above bookings, Pat gave the

address to which he was travelling as 155 East 40th Street, New York. This was then the family home of John Lally, younger brother of William, his former teammate at Ballinasloe Harriers.[208] William and his sister Bridget had left Ireland together in 1901. They had initially intended to stay a short while in Brooklyn with their older sister Kate, and then travel onwards to Los Angeles.[209] But William never got to California and was still in New York, where he had since been joined by his brother, John.

The Mauretania.

A winter crossing in steerage posed obvious risks to an elite athlete's health, and White's 'friend,' whoever he may have been, though clearly not intimately acquainted with the athlete, appears to have been anxious to protect his form. The upgrade, furthermore, is suggestive of a larger investment than just a one-way ticket to New York, as Pat would also have had to invest in a decent wardrobe. Second cabin passengers dressed for dinner, not quite as grandly as first-class, perhaps, but more formally than Pat was accustomed to doing at home.

The R.M.S. Mauretania, sister ship of the Lusitania, was the Titanic of her day. The largest and fastest ship in the world, she regularly shaved two to three days off the standard transatlantic crossing. The latest thing in luxury travel, she boasted an interior designed by Harold Peto, a series of elevators and a grand walnut staircase.

Second Cabin State Room, R.M.S. Mauretania.

Second cabin passengers were quartered aft, with recreational space on the promenade and bridge decks. These included a large dining room, a handsomely furnished social hall, a smoking room, and a ladies' parlour. Their cabins, or 'staterooms,' differed from first-class primarily in that they were furnished with berths rather than bedsteads. Apart from that, there was little significant difference. A second cabin ticket did

135

not come cheap.

An upgrade from steerage to second cabin, however, was something of a double-edged sword, for though Pat's occupation had been listed on the upgrade as a 'gentleman,' he was about as far from gently born as it was possible to get. His second-cabin companions, on the other hand came almost exclusively from the ranks of the British *petit bourgeois* – though he would not have known them by that designation – and unlikely as any of them were to be named in Debrett's, they were still many ranks above his station by the societal standards of the day. Indeed, a common labourer would never have dared pretend to first-name familiarity with such people back home, let alone risk the embarrassment of a social solecism by dining with them.

This random collection of middle-class merchants, accountants, salesmen, and ministers of religion came from a world that so rarely intersected with White's that their customs and tribal signatures, not to mention their dining room etiquette and breadth of education, would have been largely alien to him. The plump, soft hands they offered in greeting were smooth as China silk, washed by the kind of scented soap that lathered easily and was rarely seen in a labourer's cabin. They had little, if anything, in common.

These were the kind of people who spoke freely of money at the dinner table, and not with the crudity of ditch diggers, but in the jargon of commerce, by which its single-minded pursuit was somehow sanctified. To such men, who were not lacking in pretensions of their own, investment in stocks was socially acceptable, no matter what the probability of success. Betting on

136

sport, however, was frowned upon with Sunday seriousness and professional athletes, on account of their long association with gambling, about as welcome in their inner circles as an unfrocked priest.

It is unlikely White ended the journey on more than nodding terms with the majority of his fellow diners. And yet, for all of that, it must have been infinitely more satisfying to have been able to claim, when asked where he hailed from and what he 'did,' that he was a full-time professional athlete, rather than a common agricultural labourer. At the dinner table, a man was only as vulnerable as his greatest pretensions.

The Mauretania set sail from Liverpool on 23 January 1909, just three weeks after the Powderhall race. Her first port of call was at Queenstown (Cobh), where she was to pick up the majority of Irish passengers. Why White did not embark from there is unknown. Presumably, he had travelled to Liverpool to meet with someone, most likely a representative of his sponsoring 'syndicate.'

As it was still winter, an Atlantic crossing meant heavy seas and crowded balustrades. For the first couple of days, the ship's doctor, Sidney Jones, was kept busy. Meals were served thrice daily for those who found their sea legs quickly, and an orchestra provided daily entertainment. In heaving seas, pacing the decks was difficult to sustain for very long. In a swell, it was all but impossible.

White had rubbed up against all sorts in the wake of his London run of the previous year. But those encounters had been fleeting at best, and little more than introductions. On the Mauretania, however, his encounters with the white collared classes were of necessity more prolonged, especially as second-cabin passengers took their evening meals together at the long table in the second-cabin dining room. More dinner party than supper, no matter how neatly turned out he may have been, the experience would have required a degree of caution and watchfulness.

That White had not spurned the upgrade speaks much to his confidence and the direction of his pretensions. But wasn't that where his ambition lay? Wasn't that the very reason he was travelling to America, to reach for higher things? Wasn't sporting glory the only means by which a man like him could drag himself up the social ladder? It may have been uncomfortable being the solitary blue collar in a sea of white, but it was a taste of the life he aspired to.

But had it come at a cost? When boarding the Mauretania, Pat had declared himself to be carrying more than fifty dollars in personal funds. By the sixth day of the voyage, however, this had been reduced to forty, an indication, perhaps, of the cost of keeping up with the Joneses. What remained, however, was still more than sufficient, should the need arise, to find cheap accommodation for a month and to pay for a steerage ticket home.

Home! Wouldn't it just be the cruellest of humiliations if he had to return prematurely? The prospect didn't bear thinking about. The syndicate may have been carrying the financial risk, but he was carrying a reputational one. So much would hang on the result of that first race. In the gladiatorial arena of professional sport, a man's worth was measured not only in victories and personal bests but in the revolution of turnstiles, and to the good folk of New York, Pat White was about as famous as his brother's greyhound.

BROOKLYN

THE MAURETANIA REACHED New York on the morning of January 29 and sailed up the Hudson in the teeth of a snowstorm so severe that it caused a train to derail at Woodside Junction and a four-masted schooner to run into the Scotland Lightship.[210]

Skyline from the North River, 1903.

The view from the Hudson that morning was grey and forbidding. From the Syndicate Building to the Surety Building, the horizon was dominated by that uniquely American icon, the 'skyscraper,' giant vertical monoliths of twenty-plus storeys, taller than anything the majority of passengers had ever before seen. Ominously looming over the spire of Trinity Church, they appeared to mock the insignificance of the individual and to assert, in the most imperious and inhuman manner imaginable, the all-encompassing power of Mammon.

The Mauretania docked at Pier 54, at the foot of 14th Street in Chelsea, from where the third-class passengers were transferred by ferry to the American immigration station on Ellis Island.[211] The morning was bitterly cold, and more snow was forecast for later in the day. It was hardly the best preparation for an immigration check, where the merest suspicion of a contagious disease could result in a passenger being denied entry.

Second cabin passengers, however, were not obliged to travel to Ellis Island with the steerage passengers but were afforded the privilege of a cursory medical inspection aboard ship. It was assumed that if you could afford a first or second-class ticket, then you posed little risk of becoming a burden on the state and were mercifully spared the Ellis Island experience. His papers checked, and the obligatory 'six-second physical' passed, Pat disembarked with the rest of the 'quality.'

An army of horse-drawn Hansoms was queuing at the dockside. Pat understood horses, knew the smell and power of them. When holding a rein, he had always felt in control, more in control at any rate than he could have felt in that moment as he prepared to enter a professional running circus in which he would be the only man familiar with the curve of a furrow or the feel of a plough.

He took a cab to East 40th Street. Crossing the Brooklyn Bridge, the cabbie took him down Flatbush Avenue and through Prospect Park. As an introduction to New York, it was about as pleasant and sanitised as it got. But it was slow going in the snow, it was early, and it was bitterly cold – too cold to be sitting patiently on a stoop. He could only hope that the Lallys were up.

Hospitality and generosity to new arrivals were almost expected of Irish exiles at the time. The Lallys had been the beneficiaries of their sister's when they first arrived in New York, and now it was their turn to provide for others, not least because White was an old friend. It was an imposition, to be sure, but it was one that the majority of Irish exiles gladly endured, and frequently more than once.

The Cunard Dock, Pier 54, in 1907.

Four years had passed, almost to the day, since John Lally had made that same transatlantic crossing. He had been nineteen at the time, and had travelled with his sixteen-year-old wife, Josie.[212] He had been working in a draper's shop in Ballygar when he'd met her. Married on 7 January 1905, they had sailed just twelve days later from Cobh on the S.S. Baltic. At Ellis Island, each was recorded as having no more than $10 each in funds.

142

The couple had since settled in East Flatbush, an area that, just twenty years earlier, had been countryside but had by now been transformed into a densely populated neighbourhood of six-story apartment blocks housing thousands of Irish, Italian, and Jewish immigrants.[213] The area was far from salubrious, and, apart from the park, there was little left to delight the bucolic eye. Nothing grazed in Brooklyn now.

Still, it was a world away from the gang-infested West-Side ghetto of Hell's Kitchen, where innumerable Irish unfortunates continued to settle in the hope of finding work on the docks or the railroads. It had not been plain sailing since then, but the Lallys were settled now. John worked as a ticket clerk for one of the local railway companies and was the proud father of a two-year-old daughter, May. His wife, Josie, was seven months pregnant with her second child.

Given Josie's condition, it is unlikely that White stayed with the Lallys for more than a few days. With sufficient funds to rent a place of his own, he just needed help in deciding where. That he was staying, even temporarily, at John Lally's apartment and not at his brother William's would suggest that William either lived a fair distance outside of the city or that he, too, was staying at John's. Little is known about William.

In the short term, John Lally's apartment at 155 East 40th Street was ideally situated, being less than twenty minutes on foot from the Drill Hall of the 69th Regiment Armoury, where many of the professional athletes trained, and less than thirty from Madison Square Garden, where the promoter, Patrick T. Powers, had his offices. Exactly where in Brooklyn Pat eventually set up home remains unknown, but it was most likely in a 'furnished room' or at a boarding house.

THE RINGER

SON OF A Waterford father and a Derry mother, Patrick T. Powers was a significant figure in both Irish-American society and American sport. Born and raised in Trenton, New Jersey, he was intensely proud of his Irish heritage and considered Ireland his 'native country.' He maintained a permanent office at Madison Square Garden and had previously acted as secretary and general manager of a corporation formed to run the Irish Industrial Exhibitions at the Garden in 1905 and 1908.[214]

Well-connected in sporting circles, most notably in baseball, Powers had a keen interest in Irish sports and a proven track record of supporting Irish athletes in New York, where his sporting promotions would frequently exploit the commercial power of emigrant nostalgia and patriotism. During his first visit to Ireland in 1907, for example, Powers had attempted to recruit Gaelic football and hurling teams to compete against American teams at Celtic Park, as well as an Irish cycling team to compete in one of his six-day international marathons at Madison Square Garden.[215]

More recently, Powers had provided Pietri and Hayes with the opportunity to turn professional and recreate their Olympic drama in New York, where the disputed result of the 1908 race had

Johnny Hayes

become a part of an Irish-Italian rivalry that was deeply rooted in ethnic, economic, and religious conflict. This rivalry had already led to violence, most recently over access to jobs in the construction and garment industries. Recognising the commercial power of such animosity, Powers had drummed up such nationalistic fervour amongst the emigrant Italian and Irish communities in New York that, when the pair finally reprised their Olympic race, a crowd of 16,000 had crammed into the Garden to witness the little Italian redeem his reputation by defeating Hayes.

Powers had also, just a few weeks beforehand, added Tom Longboat to his stable. Allegedly embarrassed by the persistent rumours that he had secretly drugged Longboat during the London Olympics for financial gain, Tom Flanagan had suddenly decided to get out of the sport entirely and sold his contract to Powers for the princely sum of $2,000.[216]

Powers had been significantly aided in his running and cycling promotions of late by the fallout from the introduction, in June 1908, of the Hart–Agnew anti-betting legislation. This body of laws, enacted to combat gambling corruption at racetracks, had prompted California to ban betting on horses in February. New York had followed suit soon after. With the closure of racetracks, the viability of horse racing in New York collapsed, forcing many owners to move their horses out of state.

Another factor contributing to the rise in interest in professional running contests was racism. On 26 December 1908, African-American boxer Jack Johnson defeated Tommy Burns to take the world heavyweight title, seriously tarnishing the sport of professional boxing in the eyes of many white spectators. The subsequent decline of boxing and horse racing in New York had left white working-class gamblers searching for alternative entertainment, and, in steadily increasing numbers, they had turned to Powers' international sporting extravaganzas at the

Garden.[217]

On the face of it, Powers was a natural fit for an Irish professional athlete hoping to make it big in the United States. Still, Powers was also a shrewd and ruthless businessman. The extent of that ruthlessness would have been immediately apparent to White in Powers' treatment of the Olympic marathon champion, Johnny Hayes, whom White, perhaps even unknown to himself, had been brought over to replace.

Having signed for another match against Pietri at Madison Square Garden in January (a race he ultimately lost), Hayes had attempted to hold out for more money and, failing to get it, had decided to leave Powers' stable and go solo.[218] Powers then used his considerable influence to have him blacklisted. For a short while, no other promoter would touch Hayes for fear of alienating Powers.

> Hayes' advisors got him in hot water, and kept him there ever since. Johnny deserted the amateur ranks. He was beaten by Dorando, the man he conquered, in a match at the Garden. Instead of going along and getting into the best possible condition for another try, he thought he could get along without Powers. But he has found his mistake. Everywhere the door is barred. His athletic accomplishments, from an athletic standpoint, are useless to Hayes now.
>
> Powers has a new Marathon candidate in Pat White, just over from the "Ould Sod." White is the best-known long-distance professional performer in Ireland. It is said he covered the British Olympic course in 2:39, many minutes under Hayes' time. White is training at the Sixty-ninth Regiment Armory,

and will in all probability soon be given a chance to show his colors in Madison Square Garden. A deal is now on to match Shrubb, Longboat, Dorando and Maloney in a big four-cornered marathon. Maloney has some doubts about turning professional. If he will not enter, White is to be substituted. In the meantime, Pat will figure in some exhibitions in Paterson, N.J.[219]

The above article, published in the *Washington Times*, suggests a closer link between White and Powers than is evidenced elsewhere. It raises the possibility that Powers may have been more than just a promoter of White's races at this stage, but a member of the syndicate that had brought him to New York.

Exactly how William Lally entered into the equation is unclear. As John's elder brother and a former teammate of White's, it was to be expected that they would be close, but it seems unlikely that he could have been part of the syndicate that brought White to America. The most likely scenario is that Powers told White to find himself a manager so that he could concentrate on his running. And so White simply handed the job, informally, to William Lally.[220]

Contracts between athletes and managers could vary wildly in terms, from those where an athlete was bound to the manager, such as had existed between Longboat and Flanagan, and those where the manager was the hireling. Dorando Pietri, for example, once publicly threatened to fire his own manager if he could not secure a match for him against Longboat.[221]

It is not known what split of his earnings White had agreed with Lally, but it is unlikely to have been anything like the 50-50 split that Longboat had with Flanagan. A written contract was also unlikely between friends.

The Maloney mentioned in the *Washington Times* article above as a potential first opponent for White was twenty-six-year-old Matt Maloney, a native of Coolameen, in County Clare. He had left for New York at the age of twenty and settled in Yonkers. Having never participated in athletics while growing up in Ireland, he had only recently taken up running. His first race had been just two years previous.

On 26 December 1908, Maloney had won a marathon sponsored by the *New York Journal* in a time of 2:36:26, which at the time was a world amateur record.[222] The following January, he had won an indoor marathon at Madison Square Garden in 2:54, setting an amateur world indoor record for twenty-five miles en route.[223]

That Maloney had burst so unexpectedly onto the marathon scene was a problem for White, but not for Powers. A little competition from other 'Irish' athletes was good for him. It might even help to bring the recalcitrant Hayes to heel. With the next Olympic Games over three years away, however, Maloney was dithering about turning professional so early in his career.

Meanwhile, back in London, Crowhurst had returned from Paris with a list of French, Belgian, Italian, and Dutch entrants for the six-day race. There had as yet, however, been no response from aspiring Irish entrants, and rumours were rife in Dublin that White had sailed to New York, intending to partner with an American to form an Irish-American team.[224] As soon as it became apparent that White had never had any intention of competing in the six-day race, Pat Fagan and Frank Curtis offered to make up an Irish team.[225]

> What is known as a six days' foot race will commence on March 8th in the Madison Square Gardens, New York, and will end on March 13th. Teams are already entered representative of nearly every country in Europe, as well as Canada and the United States... The Irish representatives will be Pat Fagan, 20 Greek Street, Dublin, and Frank Curtis, Ashbourne, Co. Meath... It was hoped that Pat White, the Donabate, Co. Dublin, champion, would take part in the six days' contest, but he is on more serious business. He has gone to America to arrange a match with Dorando, Longboat, Hayes, and other long-distance runners.[226]

Less than two weeks after he arrived in Brooklyn, White was assigned a publicist who arranged interviews and photographic sessions with the local press. In a city filled with bright lights and incessant clamour, the hidden lamp was quickly extinguished, the softly spoken word too easily muffled. As an unknown quantity in America, his arrival had to be trumpeted if the sporting public were to be enticed to part with their hard-earned cash to watch him run.

The *Buffalo Courier* was the first to interview him:

> A ruddy faced, healthy looking Irishman arrived in town the other day. He is Patrick White of Dublin, the champion distance runner of the Green Isle, and has come to this country to grab off some titles and the accompanying gold. He says he can beat all the Longboats, Shrubbs,

Dorandos and Hayes in the world and is willing to bet that he can.

Patrick is twenty-six years old and weighs eleven stones eight, which in plain English means 162 pounds. He ran nine races last year at distances ranging from ten to twenty-six miles. He had travelled all over Ireland and defeated the best professionals there.[227]

Before any match could be finalised, however, the syndicate that had brought Pat to New York needed to ascertain how soon and how far they could run him. So Pat was hastily entered in the Brooklyn-Seagate Marathon, a strictly amateur event scheduled to take place on 12 February 1909 as part of the Abraham Lincoln birthday celebrations. The race would run from the 69th Regiment Armoury to Coney Island and back.

To conceal his form from the bookies and his identity from race officials, Pat was entered under a pseudonym. It was not uncommon at the time for amateurs to enter professional contests under an alias, but a professional entering an amateur contest was about as rare and conspicuous as a Chinaman in a Harlem tearoom, and the deception was quickly exposed:

> Many amusing incidents marked the running of the Marathon race yesterday, perhaps the most interesting of which was the discovery of a "ringer" in the person of Pat White, the Irish pro, who ran second to St. Ives in the big professional Marathon in England last year. White entered the race under the name of Leonard Rhodes, unattached, with the registry number 14015, and he was No. 106 on the list of entries.
>
> White, who is here to meet some of the stars

in the local professional field and possesses a press agent, lined up with the starters right under the noses of a host of A.A.U. officials, who failed to recognize him. In fact, it was not until White had gone six miles of the distance and was among the first flight, apparently going easily, that his identity became known. It remained for the newspaper men in the press car to discover White's identity. It passed within a few feet of the foreigner, who was decked out in a neat running suit of white, trimmed with green material, which set off his sturdy form to excellent effect, winning many favorable comments from the crowd that lined the course. As the car passed him one of its occupants shouted:

"Hullo, Pat!"

Around came his head with a jerk and he grinned sheepishly at the man who recognized him. An expression of woe crossed his face immediately, which said without words: "The jig is up." But White did not quit at once. He continued on to Surf Avenue, where he was forced to give up owing to bad feet. He had worn no stockings, and an examination of his feet showed that his shoes had rubbed off the skin in ribbons and he was practically unable to walk.

Later it was said by his backers that he had entered the race merely for practice, and he had no intention of claiming a prize. There was no athlete by the name of Leonard Rhodes, according to the athletic authorities, it was merely a name White's managers had invented for the occasion. How they secured an official registration number, however, remains a mystery.[228]

Shortly after the Brooklyn Marathon, Matt Maloney finally agreed to turn professional. Unable to secure a match against Shrubb or Longboat, he offered instead to 'run a marathon

Start of the Brooklyn Marathon 1909.

race with any man in the world' for $1000. The offer was quickly snapped up by William Lally on behalf of White and his syndicate. Maloney was a raw young talent with a strong local following. The match would surely appeal to the Irish community and provide White with an opportunity to race for the first time on an indoor track.

Following negotiations between the two camps, the purse was doubled to $2,000, of which $1500 would go to the winner and $500 to the loser. By the time the match was announced in the Irish papers, however, Chinese whispers had inflated that amount to a staggering $2,800, fuelling all manner of wonder and envy at home. At the exchange rate of the time, the $1,500 and $500 split would have translated to approximately £308 and £102 sterling, or, in 2025, to approximately £46,000 and £15,000 sterling. A professional free-for-all five-mile race would also be on the programme for a prize of $100.

> The matter of a side bet was suggested, but Maloney's sponsor readily agreed to race for the fat purse alone. It appears that the $1000 forfeit has caused several of the "pro" Marathoners to back out of the contest.[229]

MARATHON MANIA

THE WHOLE COUNTRY had gone crazy. Such was
the hunger for tests of endurance that all manner
of enthusiasts were now to be seen on public
greens testing their limits.[230] Back in December
1908, a letter writer to the Washington Post
described the fad as 'the expression of a national
symptom' and claimed, somewhat prophetically,
that it was only a matter of time before all
manner of marathon merchandise would saturate
the market 'like a cloud of locusts in a Kansas
wheat field'.[231]

Marathon Mania Cartoon, in *Puck*, 20 January 1909.

Four days after the Brooklyn Marathon, the

craze was further satirised in *Collier's Weekly*. By May, a silent movie would have been released lampooning the craze, in which a man reading a newspaper report of a marathon race starts to jog around the kitchen table, so engrossed in his daydream of marathon glory that he neglects the crying child he is supposed to be caring for.[232] The craze would also see a mad rush to apply the formula to other activities such as dancing, cycling, ditch digging and even novel writing! [233]

'Effect of the Marathon Craze.' Satirical cartoon published in *Collier's Weekly*, 6 February 1909.

For as long as the craze lasted, there was a small fortune to be made, and Pat White wanted a slice of the pie. Unfortunately, the time he needed to get back into racing shape and adjust to the life and diet of an American was not granted by his backers. They had already invested a fair amount in bringing him over and were impatient to see that investment repaid. Between his board and lodgings, and the cost of a publicity campaign, every day of delay was costing them money.

White's adaptation to life in Brooklyn was not without its athletic challenges. Running outdoors, especially on city streets, was not the common occurrence it is today. Beyond the park and the track, it attracted stares and, occasionally, alarm. It was a far cry from Richardstown and Ballyboughal, where everyone knew him by name, where the roads were mostly empty, and eccentric pursuits such as running might well be remarked upon, but were nevertheless accepted as being part of the rich tapestry of rural life.

At home, the most White might chance upon during a Sunday morning run would be a rabbit scuttling for the undergrowth or a fox returning from the hunt; the most he might hear, the ruckus of crows and ravens, the rustle of a robin or sparrow in the hedgerows or a whisper of wind in the whitethorn. The peal of bells from a distant spire might occasionally break his concentration, or an affectionate hail from a passing neighbour. Mostly, though, his country runs were quiet and contemplative. But this was New York, the city that never sleeps. Quiet and contemplative it was not.

Unable to train as he was accustomed, Pat's regimen underwent a dramatic change. Training now took place indoors, and the skipping rope became a staple of his daily routine – an innovation suggestive of the influence of Ernie Hertberg (Ernst Hjertberg), a fitness guru believed at the time to be one of the finest coaches in the world. Hertberg had recently surrendered his amateur status as trainer of the Irish American Athletic Club to train and manage professional athletes. Among his stable, he counted the Olympic marathon champion, Johnny Hayes, and the Swedish Olympic silver medallist and world record holder over 3000m, Johan 'John' Svanberg.

Hertberg believed Marathon runners needed to do 'much work on the toes, to get the ankles and toes elastic and strong.' He also believed in changing the style of running now and then to 'give the muscles variation in work.' His athletes ran just three times a week, and supplemented their runs with long walks taken with 'short, quick, and easy steps.' [234]

A few days before the head-to-head with Maloney, White's publicist arranged an interview for him with Vincent Treanor of the *Evening World*. Treanor, a thirty-one-year-old sports reporter, whose expertise lay not in track and field but in professional boxing and horse racing, was quicker than most to spot the obvious:

> Maybe Patrick isn't fit and ready for his race with Maloney. One look at him shows that. His ideas of training are novel and original. He doesn't go out and run his head off in daily training like the rest of them do. Paddy walks, running very rarely. He says that's better. He does five miles before breakfast, five miles before dinner, and seven before what he calls supper. "I'll save my running for Friday night," he says.
>
> Paddy's favourite way of training is in the "gym" – something after the way fighters condition themselves. He puts in a couple of hours a day skipping around, swinging on the rings, and playing handball. "This saves my feet and improves my wind," he explains. Long runs before a Marathon race aren't half as good as

long walks, according to White.

White says he's as right as a clock, and believes he will beat Maloney sure. The mere defeat of Maloney, however, is not what he is after. He wants to run faster than Hayes, Dorando or Longboat and create new figures that will keep them all hustling to better. He says he will have no trouble going the route. He has a schedule all mapped out that he will follow closely. He figures Maloney can't beat it.

White takes great care of his feet. Every other day he bathes them in hot salt water to harden them. He puts no alcohol on them at all, although he uses this rubbing fluid on his body every day after his gymnasium work.

White has a nice easy-going style, reminding one very much of Tommy Conneff, the greatest middle-distance runner ever seen in this country. He has a stride of five and a half feet, and when in full swing lifts his feet not more than four inches from the ground. Since he has been here, he has given himself two time trials on the hard boards of the Sixty-ninth Regiment armory, one of three miles in less than 15 minutes and another of ten miles in better than 55 minutes.

Sparrow Robertson will lay a specially made loam and dirt track for the race. It will be eleven laps to the mile, and as fast as can be constructed.[235]

When questioned about his diet by another interviewer, Pat, who had recently claimed to abstain from tobacco and alcohol completely, indicated that he derived his energy primarily from potatoes, a food many runners at the time considered far too starchy for athletes.[236] Carbohydrate loading had yet to be discovered, or adopted, by the marathon community. He stood out, did White, outwardly confident in his talent, but inwardly insecure as to his knowledge. A new life, a new training regimen, and a new culture. It was enough for any man to be adapting to, without the pressure to perform.

NEW BEGINNINGS

WHEN IT CAME to new beginnings, the inauguration of William Howard Taft as the 27th president of the United States was hardly auspicious. Held on Thursday, March 4, 1909, it had to be moved indoors when an overnight blizzard covered Washington with ten inches of snow. The same storm hit New York later that afternoon, covering the streets with a three-and-a-half-inch carpet of snow. By 7 p.m., that carpet had acquired a jaundiced hue as the gas lights came on. By 9 p.m., the temperature had dipped a couple of degrees below zero, and the carpet began to freeze. Walking became treacherous.

At 6 o'clock the following morning, an army of six thousand soldiers armed with shovels descended on the city to clear the snow from the principal arteries between the Battery and Twenty-third Street.[237] But it was slower going elsewhere, as only one snow removal contractor remained licensed in New York State following recent investigations into political corruption in the awarding of public contracts. It was hardly the best of conditions to be going out in, and it augured badly for attendance figures for that night's contest between White and Maloney, most especially for those reliant on public transport to get there.

The match against Maloney was due to take place on an indoor track, of which White had limited

162

experience, apart from the ten-mile exhibition runs he had recently undertaken in New Jersey to earn some pocket money and generate much-needed publicity.[238] Such tracks were small and narrow, even at Madison Square Garden, the largest auditorium in the world. The previous November, for example, the Dorando vs. Hayes rematch had seen the organisers construct a track measuring just one tenth of a mile, or 161 metres, in circumference for a race of 262 laps. Modern indoor tracks, by way of comparison, are 200m in circumference.

The White vs. Maloney race, however, was scheduled to take place not at the Garden, but on a specially laid oval track in the Drill Shed of the Sixty-Ninth Regiment Armoury, home of New York's Irish Guard.[239] The match would be promoted, not by Powers, who was tied up with the organisation of the six-day race at the Garden, but by Monty Pike, president of the North Beach Athletic Club, under whose auspices the armoury had been booked.[240]

As the drill shed was a much smaller venue than the Garden, the track would be considerably shorter, and the bends would be exceptionally tight. At 146m in length, it would be just three-quarters the size of a modern indoor track and lacking in banked curves. Instead of ten laps to the mile, there would now be eleven. The smaller venue would also mean seating for only 6,000 spectators. On a positive note, smoking would be prohibited during the race. This new departure would follow the introduction of a law banning smoking on the subways, a law that was due to come into force for the first time on race day.

The *Brooklyn Daily Eagle* did its best to

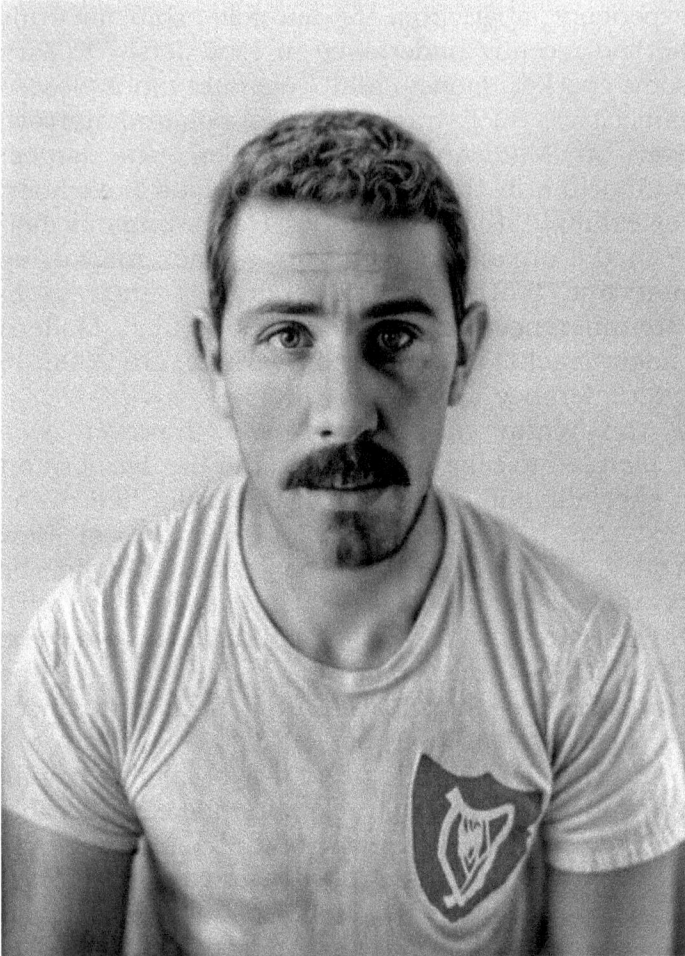

Pat White's publicity photograph from the front page of the
Brooklyn Daily Eagle, 13 February 1909.

generate enthusiasm for a contest between two Irishmen who, at the time, were largely unknown to the sporting and gambling public.

The race is the greatest betting proposition New

York has had in many a day, and it should be the sporting feature of the week. There are no big fights at the fighting clubs, and it is a month since the last Marathon race was run at Madison Square Garden.

In the meanwhile the two Brooklyn amateur Marathons have added further to the excitement. White himself, although a professional, ran in the Thirteenth Regiment, Lincoln's Birthday Marathon, not as a competitor, but just as a try out. He was running easily at Sea Gate, having covered at an average of 10 to 11 miles an hour with the leaders Lee and Miller, when his backers were satisfied that he was a goer and a stayer, too, and stopped him.[241]

On 5 March 1909, shortly before 9 p.m., Maloney and White lined up at the start to be introduced like championship prize fighters. Then, at the striking of the hour, Big Tim Sullivan, the Tammany Hall political boss and self-proclaimed 'King of the Bowery,' sent White and Maloney on their way. A confident Maloney went immediately to the front.[242] White allowed him to lead for three miles before, in a change from his customary tactics, he took the lead and raised the tempo.

Maloney continued in the lead for three miles, but a few yards below the three-mile mark White forged ahead of him and at the five miles was ten yards ahead. During the seventh mile White spurted and gained a lap. This lead he continued to increase until at the tenth mile he was a lap and a half in front of his rival. Time for ten miles: 59:03.

This was what the crowd had come to see, a

genuine scrap, but with the athletes trading surges instead of punches, gaining a lap or two and then sitting in behind and letting the other fella do the work. They had not come to see a plodder let his opponent go, only to start racing after a couple of hours had passed. They wanted to be entertained, to see each man battle for the inside line, head-to-head, man against man. It was all so very different from road racing.

But then White ran into trouble. British tracks at that time ran in a clockwise direction. Unaccustomed to running in the opposite direction and on an impossibly tight track, his left calf began to cramp, forcing him to stop and walk.[243]

> Up to and after the fifteenth mile White maintained his lead, but then he faltered a trifle and Maloney went after him and gradually cut down his lead. At the end of the eighteenth mile Maloney was only thirty yards behind White, whom he soon passed. Another mile saw Maloney two laps in the lead, the little Dublin runner having stopped almost to a walk. During the twentieth mile Maloney went farther ahead, so that when the twenty miles were completed he was eight laps ahead.[244]

White managed to struggle on for a couple of more laps, but at mile twenty, he was finally forced to retire, and Maloney was gifted the easiest of victories.[245]

> White was obliged to quit in the twentieth mile, Maloney at that stage being three-quarters of a mile in the lead. White was taken to his dressing room suffering from contracted muscles of his left leg. He said that this was caused by his

166

continual turning to his left side. He is not used to running on an oval track, all his previous work having been done in the open. The prizes for this race were $1,500 to the winner and $500 to the loser.[246]

Not everyone watching believed the story about cramp. The *Boston Daily Globe* report described White variously as being 'all in' and 'fagged out' at the end of the race. In short, he wasn't fit. Maloney, he wrote, had simply 'ran the legs from under Paddy White.'[247] The defeat was a competitive disaster for White, and the syndicate took a serious tumble. Their losses were all the more upsetting for having come on a 'sure thing.' It would not have been accepted gracefully.

The defeat, however, was not without the possibility of redemption, and Pat had still achieved an enormous payday by Irish standards, though exactly how much of that $500 he got to keep is anybody's guess. There was no need to panic just yet, but there *was* ample cause for concern. The gate receipts, even allowing for the weather, had been disappointing. Neither man had proved to be a box-office draw, even among the Irish community.

The Marathon craze seems to be subsiding, though this can better be determined after the Hayes-Dorando match Monday night. There was a very small crowd to see Matt Maloney beat Paddy White, the Irish champion, last week and there was not a great deal of enthusiasm. It is true neither of these men has the drawing power of Longboat, Shrubb and some of the others, but it is doubtful if even these stars could fill Madison Square Garden again unless a crowd of them should race.[248]

Truth be told, it was always going to be difficult to replace Johnny Hayes in the affections of the Irish community. Hayes' ruddy appearance, boyish charm and healthy lifestyle had such broad appeal that his employers, Bloomingdales, had not only built a cinder track for him on the roof of their New York department store, but had fast-tracked his promotion from an assistant in the superintendent's office to manager of the sporting goods department.[249]

Johnny Hayes had what Maloney and White lacked. He had name recognition, an Olympic title, and a winning personality. Professional sport was theatre, and spectators demanded a spectacle, or at the very least, the chance to get up close to a celebrity. Johnny Hayes had what it took to entice people out of their homes on a cold winter's night. White and Maloney did not.

Not every report of the race, however, was pessimistic regarding their prospects in the professional circus. The *New York Tribune*, for instance, was surprisingly supportive:

It may take Pat White, the Irish champion, some time to establish himself in this country as a long distance runner after his defeat by Maloney on Friday night, in the race over the full Marathon distance. I agree, however, with Al Copeland, the Princeton trainer, that White will yet make his mark, if he gets the opportunity, as there can be no question about his being a clever runner.

He has not been feeling just right since his arrival in this country four weeks ago, and in all probability he needs another month or two to get

168

fully acclimated. Maloney's stock has gone up, and those interested in Marathon running will not be satisfied until he is matched with Longboat, Dorando or Hayes. There are many who would not hesitate to back him to win.[250]

At Madison Square Garden, Frank Curtis and Pat Fagan set off two days later in the six-day indoor race, relentlessly running in circles in a task that was to prove as punishing on their sanity as on their physical well-being. By the third day, they were one of only twelve teams still running. The second day had proved particularly brutal. Two men had fainted during the night. One had been carried from the track, and the other, recovering consciousness, had resumed the race and run until midday the following day, when he, too, was forced to retire.

At this point, Curtis and Fagan were running in third place, twenty-three miles behind the leaders, Edouard Cibot and Louis Orphée of

France, who had broken the world record for 24 hours en route. By the fourth day, the Irish pair had been overtaken for third by the Americans, Dinner, and Prouty, who led them by two miles. By the fifth day, with only ten teams remaining in the race, the Irish pair were lying seventh, with Curtis reportedly in terrible shape.[251]

Madison Square Garden during a six-day cycle race organised by Powers in 1908.

That same afternoon, Pat was given the chance to test his calf in an exhibition race over ten miles. Running on the same track and at the same time as the six-day event, he was paced by the Welsh professional Percy Smallwood of Conwy for the first two miles before some of the competitors in the six-day race decided to join him to relieve the pain and the unremitting boredom.

White's easy graceful stride was admired by

those in attendance, and some of the sharps predicted once more that he would be heard from before the season is over. Pallanti, of the Italian team, surprised the onlookers by following the pace set by White for a full half mile and then sprinted by him on one of the straights before slowing down to the regulation jog. It was a remarkable piece of running for a man who had been plodding away since early Monday morning. Orphée, of the French team, also followed White's pace for three or four laps, just to satisfy himself, as he said, that he had not lost his speed.[252]

Pat's time for the distance was 58:14, good enough, it seemed, to convince Powers that he had not lost his form. Later that evening, contracts were signed for a ten-mile indoor head-to-head between Pat White and Johan Svanberg, the race to take place on the final day of the six-day race at the Garden.[253]

While the crowds that have turned out to see the six-day go-as-you-please race in Madison Square Garden have been woefully small, the big amphitheatre should be filled to overflowing tonight, as in addition to the finish of the long grind, one of the best ten-mile match races of the winter will be decided as an extra attraction.

Pat White, the Irish champion, who was beaten by Matt Maloney in a Marathon run a few days ago, due partly to his straining a tendon early in the race, will meet John Svanberg, the five-mile record holder of Sweden, who won his heat in the five-mile Olympic championship last summer and finished well up in the final.

Svanberg won a relay race at ten miles two or three nights ago in 58 minutes, 14⅖ seconds.

Svanberg had the pole all the way in his race, while White had to work his way in and out of the six-day runners, so that to all appearances the men are well matched. In all probability, the winner will have to run in 55 minutes or better, and the contest should be worth going to see.

The race will begin at 9 o'clock, and the men will run for a $1,000 purse.[254]

The race between White and Svanberg took place on the day of John Francis Lally's baptism, which had been celebrated that afternoon at the Church of Our Lady of the Scapular of Mount Carmel on East 28th Street. Baptisms fell somewhere between weddings and funerals on the scale of social obligations in New York, and it would have been a poor friend who did not join the celebrations. The timing was unfortunate, but it also served as a reminder, if further motivation were needed, of all that he was sacrificing to be part of the show, racing against the best distance runners in the world.

The final race of Pat White's twenties began at 10:03 p.m. on Saturday, 13 March 1909. By all accounts, it was a cagey affair:

Both men were lustily cheered when they jogged the track by a crowd numbering four thousand persons. After a little warming up, a coin was tossed. White called the turn and drew the pole. Both men hit up a lively pace at the start, with White in the lead and Svanberg a stride behind. The latter then put on speed and, passing White, opened up a lead of fifty feet. After the sixth lap, the Irishman hit up the pace, and in turn, took the lead...[255]

172

Svanberg, Athens 1906.

The second and third miles were run at a good gallop, with the lead constantly changing hands, and neither man succeeding in gaining more than three or four strides on his opponent. In the middle of mile four, White brought his supporters to their feet by going to the front, a lead he held for the next two miles. Svanberg eventually overtook him when, after 'several lively brushes,' White lost the battle to deny him the advantage of the inside line.

Shortly after mile eight, White again attempted to pass the Swede, but Svanberg always seemed to have enough to deny him. At mile nine, however, to the wild applause of his supporters, he finally succeeded in overtaking him. The Swede appeared to have shot his bolt, and White quickly opened a six-yard gap. Svanberg gamely fought back and, going into the final mile, was hanging onto White's shoulders.

> The final mile was an eventful one. White turned into it in the lead, with the Swede a single stride behind him. Both men were running strongly and both men appeared to have plenty in reserve for the final sprint. This relative position was maintained during the mile until the last quarter of the ninth lap. Here Svanberg lengthened out his stride, and in the twinkling of an eye was on even terms with the man from the land of the shamrock. Another moment and the Swede was in the lead.
>
> The spectators were on their feet, yelling and cheering, for the determining sprint was on, and they knew it. White's friends, who were largely in the majority, implored him to come on and "Get him." White responded to the best of his ability and the race was still in doubt when Svanberg stumbled and went sprawling. There were cries of "Foul" but none was apparent, and Tim Hurst, the referee, was not called on to entertain a complaint. After getting to his feet, Svanberg pluckily finished the race... one of the hardest fought that has yet been seen at the Garden.[256]

Having emerged victorious in a time of 57:17.4, Pat took home the lion's share of the $1000 purse.[257] Negotiations began immediately for a rematch, this time over Pat's preferred distance – the marathon.

Out of sight, out of mind, and no longer embarrassing the best of the English runners, the unconditional adoration of the Irish press had

174

cooled somewhat in White's absence. Having exhausted their fascination with him in 1908, now less fulsome in their praise, the sports reporter of the *Irish Independent* even went so far as to somewhat cheekily compare Pat's recent time against Svanberg with the current amateur world record.

> A big crowd (cables our New York correspondent) was attracted to the ten mile race here yesterday (Saturday) between Pat White, who is programmed here as the Irish professional champion, and Svenberg, the champion of Sweden. The latter has earned a big reputation as a runner in the States.
>
> White was stronger and fleeter than when he ran against Pat Maloney recently. He did most of the pacing. And had the Swede well worn out before the finish. White's time was 57 min. 12 2-5 secs. This is 20 secs better than Alfred Shrubb's time for ten miles in his Marathon race against Longboat on February 9th, when the Indian won. In that race Shrubb led at ten miles in 57 min, 32 2-5 secs. The amateur record is held by W. D. Day at 52 mins. 38 2-5 secs.
>
> Pat White is the well-known long distance champion from Donabate, Co. Dublin. He ran second in the English Professional Marathon last autumn, and was second again in the Scottish Marathon on New Year's Day. He has twice won the "Herald" race.[258]

Curtis and Fagan would not improve on their placing in the six-day race and would ultimately finish seventh, having covered 562 miles – 78 miles behind the winners, Cibot and Orphée. But it was not the defeat that dismayed the Irish pair, so much as the discovery that they had never been part of a sporting contest, but merely players in a show.[259]

At one stage during the race, with the number of surviving teams dwindling daily and public interest falling, Powers had introduced a new rule, allowing teams to run a substitute should one or other team members retire. Most of the competitors objected to the new rule, but Powers waved away their objections, claiming that it was necessary 'in the interests of competition.'

The result was chaos, with many competitors forming new teams during the race. Had the race finished under the original rules, Fagan and Curtis would have finished third. Before the race was even over, the scales had fallen from their eyes, and the professional circuit revealed to be little more than a circus. Exhausted and disillusioned, they took the first boat home.

SNUBBED!

FIVE DAYS AFTER the Svanberg race, Pat White turned thirty: not old in the scheme of athletic careers, but no longer young. Little is known about his life in Brooklyn, and it would be wrong to speculate too wildly, but he was a young man alone in a big city with few friends, no family, and his pockets bulging with more money than he had ever possessed in his life. It would perhaps be unreasonable to imagine that he resisted the temptation to indulge himself.

In just two months, White had won up to $1,000 in prizemoney, though how much of that he got to keep and how much went to repay his backers is difficult to say. Nevertheless, just two days after the New York race, the first full marathon to be held in Ireland took place at Jones' Road, Dublin. Organised by Surgeon John Stephen McArdle, it was run over 60 laps and 425 yards of a track that was just under half a mile in circumference. The race was won by Tom Hynes in a time that was just nine seconds under 2:52 (i.e. four and a half minutes slower than White had run at the Powderhall the previous January). Hynes' prize was a meagre £30, or $136, large by Irish standards, but a pittance by American. Pat White may not have been getting rich, but he was certainly earning more than Hynes.

On the day after White's victory over Svanberg,

177

a penitent Hayes, finally shaken out of his complacency, put his dispute with Powers behind him and ran a third match against Pietri at the Garden. Pietri emerged victorious, lapping his opponent no less than five times and leaving Hayes' supporters searching for a new Irish hero to replace the old. The pressing question now was, would that be White or Maloney?

Thus far, the fashion had been for head-to-head races, but the disappointing attendance for the latest Pietri-Hayes rematch forced Powers to change tack. For his next promotion, he decided to organise an unofficial world championship race featuring six of the best professional distance runners currently on the American circuit. This 'Grand Marathon Derby' was arranged for 3 April 1909 at the Polo Grounds in New York. The purse would be in excess of $5000.

But why only six competitors? Well, this was allegedly at the insistence of Longboat and Shrubb's managers, who were reluctant to dilute either the prize fund or their clients' chances. And so White and Svanberg, both of whom had appeared to be rounding into excellent form, were barred from entering. That Powers had so readily favoured Maloney over White suggested he had been less than impressed with both the Irishman's pulling power and his loss to Maloney.

White was devastated. Snubbed by Powers, he decided he'd had enough and was ready to return home. Lally, however, had already arranged a match for him on 10 April in Boston and persuaded him to wait at least until after that before making a decision. As for the Grand Marathon Derby, the local press were not slow in protesting White's omission.

There is only one cause for complaint in the make-up of the field, that being the bars that are up against Pat White, the Irish Champion, who in my opinion is deserving of a chance of proving himself against the best runners in the country.

It would have been interesting, also, to see whether Svanberg, the Swedish five-mile champion, who was second to Sherring in the Athens Marathon in 1906, is as good as ever. White defeated him over ten miles in Madison Square Garden. An accident marred this race, it is true, and there are many that believe that the Swede is White's superior at any distance, but I am not convinced.

White was defeated over the Marathon distance several weeks ago by Matt Maloney, but in that race, White sprained the tendons in his foot early in the contest, and showed remarkable pluck and courage to stay as long as he did.[260]

Start of the Grand Marathon Derby, 3 April 1909.

The Grand Marathon Derby went ahead as planned on 3 April. A crowd of 25,000 squeezed into the grounds, with thousands more gathering to watch from vantage points on the Speedway, Coogan's Bluff, and every tree and chimney that offered even a partial view of the track. At Times Square, hundreds more congregated around the *New York Times* bulletin board to read live reports from the track.

Pat White may not have been on the starting line for the Grand Marathon Derby, but that did not necessarily mean he was without skin in the game. Longboat was the bookie's favourite at odds of 6/5, with Pietri starting at odds of 11/5 and Shrubb at 8/5. Hayes and Maloney, regarded as rank outsiders, were being offered at better odds.

The longest odds of all, however, were being offered against Henri St. Yves, an unknown quantity to most Americans, but not to Pat White, nor indeed to the Princeton cross-country team with whom he had been recently training. And so, when the Frenchman, to the surprise of almost all present, ran out a convincing winner, the band played the Marseillaise and the Princeton boys celebrated wildly, having backed him at exceptionally long odds. It would have been surprising if Pat White's wallet had not sat a little heavier in his pocket after that race.

White and Svanberg were not the only athletes to be overlooked for the Grand Marathon Derby. Also rebuffed were Frenchmen Eduard Cibet and Louis Orphée, the latter of whom Pat was contracted to race on 10 April over a full marathon at Huntington Avenue, grounds of the Boston Red Sox.[261] White had previously committed to a head-to-head rematch against Svanberg a week later at Celtic Park, home of the New York Gaelic Athletic Association, but withdrew from that in favour of a chance to race over a full marathon against Orphée and Pat Dineen on the weekend before the Boston Marathon.[262] Two days after the Grand Marathon Derby, he left New York for Boston.

> Boston, April 7. – Pat White, who will meet Orphée and Dinneen in the Marathon race at the American League grounds Saturday, arrived in town yesterday morning and looks like a likely chap. He says that he is not afraid of Dinneen, but fears the Frenchman Orphée. White had a clipping in his pocket from a French paper, which was translated, by extreme effort, and showed that Ophee had covered a distance, approximately 25 miles, in two hours twenty-five minutes nineteen seconds and the Irishman remarked:
>
> "I believe Orphée did it and will prove to be another St. Yves, and I am going to plan my race to consider him, although Dinneen may fool us both."
>
> White claims that the climate in this country affected him greatly in his race against Matt Maloney, but he recovered somewhat when he beat Svanberg, and predicted that the winner Saturday would have to do close to two hours 40 minutes to win the race. The Irishman, who had not seen Boston but a few hours, added:
>
> "Say, this is the greatest town ever." [263]

For this race, White made a point of completing his training in Boston, the city which boasted the largest Irish population in the U.S. By being conspicuous in the expat community, he helped

RUNNERS' RECORD MAKE RACE
SATURDAY MOST PROMISING

PAT DINEEN OF SOUTH BOSTON. PAT WHITE OF IRELAND, LOUIS ORPHEE OF FRANCE.

to promote the event, garner valuable column inches for the promoters, and increase the gate money.

White has won many friends and admirers during his short stay in Boston, and the form he has been displaying augurs ill for his rivals. Since he has become acclimated he has steadily improved until now he claims to be as fit as he ever was in his life. After today's race White intends to go after Maloney, for he is satisfied that the New York lad's victory over him was due to lack of condition.[264]

Orphée's manager would later confess that he had only taken the match in Boston so soon after the six-day event at Madison Square Garden, in the hope that, by winning it, he could force a match against St. Yves and prove once and for all who was the greatest Marathon runner in the world. He had little doubt but that his man would win.[265]

Come the day of the race, weather conditions at Huntington Avenue were cold and windy and not conducive to fast times.[266] Pat Dineen, the South Boston baker, forced the pace from the start and took an early lead. The others allowed him his moment. At the end of the first mile, however, Orphée and White took control, a state of affairs that would continue for the next ten miles.

> From the start White had been running close to the stakes marking the track, and on the seventh mile he struck his left knee against one of the stakes, cutting a gash that hindered him very little. He seemed to be having trouble with his right leg and ankle and limped noticeably.[267]

From mile eleven to mile twelve, Dineen made several unsuccessful attempts to close the gap on them, but by mile eighteen he had fallen two hundred yards adrift.

There was a bit of argy-bargy during the next mile as White tried to retake the lead from Orphée. The Frenchman, however, refused to yield the inside line, and White was forced to drop in behind him and sit there until the twenty-second mile, when, first one, and then the other, would go in front, the lead continuously

From left to right: Louis Orphée, James Gallivan starter, Pat Dineen, and Pat White at the Huntington Avenue race.

alternating until the twenty-second mile when Pat hit another stake and fell heavily. Rising gingerly to his feet, he was forced to walk a few steps to catch his breath. He quickly resumed the race, but Orphée had gone.

During the twenty-fifth mile, with the race all but over and White still secure in second position, his ankle gave way for a second time, forcing him to retire. Orphée went on to win in a little under 2:54.[268] Dineen, like White, would also fail to finish, dropping out as the Frenchman crossed the finish line two and a half laps ahead.[269] White had now failed to finish in two of his first three races on the American circuit. Not everyone bought his excuses.

White found the distance too much for him. He

184

dropped behind gradually and in the 25th mile he was compelled by exhaustion to drop out of the race.[270]

Sometime between his omission from the Grand Marathon Derby and the outcome of his race against Orphée, White came to the decision that he'd had enough of America. He fired off a telegram to Dublin, asking to be entered in the 'Irish Marathon Race,' which was due to take place at Jones' Road on 16 May.[271] But once again, he was persuaded to stay and to give himself time. Win, lose, or draw, Lally was making money.

Pat White may have been brought to New York to replace Johnny Hayes, but he had proved to be an inconsistent performer, ill at ease as a public figure and a total loss as a crowd-puller. Having shown little to suggest that he was capable of cutting any ice in the professional ranks, he was promptly dropped by Powers.

There was nothing personal in Powers' decision. It was just business. He had recently done worse to Longboat, whom he actually managed, by selling his contract to an Ontario businessman for $700, considerably less than half of what he had bought it for. One had to be practical about such things. Maloney at least had a local following. Sentiment could only be indulged so far in business.

Prior to the Maloney race, the Pittsburgh-based Italian-American, Hughie Brusse, had offered to race the winner for a side bet of $500 or $1000.[272] Maloney does not appear to have taken the bait, but White eventually did. Details of that race are hard to find, but it appears to have taken place some weeks later in Atlantic City, New Jersey, and over fifteen miles rather than a full marathon. White would lose that race, too.[273]

DECLINE AND FALL

RAGAMUFFINS LOAFED ON street corners in their summer haircuts, games of potsy broke out at random intervals on the colourfully chalked sidewalks, and organ grinders pushed their carts around the multi-ethnic blocks in search of appreciative outdoor audiences. Summer had arrived in Brooklyn.[274]

With rising temperatures, careworn mothers crowded the tenement stoops, desperate for adult conversation and the comfort of the tepid breeze that would occasionally waft in from the East River. Overhead, feather mattresses aired, half-in and half-out of bedroom windows, and row after row of white shirts and bedsheets hung limply from the clotheslines that bridged the alleys like so much celebratory bunting.

For Pat White, the arrival of summer did little to brighten his prospects. Snubbed by Powers and dropped by his sponsoring syndicate, he found himself cast adrift, relegated from headliner to supporting cast, rooted in the summer heat like a parched weed in a vacant lot.

There was still, occasionally, money to be made in a supporting role, but the larger purses for now lay beyond his grasp. In need of a new manager to reverse his misfortune, he dropped Lally and turned to 'Monty' Pike, president of the North Shore Athletic Club and erstwhile promoter of his race against Maloney.

More accustomed to promoting boxing matches than athletic contests, Pike ran a private 'fight club' out at Coney Island.[275] He was familiar, if not exactly intimate, with those managers and promoters who plied their trade in New York,[276] and was quick to find White races: perhaps a little too quick, given the Irishman's recent injuries. White may well have needed to give his ankle time to heal, but he also needed to earn a living and to maintain his relevance on the professional circuit.

And so it was, just five days after the Boston race, that Pike entered into negotiations to match White against Henri St. Yves. Scheduled to take place the following Sunday at the old horse racing track at Clifton, New Jersey,[277] the match would be promoted as 'the Gaul vs the Gael.' [278] It was to prove a reckless engagement.

Pat before his race at Clifton Stadium. The unidentified gentleman to his left is possibly Monty Pike.

Clifton, a small New Jersey town, lay approximately twenty-two miles north-west of Brooklyn on the western side of the Hudson River. It was a low-lying and dullish place, open to a domed sky, the kind of place where the sun sets behind the treeline rather than tall buildings or distant mountains. The old racetrack, situated on what is now the site of Memorial Park and Clifton High School, had a large grandstand, the greater portion of which was enclosed with glass, ensuring that spectators had a comfortable view of the entire course.

> St Yves, it may be remembered, was the French waiter who defeated Pat White of Donabate in the Edinburgh Marathon last year. White ran second to him, and it was thought if White had managed to hang on to him, and rallied his men, who finished 3rd, 4th, and 5th, he would have him. Opinions have been reversed since then by St. Yves' performance on Saturday, when he ran Longboat, Scrubb, Hayes, etc. off their feet. Dorando ran second and Hayes third. Matt Moloney, the Irish American, who defeated Pat White in a trial Marathon only got fourth place. Hayes passed him in the 25th mile.[279]

There was something odd about this match that didn't sit right with many of the sporting public. St. Yves was scheduled to race Alfie Shrubb, perhaps the greatest distance runner of his generation, just five days later.[280] Why would the Frenchman risk a gruelling battle, let alone a possible loss to White, just five days before it? Were White to push him hard, he'd be fatigued entering the race against Shrubb. Were White actually to win, St. Yves would have killed the gate. This was the marathon equivalent of a boxer risking a handshake from a total stranger in the lead-up to a championship fight.

The suspicion was that Pike was hiring White out as a trial horse. In the space of just a couple of months, White had gone from being seen as a dangerous opponent to being little more than a sparring partner for more promising prospects looking for easy wins. White, however, was in no position to be picky. At the end of the day, even a trial horse got paid.

As a potential shortcut out of poverty, professional running was a lot less dangerous than professional boxing, but it was no less dog-eat-dog and, compelled by a combination of financial circumstances and diminishing purse sizes to race more often than he might otherwise have wished, White had little option but to take races wherever and whenever he could, and to be discreetly stinting in his efforts when there was nothing to be gained.

This was a dangerous game to play. If he had too many bad races, the offers would stop coming in: if he took on too many, his ankle might never heal. In Ireland, he'd had a job and a home to fall back on. He could choose when and where he raced. Now, he either ran, or the promoters found someone else. For better or for worse, this was now his reality: a brittle, diminished figure, living out of a suitcase, lost in crowded bus stations and railway halls, dwarfed, unnoted and insignificant, his unbuttressed pretensions approaching the point of collapse, no longer somebody, but anybody.

Well-paid match-ups were becoming increasingly difficult to find. By the time the Clifton race took place, there had been so many 'marathons' in so short a time that public interest had become jaded and cynical. Gates had fallen, and fallen significantly. The question was never fully put, but it was certainly hinted that many of these 'races' had been little more than assisted time trials.

Pat White at Clifton Racetrack.

There is a suspicion that the "Marathon" game, especially that of the professional brand, is being overworked. The promoters, however, have been able to instil into it that variety so necessary to make it acceptable to American crowds, and it may be that, with the advent of St. Yves the sport is due to retain its popularity...

Tomorrow afternoon's race in Clifton will not be regarded by anyone as a serious contest. St. Yves can surely beat Pat White. The sports will merely visit the track to get a line on just how good St. Yves is. The distance being the same as

191

that agreed upon for his race with Shrubb, it is believed that St. Yves will endeavour to run on a schedule which he hopes will be the correct one to try against the English man.[281]

And that was precisely how it turned out. When St. Yves finally began to force the pace, White struggled to keep up and, much to the annoyance of the crowd, dropped out of the race. Truth be told, even without the injury, the Frenchman probably had too much for him.[282]

Whether the result had been pre-arranged or not, St. Yves had succeeded in harvesting the kind of positive publicity that could only improve public interest in his race against Shrubb. As for White, the pejorative brickbats of the American press were becoming increasingly difficult to ignore, and it is unlikely he came away from the Clifton race unscathed. A professional athlete's prospects, after all, were hardly enhanced when the press corps, upon whose cooperation promoters relied almost entirely for advance publicity, found itself roused to indignation by a furious crowd that felt conned out of their hard-earned cash.

CLIFTON, N.J., April 19. Running the legs off Pat White, the Irish Marathoner, Henri St. Yves, the little Frenchman who won the New York Marathon Derby, made White quit yesterday in the eleventh mile of their scheduled fifteen-mile race in the Clifton Stadium.

The race was disappointing to the large crowd, which hurled uncomplimentary remarks at White when he walked off the track at the end of the tenth mile, saying his ankle, which he sprained in his Marathon with Mat Maloney,

192

pained him. After staying off the track for a few minutes, White came back and resumed running. Setting a terrific clip, he led St. Yves for two laps around the six-lap track and then, winded, quit again in the third lap of the eleventh mile to the jeers and hoots of the crowd. St. Yves continued the race and finished the fifteen miles in 1:27:05.[283]

A few days later, yet another marathon was announced for New York's Polo Grounds, sponsored in part by Patrick T. Powers. It was scheduled for May 8. Once again, disregarding the evidence of his client's loss of form, Pike accepted an invitation on Pat's behalf.[284] The prize fund was just too substantial to ignore. The winner would receive $5,000; seventh place would earn $200.[285] It was worth a shot, perhaps even a flutter, especially as Pat's recent form had been reflected in bookies' odds of 15/1. St. Yves, by way of contrast, was being offered at 8/5.[286]

> Pat White of Ireland would be a dangerous contender if he was in good shape, but his leg is bad and it is doubtful whether he will finish.[287]

The fine weather had held, and the grass track was dry and heavily sanded. A crowd of 15,000 people had crammed into the stadium, 10,000 fewer than had attended the 'Grand Marathon Derby' on April 3, but still a hugely profitable gate. To encourage attendance, the kick-off for the football game at American League Park was moved to allow fans to watch the race.[288]

The opening pace proved almost as hot as the weather, and several competitors struggled to

193

keep pace. Nevertheless, as they entered the fifth mile, Pat emerged from the pack, surged past the pacesetter, Marsh, and took the lead. He was immediately followed by St. Ives.

The Irishman's time at the front, however, was to prove short-lived, and by mile seven, St. Ives was leading Marsh by fifty yards, with Pat two laps behind in sixth place. At the ten-mile mark, St. Ives would be seventy-seven seconds ahead of his previous best for the distance.

Polo Grounds Marathon, 8 May 1909. Left to right: Simpson, White (11), Svanberg, Crook, Pietri, Cibot, Morrissey, Carvajal, Orphée, Appleby, Marsh, St. Yves and Maloney.

But then, the conditions began to tell on the field. At ten and a half miles, Marsh would stop to have his left leg massaged. At mile sixteen, Pietri and Morrissey would do the same. At mile seventeen, Pietri would stop briefly as if debating whether to call it a day, and White would stop for a rubdown. The combination of the blistering heat and a fast early pace was taking a heavy toll on the competitors.

Shortly after mile seventeen, Morrissey

194

collapsed and had to be carried away. St. Ives, by then, was two laps ahead of Svanberg, but both were slowing. At nineteen miles, Svanberg collapsed and had to be revived with splashes of cold water. Concerned for his health, the crowd yelled for him to be removed from the race, but the Swede insisted on continuing.

There wasn't a runner on the track now who wasn't struggling, and by mile twenty-three, St. Ives had extended his lead to a whopping five laps. The prospect of *none* of the athletes actually finishing the race seemed increasingly likely with every passing lap.

White, Orphée, and Carvajal were now in survival mode and so far behind the leaders that they attracted little or no attention. Nevertheless, due to the rate of attrition, even the backmarkers considered themselves to be still in contention for the seventh-place prize of $200. When Marsh and Maloney dropped out, it even seemed for a time that simply finishing the race might be enough to guarantee a decent payday.

As St Yves entered the final three miles, Pietri began to behave erratically, sprinting and walking by turns, raising suspicions that his handlers were feeding him a powerful stimulant.[289] His erratic surges, however, were to little avail, and St. Yves hung on to win in 2:44, six minutes ahead of Svanberg and eight ahead of Crook.

When Cibot, in seventh place, crossed the finish line, twenty-one minutes after the winner, the last of the prizemoney had been claimed and, with nothing left to compete for, the remaining runners, White included, dropped out.[290] The decision to race, in retrospect, had proved to be a poor one. Not only had it set back his recovery, it

195

had accelerated the decline of an already crumbling reputation. The *New York Tribune* called it as many saw it:

Pat White, the erstwhile Irish Champion, never figured prominently, and ran his usual poor race.[291]

His 'usual' poor race! That had to have stung. It may even help to explain why White did not race again for the next three weeks. On 28 May, however, reports began to appear in the papers that he was showing form, having completed a time trial over the full marathon distance in 2:50. The time was a good ten minutes off his best, but it was still more than a minute faster than Hynes had run in taking the Irish title in March, and indicative, at the very least, of a partial return to form. Four days later, he lined up for a marathon at Brooklyn's Brighton Beach.

An early fog on the Hudson River had given way, as the hours progressed, to a hot and humid day. Long before the competitors reached the halfway point, many of them were observed to be in distress. No less than seven of the fifteen starters were forced to abandon the race 'from the strain.' The contest, on a course that measured six laps to the mile, was said, at times, to have resembled a walking race.[292]

The race was a slow affair and relieved only occasionally by occasional sprints. The most exciting thing was near the finish when White by a vigorous spurt beat out Davis for fourth money. White was the favorite, but his running was a disappointment. At the end of the eighteenth mile he stopped to a walk. The rest did him a lot of good, for at the twenty-first mile he was fighting every inch of ground with the leaders...[293]

The winner, Orphée, crossed the line a few seconds under three hours,[294] and in finishing, White had managed to secure a decent payday. He had earned precious little prizemoney since his head-to-head with Svanberg in March.

As the summer heat climbed to 36°C, Pike next secured a place for White in yet another full Marathon. It took place at Point Breeze, Philadelphia, on 5 June.[295] Despite the heat, race day proved to be miserable and wet, with the ground so soft that the organisers were, at one point, prepared to postpone the contest. Persuaded by one of the athletes' managers not to disappoint the crowd or deny the athletes their chance of a prize, the race was allowed to proceed, albeit over a distance of ten miles. Thirteen runners started.

On a very muddy and slippery course, the pace set by the Ojibwe runner, Red Hawk, was so fast that athletes were quitting the race as early as the end of the first mile. Pat managed to last as far as mile seven, when, having slipped to his knees on the backstretch, he too decided to drop out. In the heel of the hunt, Red Hawk won by a half mile from the Mohawk athlete, William Davis.[296]

Two weeks later, Pat was back in Philadelphia for the annual sports day of the United Lodges of the Sons of Saint George. I could find no results for this event, for which the professionals were to compete for a share of the gate receipts, but an example of how difficult it was becoming to earn a living as a full-time professional was evidenced by the fact that two of the French runners, Cibot and Orphée, were forced to pull out of the event on account of an attachment being issued against their share of the receipts.[297]

MARATHONER SHOWS FORM

PAT WHITE.

There was an air of desperation about the manner in which Pat was now chasing races and the next prospective payday would not occur until the Fourth of July holiday weekend, a fortnight hence. As the fourth fell that year on a Sunday, the public holiday would be celebrated on the following Monday, extending the celebrations into a long weekend. There would be no shortage of professional races that day, and Pat initially agreed to race Johnny Hayes in Burlington, Virginia. Contracts had yet to be signed, however, when Pat changed his mind. A more attractive proposition had been brought to his attention.

In direct competition with an amateur sports day organised for that morning by the City of Philadelphia at Belmont Plateau, the United Irish Societies of Philadelphia announced that they would host their annual games at Washington Park, with the amateur games taking place in the morning and the professional contests, sponsored by Clan na Gael, a sister organisation of the Irish Republican Brotherhood, taking place in the afternoon.

Given his family's political sympathies, Pat was never going to turn down an opportunity to spend a day in the company of like-minded Irishmen. And so, with Philadelphia less than two hours from New York by bus or train, he decided, despite having previously agreed to race in Virginia, to travel instead to the Clan na Gael event on July 5.[298]

At Washington Park, the professional games ran continuously from midday to 7 p.m. In addition to the usual track and field events, there were Irish dancing competitions and an obstacle sack race. The atmosphere was more akin to a

199

county fair back home than a professional track meet, but there was still prizemoney to be won, and races to be taken seriously.

Pat raced three times that day, winning the two-mile and five-mile races and finishing as runner-up in the mile to Scottish professional Jimmy Curran. By the end of the day, he had accumulated $112 in prizemoney, a decent pay day by any standards.[299]

His thunder, however, was stolen somewhat by the news, reported later that day, that at Celtic Park, New York, fellow Irishman, Martin Sheridan, of Boholo, County Mayo, had won the American "All-Around" Championship (the precursor of the Decathlon), and set a new world record in the process.

That same day, back home in Dublin, the organisers of the latest *Evening Herald* race, from Drogheda to Navan, held a celebratory dinner to reward the officials, committees and stewards who had given their time to the event.[300] A toast to the company invoked the name of Pat White as the prime example of what the race had done for Irish sport. There were no flags in the professional game, but there did not need to be, for every time Pat White competed on the international stage these days, with very few exceptions, he was referred to as Irish, rather than British. In the current political climate, that mattered. It mattered a lot.

Mr. Christopher J. Murphy presided. In proposing the toast of "The Guests" on behalf of the proprietors of the "Independent", he referred to the success of Pat White in Ireland and America since their race last year. They could, he said, fairly claim that they have brought White out, and in doing so they have shown that the people of this country could hold their own in long-distance running as in other branches of sport.

As the summer heat intensified, Pat decided to compete in one last marathon, this time in Atlantic City, New Jersey, on 17 July. The race was won by Hans Holmer of Quebec in a time of 2:50. Pat finished second, two minutes adrift of Holmer and well outside his best for the distance, but still comfortably ahead of Dineen and Maloney.[301] His form had not improved significantly, but at least his coffers had been replenished, and he'd had his revenge over Maloney.

With the marathon season more or less suspended for the summer, White next took a notion to chase what little money was to be had in professional track meets. On Sunday, 26 July, at the United Brewers track and field meeting at Celtic Park, he finished second in a one-mile race won in a time of just 5:10.[302] For the remainder of the summer, however, he was idle, obliged to live off his savings and reflect, with a sinking heart, on his prospects.

Sometime in early August, White decided for a second time that he'd had enough. He wrote home, possibly to Bernard Colgan, stating his intention to sail for Queenstown on August 14, and challenging Tom Hynes to a race over a full marathon at Jones' Road on September 5. The proprietor of the Jones' Road sportsgrounds promptly offered to put up prizes equal to those awarded at the Irish professional marathon

201

championships on May 16, on condition that the race would be open to all-comers, and that White would confirm his intention to compete. If White did not sign up, there would be no contest.[303]

Hynes accepted the challenge, but White failed to reply. Three times now he had attempted to return home, and each time his resolve had failed him. It was hard to break the habit, to lose the desire to be out in front of enormous crowds, the subject of their attention and set apart from the ordinary, even if it was only by the lower steps of a pedestal. In the circus maximus, Pat White was neither a small nor an ordinary man, but an exceptional one.

It mattered little to White if to the spectators he was just another wager, another horse on the downs, his value measured not in his worth as a man but by the length of his odds. What mattered was that he was still out there, still in the arena, every week a part of the game. To return home would not just be to abandon the hope of a different life: it would be an admission of failure. Purses back home were simply too small and races too infrequent to sustain a man. In no time at all, he would be back scratching a living as a farmhand.

There was to be no Indian summer in New York that year, and temperatures plummeted from a high of 33°C in August to mid-twenties by early September. This should have been an ideal climate for White, and on 5 September, before a crowd of 10,000 spectators at Washington Park, he ran in a five-mile race that was billed as the feature event of the New York Caledonian Club's annual games. That race, organised to announce the professional debuts of several local amateurs, was won by Charles Muller of Mohawk A.C, who ran the seasoned pros off their feet and took the winner's purse of $125.[304] Pat did not feature among the prize winners. Four days later, in a full marathon in Lowell, Massachusetts, won by Hans Holmer in a new world record, he dropped out during the twelfth mile, complaining of a foot injury, just as he was being passed by the Olympic Champion, Johnny Hayes.[305]

Lowell Marathon Grandstand, with Mayor Brown coming up the course in a hot air balloon.

The trees in Central Park slowly became a tapestry of copper and brass, Halloween pumpkins began to appear in the shops, and Pat White suddenly found himself struggling to find races. With winter fast approaching, he broke with Monty Pike and signed instead with fitness guru Ernie Hertberg, who at the time was also managing and coaching Johnny Hayes and Johan Svanberg.

If the publicity photograph for that race is a

TWO LEADING CANDIDATES ENTERED IN MARATHON TO BE HELD IN NEW JERSEY

MALONEY — WHITE

Publicity photo for the Wakefield Park Marathon.

true likeness, then the last nine months of professional racing had taken a heavy toll on White. He appears gaunt and prematurely aged. Older, at any rate, than his thirty years.

Apart from the Wakefield marathon, White was

also entered in an indoor fifteen-mile race at the 4th Regiment Armoury in Jersey City on 4 December.[306] In the Wakefield race, which was won by Pat Dineen, White dropped out after eighteen miles.[307] In the Jersey City race, won convincingly by Holmer, he dropped out during the fourth mile.[308] The dream of a life-changing purse was splintering, his health clearly suffering. But what was he to do? He needed the money.

Newspaper reports were scathing. One report even went so far as to describe the man from Richardstown as 'Pat White, who starts so often but seldom finishes' and to accuse him of having pulled his 'usual retiring act.' [309] His reputation was diminishing almost as quickly as race attendance figures. He may have run to feel more alive, but he raced only for money and prestige, and, when the effort was no longer profitable, he more often than not stopped racing. What was the point of continuing? Was it not better to save his effort for when it *could* be profitable? This was, after all, a business. There was nothing noble about poverty.

The professional racing circuit, however, was a small and mutually dependent community, a brotherhood forged in repeated battles against oneself and each other. Its very existence relied on decent attendance figures, and these in turn were dependent on the credibility of the contests. Pat White's growing reputation as a quitter threatened that, and posed a significant challenge to the general bonhomie. He might still be considered as a makeweight in a large field, but he was now a risky challenge in a head-to-head contest. With attendances already falling, his reputation could quite feasibly tank the gate.

It must have been difficult for Pat to be part of such a small community and find that there was no longer a place for him at the top table. It had been less than a year since his run in Edinburgh, and while promoters had not entirely lost interest in him, nobody was prepared to take him any longer at his own estimation. In the professional arena, he was only as good as his last race, and with the gaps getting longer and longer between them, his pockets began to empty, and the days began to drag.

Thanksgiving came and went. Children put away their penny masks and tin horns and began to focus on Christmas. Purse strings tightened, attendances fell dramatically, and a bitter wind blew in from the New Jersey Palisades.

Offered the opportunity of one last race before the weather turned and the holiday season began in earnest, Pat accepted a match over a half-marathon against the Canadian, Ted Crook. It took place at the State Armoury in Auburn, New York, on 13 December.

By all accounts, it was a close run affair, the Irishman losing by just 'four and a half lengths.' He had managed to stay with Crook until the final 400m, when Crook finally edged ahead to win in 1:24:24.[310] The race, however, was sparsely attended, and both the result, and the fact that White had managed to complete the race, received little publicity.

Pat no longer had the speed or the motivation to be successful at the shorter distances, and interest in full marathons was waning in America. The bubble had burst; the craze had run its course. Pietri, for example, had recently travelled to London where, on 18 December, and to the

The Albert Hall Marathon, 18 December 1909.

accompaniment of an Italian tenor, he had raced the English champion, C. W. Gardiner, on a ninety-yard track of coconut matting in London's

Royal Albert Hall. Gardiner won that race in 2:37, Pietri having retired with blisters during the four hundred-and-eighty-second lap.

Back in Brooklyn, with storefront windows full of toys, the grocery stores redolent with the scent of tangerines, and the sidewalks heady with the aroma of spruce trees and roasting chestnuts, White began once again to ponder the possibility of returning home and making another assault on the Powderhall Marathon, due to take place in Edinburgh on New Year's Day.[311]

Athletes are essentially creatures of hope, and eternally susceptible to the kind of self-deception in which past defeats are rationalised into oblivion by the expectation that better days are still to come. Indeed, no sooner had White sent off his entry for the Powderhall than his resolve to return to Ireland failed him for a third time. One more race. Just one more race. His luck was bound to change.

On Christmas Day, seven inches of snow fell in Brooklyn. A bitterly cold night turned it to ice, making the roads impassable and keeping people indoors. Fourteen days into the New Year, with the snow and ice still to melt, the city was hit with another dump of snow that in places measured ten inches in depth. Temperatures fell to -6°C, too cold and too slippery for either running or long walks. Over the next twenty-four hours a total of twenty-six inches of snow fell on the city's streets, crippling transportation. Unable to train, White gained a few pounds.

Interest in full marathons over 'the London distance' was waning so rapidly now that when Hayes and Pietri met for a third head-to-head in San Francisco on 30 January, the public response was decidedly lukewarm. Former All-American football star and renowned sportswriter, Franklin Morse, described the race as having been about 'as spectacular and exciting as the sight of two old ladies engaged in a long-distance knitting contest.'

By the time the snow had disappeared from the crosstown streets, the Powderhall race had come and gone, and White was still in New York and itching to race. He would be thirty-one in March, an age at which most men had settled down, found steady employment, and started families. The fire of ambition, however, still pulsed in his blood. Life on the professional circuit was a challenging, lonely, and somewhat pernicious addiction, but he remained, nevertheless, convinced that he had yet to show what he was capable of. And yet, for all of that, those niggling doubts, that yearning for home, the promises to return that had so frequently been put on the long finger, these were, of late, being met with an increasingly faltering resolve. One more race. Just one more race!

On 5 February 1910, a Marathon relay was announced for Fairhill Baseball Park in Philadelphia and scheduled to take place just one week later. Teams of two would compete over the full marathon distance, with one runner on track at all times. Teams could alternate their runners at any time according to their chosen strategies, as long as neither man ran more than half the full distance.

Pat White was initially selected to partner with Jimmie Curran of Scotland, with Pat Dineen partnering with the newest Irish professional, J.J. Goff. White and Dineen, however, quickly realised that they stood a far better chance if they partnered with each other and promptly abandoned their original partners.[312] At the end of the day, professional running was a job like any other; the race just another form of theatre. It was all about the money.

The marathon relay, however, never took place. Following a further spell of bad weather, the ground had turned muddy and, despite the large crowd that turned up, the organisers postponed the contest until the following week, which ruled out White as he was contracted to race in New York two days later in a fifteen-mile race at Madison Square Garden, where he would find himself relegated to a five-mile handicap on the undercard.[313] In this race, a new Irish professional, John C. Hayes, was listed amongst the competitors.[314]

Hayes was just another earnest kid, fresh off the boat and on the back of a reasonably successful cross-country season in Ireland, convinced that the professional circuit would bring him on. In May of the previous year, he had run a marathon in London over the 1908 Olympic course. He had finished twenty-seventh in a time of 3:19.17, almost forty minutes slower than White's time over the same course. He would not last long in America.

It had to have injured White's pride to find himself in such company. It was perhaps the starkest illustration yet of how far his stock had fallen, but maybe not half as humiliating as the prospect that Hayes would bring the story of it back to Dublin when he left.

Twenty-one athletes started that race at Madison Square Garden, with Jimmy Lee of

Boston starting off scratch and Pat off twenty seconds alongside Al Raines. Raines won that race, Lee took second, and Pat finished third. It was far from the box-office performance he so badly needed, but it was not his best distance.

Hope, nevertheless, sprang eternal, and a week later, as part of the George Washington birthday celebrations, a full marathon was advertised for Washington Park, home of the Brooklyn Superbas.[315] Going into the race, Pat expressed confidence. He could hardly do otherwise.

> All the men entered in the race are known for their ability to go the Marathon distance. Pat White says he will show the form in this race that won for him the long-distance championship of Ireland. There will be another son of the Emerald Isle competing at Washington Park on the same day, but not in the Marathon race, who is rated a wonder up to five miles. He is Michael Doyle, and he is entered in the two-mile event.[316]

In anticipation of a race that listed eleven competitors, including the 'Terrible Swede', Karl Nieminen, and the Canadian Ted Crook, only the *New York Tribune* dared to suggest Pat as one of the favourites. His local paper, the *Brooklyn Daily Eagle*, did not even mention his name among the potential dark horses.

> The early betting on the race made Crook a favorite but Maloney's entry has made the Crook supporters a bit wary. Matt has had a long rest and has shown up well in training. Lone Fox is the dark horse of the race. The Sioux Indian has never before run in this part of the country so

that no line can be had on his form.[317]

Once again, torrential rain and concerns about poor attendance led to the race being postponed. Pat was livid. 'I'm a good mudder,' he complained to a journalist from the *New York Daily Tribune*, despite all recent evidence to the contrary, 'and they've called the race off.' [318]

Pat in his pre-race attire.

The rearranged race was re-run on 5 March at the Brooklyn ball grounds, and on ground so heavy that it was described in some papers as the 'Death Race'. It was won by the Swede, Karl

Nieminen, who finished three laps ahead of Pat Dineen in a time of 3:15:25. Once again, Pat failed to finish.[319]

Spring was soon upon him. The trees were budding, crocuses were blooming in Central Park, and janitors were beginning to shut down their boilers. On Tuesday, 27 March 1910, Pat ran his last indoor race of the winter season, a fifteen-mile contest at the Armoury against Nieminen, Jimmy Lee, and the journalist and former Olympian, Harvey Cohn. It was a low-key affair watched by just five hundred spectators.[320] Not a single newspaper carried the results.[321]

Pat would next compete on Sunday, 10 April, at Celtic Park, New York, in a race billed as a full marathon but shortened on the day to twenty miles due to the stiff breeze. The purse was to be a percentage of the gate receipts. Pat finished fourth of eleven competitors, behind Raines, Dineen, and Maloney.[322]

At the end of the race, embarrassed to have been beaten by Maloney, White's frustration finally boiled over. In a less-than-dignified tirade, he remonstrated with the judges, insisting that the scorers had miscounted the laps and that he had finished ahead of Maloney. His appeal was dismissed and the result stood,[323] but he fell a little further in his colleagues' estimation for having questioned the competence and integrity of the judges. It just wasn't done.

That was the last straw for White, and his last race on American soil. Floundering in an emotional and physical slump, he had drained his reservoir of hope and was no longer earning enough to justify remaining. Nor was he the only one of the class of 1909 who had begun to consider calling time on his career. Henri St. Yves and his manager, John D. Marsh, were also thinking of getting out of the game and going into business together ... as skywriters!

> After watching Charles K. Hamilton get some thousands of dollars for operating his aeroplanes at San Francisco, St. Yves and Marsh decided that it was the air for them in the future.
> "It's a cinch," said Marsh to a "Province" Reporter. " Just like running an automobile. You start the engine and the machine flies. Nothing simpler, nothing easier, and it gets the money. Henri and I are going to buy an aeroplane as soon as we go east. Henri will be the driver, I will be the manager and take the money. No more 'Marathons' for us.[324]

Charles K. Hamilton, in 1910.

Before the money ran out completely, or he landed himself in debt, Pat White strolled down to the Cunard offices on State Street and purchased a third-class ticket on the S.S. Caronia, a cruise liner bound for Cobh. And with that, he closed the doors on his American dream, said goodbye to friends old and new, and set sail, finally, for home.

THE RETURNED YANK

THE 'RETURNED YANK' was a figurative expression common in Ireland in the 1900s. Loaded with all manner of expectations and preconceptions, it could, for example, depending upon its usage, describe a staple figure of romantic fiction or a figure of envy and fun. It could even, on rare occasions, be used to attach a sense of failure and shame.

For those who had been forced by circumstance to emigrate, the stigma was perhaps not quite so great. But Pat White had left Dublin to a glorious fanfare of publicity and had sailed to New York in relative luxury. A third-class return on the S.S. Caronia was bound to raise eyebrows. There would be no avoiding the scrutiny and speculation, especially as the amount of prizemoney he had earned in his first months in America – a small fortune by Irish standards – had been widely reported in the Irish papers. People would be curious to see how much of it remained. Far from a triumphant return, it might even prove a tad awkward.

The departure of the Caronia was delayed for several days because a terrifying storm had battered the ship during her crossing from Liverpool, carrying away the forward deckhouse and a member of the crew. After repairs were made and the usual obsequies observed, the ship left New York on Saturday, 14 May.[325] She docked

216

at Cobh (Queenstown) seven days later.[326]

> Pat White of Donabate, the victor of two "Herald"
> races, has just arrived back from America after a
> stay lasting over sixteen months. He reached
> Queenstown on Saturday morning per the s.s.
> Corunna... He looked fit and well and seems to
> have filled in a bit.[327]

White's arrival in Cobh could not have been faced without a degree of trepidation, his brief pilgrimage to the Land of Opportunity having ended in humiliation. But there was no need to advertise a fact that was not generally known outside of the American professional circuit, and so, before he could be reported to have returned with his tail between his legs, he hurried to Dublin, where, on the morning following his arrival in Cobh, he cut an haughty swath at Jones' Road as he watched his old rival Tom Hynes win the Bovril-sponsored Irish Marathon.

White's presence, fresh off the boat and in his finest American clobber, was widely perceived as an attempt to reassert his dominance and to profit from the inevitable publicity his presence was bound to generate. Never the most loquacious of men before he left, America had at least cured him of his diffidence. He hadn't come to watch Hayes, so much as to attract the attention of the working press.

Finishing fourth that day, in a time of 3:12:26, was John C. Hayes, perhaps the only man present to have witnessed Pat's American humiliation firsthand. If there was a story to be got in front of before it gained legs, it was probably Hayes.' The pre-emptive flavour to

White's finish line bravado and his unseemly haste to announce his return, however, was to pale in comparison to the brashness of the challenge that was reported in the following morning's *Irish Independent.*

> White was a keen watcher in the doings of Hynes, Fagan, and the others in yesterday's contest and he expressed a wish to meet the winner (Hynes) over a similar distance for £200, the match if arranged, to take place at any time after three weeks. White has also the offer of a match with C. W. Gardiner, the English Champion, and should matters be fixed up promptly, the race will probably be decided in South Wales.[328]

That White might be anxious to dispel the impression of failure by appearing conspicuous in his prosperity was perhaps understandable. But two hundred pounds! It took real Brooklyn *Chutzpah* to post a challenge like that, and one can only wonder at the potential consequences had it actually been accepted. There was no way that Hynes, or any other Irish professional, could afford so great a sum, and White knew it.

And maybe that was the point – to make an offer so outrageously large that no one could afford to match it, or even question that he had it to stake. It sent a message, and it got people talking, if not always favourably. To many, it came across as an act of swaggering conceit.

Two days later, Hynes accepted White's challenge, but over a distance of sixteen miles rather than a full marathon, and for a £25 stake per side rather than £200. He also offered to race White over a series of races at ten, fifteen and twenty miles for the best purse offered, the winner of the rubber to take all.[329] White did not respond. He was not in any shape to race a man of Hyne's quality, let alone over Hynes' favoured distances.

After just sixteen months in America, Pat's accent is unlikely to have changed much, but his wardrobe almost certainly had. He would by now have possessed a pocket watch, a mundane possession on the far side of the Atlantic, but one that in Ireland was very much associated with the middle classes. He had left Ireland as a common labourer and returned as a cynical and hard-bitten professional.

How strange, it must have felt to be home again, to be surrounded by fields green with crops, and in a place where the landscape was mapped in townlands rather than neighbourhoods, to be comforted by the familiar and yet surprised by the unfamiliar. He had changed in those sixteen months, but so too had his home. Little was as he had left it. All the old outbuildings, bar the hen house, had been demolished, the cabin had been extended, and the gloomy interior brightened by the addition of a second window at the front. Peter and Bridget, furthermore, had returned home.[330]

And yet, for all that, it was still somewhat primitive compared to the newer buildings he had experienced in New York. It lacked running water and an inside toilet. In America, plumbing had been commonplace.

And therein lay the rub. During his time in America, White had become accustomed to a standard of living far in excess of that his family currently enjoyed. There was, furthermore, little sign that those conditions were likely to improve anytime soon. His father appears to have still nourished visions of bequeathing the farm to his eldest son, in the hope that land reform would eventually see him gain total ownership of it. But Pat wanted nothing to do with it. The lease on that farm had been a millstone around his father's neck for eight years, and the family's living conditions had not improved one iota. His father had bought his independence, but at what cost?

For part-time professionals like Hynes and Fagan, the size of a purse was not a matter of life and death. They had other professions to fall back on, professions they were proud to pursue and happy enough to remain in. Following his return from America, however, and the bursting of the marathon bubble, it appears that White was determined to stave off the inevitable return to labouring, be it for his father or anyone else, for as long as possible. Having issued a £200 challenge while he was still fresh off the boat, a return to manual labour would simply accelerate the humiliation he was anxious to forestall.

It is only too easy to form the impression that Pat White's attitude to sport had become distastefully mercenary since his time in America, but such an assumption would be unjust. Like it or not, running was not just his life now; it was his profession. A single payday would often have to sustain him for months. Money mattered. He had plans of his own. He would not be spancelled by his father's ambition, or made responsible for debts that weren't his own.

In such a small country, there was no avoiding Tom Hynes and, later that summer, Pat finally

220

consented to face him in a charity fundraiser over fifteen miles. The race took place on 14 August 1910, at the grounds of Galway Grammar School. It did not go well.

> Tom Hynes, Galway, winner of the "Herald" Race in 1903, and the winner of the principal Irish Marathons for the past two years, outclassed four other "Herald Race winners in a fifteen miles Marathon, before 2,000 spectators, at the Grammar School grounds, Galway, on Monday.
>
> The Marathon was got up in aid of the new Cathedral and College. Many came by excursion from Athlone and other Western stations to witness the race. As the pistol shot, the following started – T. Hynes (Galway), Pat White (Donabate), Pat Fagan (Dublin), J. Lynch and P. Walsh (Dublin), J. Timmons (Oldcastle), J. Steele (Moate) and O'Brien (Moate).
>
> White made the pace for the first few miles, when Fagan, who had been running second, came abreast for a few minutes. Hynes dashed out between the two, and held the lead from that to the finish, winning easily. Three miles from home the Oldcastle man dropped out. The finish was as follows: Hynes, 1 hr. 25 mins. 55s, White, 1 hr. 26 mins. 50 secs. Walsh, 1 hr. 27 mins. 20 secs.[331]

It is doubtful that Pat made much, if anything, from what was essentially a charity event, or that he put much effort into it. No purse was on offer, or at least none that was ever made public. His first real professional engagement would not come until September, when he was matched to race Pat Fagan from Swords to Gormanston, a distance of fifteen miles.[332] Alas, if that race ever took place, the result was never published.

The first recorded instance of Pat actually

winning prizemoney following his return from New York would not come until the Castlerea Bazaar on 21 September 1910, when he would beat a field of seven in a fifteen-mile race to take home the sum of £15. Approximately half of what he could earn annually as an agricultural labourer,[333] it was enough to tide him over until the following year's Powderhall. Nothing more would be heard of him that autumn.

THE WORLD RECORD
RACE

PAT WHITE HAD good reason to fancy his chances at Edinburgh in 1911. He had finished second in the inaugural Powderhall Marathon, behind a man who had proved himself the best in the world in the months that followed. Having returned to Richardstown, furthermore, he was back among the domestic cram and clutter, wrapped in the comforting embrace of the familiar, running again on his native ground and in clean country air.

There had been so much to talk about at first, but once the fuss had died down and the demands on his time had diminished, Pat had settled back into his old routines. He had a clear sense of time and distance at home, knew when training was going well and when it was not, knew when to run and when to rest. By Christmas, he was in the shape of his life and looking forward with renewed confidence to Powderhall.

There was, however, a fly in the ointment. A Frenchman, Louis Bouchard, had entered the race, and Pat had learned by hard experience to be wary of the French. Bouchard had run 2:36 in London the previous March, just two minutes less than Ljungstrom's world record of 2:34. Also entered was British-born Hans Holmer, who had run 2:35 in Toronto the previous May, but on an unverified course. Holmer, too, was a threat. The last time they had met, at Wakefield, New Jersey, Holmer had beaten White convincingly.

On the positive side, the 1911 race was to be held on the quarter-mile cinder track at the Powderhall Athletic Grounds rather than on the Falkirk to Edinburgh Road. There would be no interference from spectators or cyclists to contend with, and no hills. A fast, flat race was promised, and that was very much in Pat's favour.

The weather gods smiled, and a chilly but windless winter morning greeted competitors on race day. One could not have asked for more. Despite it being a Sunday, and the race publicly condemned as a 'new and most reprehensible form of Sabbath desecration,' a crowd of 12,000 spectators turned out to watch.[334] Reminiscent of the Garden on a good night, the stadium was abuzz with heated debates, bellowing bookies and excited banter.

From the forty entrants, twenty-six runners started prompt to time, G. Bradley (Alfreton) taking the lead for the opening two laps. Antoine Rives (Brussels) and Louis Bouchard (France) were soon at the head of affairs, keeping there at the end of the first mile, separated by a yard, with J.W. Kitchener (Kent) a few yards away, P.J. White (Dublin) lying next, and Hans Holmer (America) in fine pace behind...

Bouchard led throughout the next mile, with Rives in close attendance. The Frenchman set a cracking pace in these four laps, but could not shake off Rives, and when the third mile had been completed these two were abreast. The opening three miles were covered in 15 min 51 sec...

Bouchard was running a great race and shook

off Rives and Holmer. The latter had been improving his position, and set away on his own in the fourth mile, lapping Jack Price (Birmingham), the holder, in a common canter...

Bouchard was well in front during the fourth, fifth and sixth miles, which were done in 21min 15sec, 27min, and 31min 47sec, respectively. This was a warm beginning but Bouchard never flagged in his hot pace.[335]

By the time the runners reached mile six, White was sitting back in sixth place, well behind Bouchard, who was leading Holmer by 120 yards. Little of note happened over the next four miles, but during mile eleven, Bouchard made a surge, during which he managed to lap every competitor bar Holmer. Ignored by spectators and bookmakers alike, White stuck to his race plan, steadfast in his refusal to engage with the drama unfolding at the front.

By mile fourteen, only nineteen competitors remained in the race, and Holmer had reduced Bouchard's advantage to seventy-five yards. Bouchard, nevertheless, persisted with his blistering pace, setting world professional records at fifteen and sixteen miles. No one in the stadium was focused on anyone but these two. At the age of thirty-one, White could no longer keep up with the top two for pure speed, but he was still running strongly and appeared comfortable.

At mile seventeen, Holmer closed to within ten yards of the Frenchman and, sensing his presence, Bouchard put in another surge and increased the gap to twenty-four yards. Of the other competitors, only Gardiner and Clarke appeared to be in the hunt.

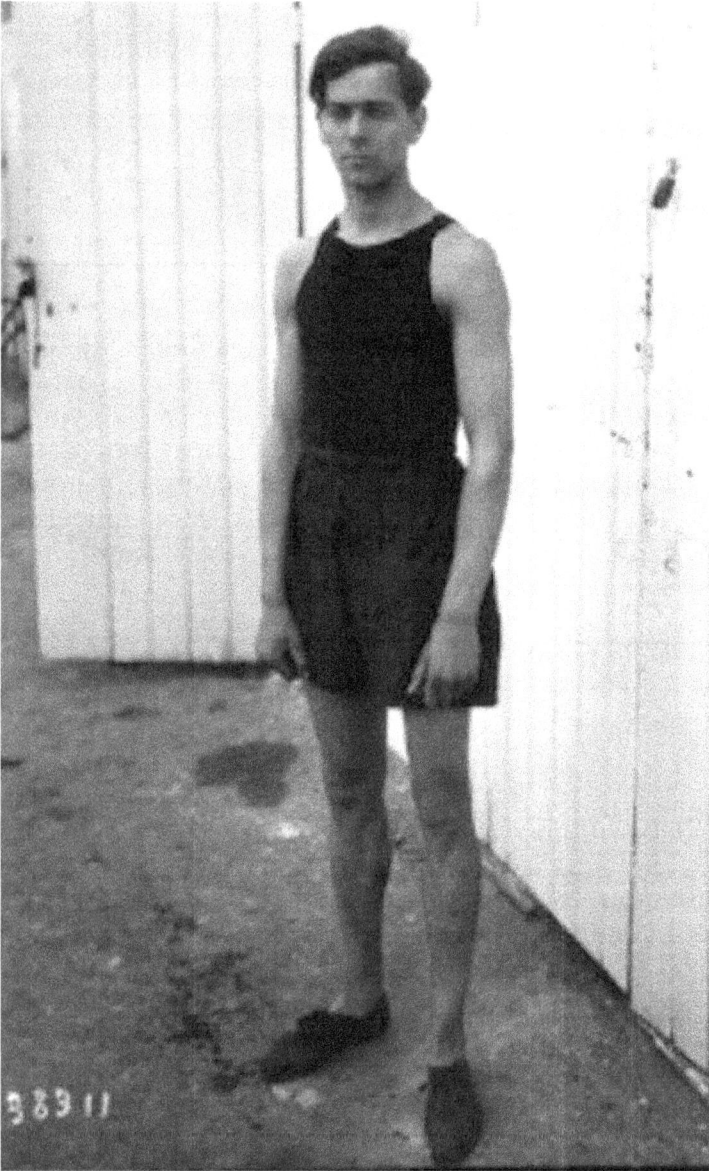

Hans Holmer.

A mile further on, Bouchard paid the price for his exuberance and began to wilt. Holmer overtook him, waving his hands in celebration as he passed. Demoralised, Bouchard eased up and walked a lap of the track, surrendering, in the process, his lap-and-a-half advantage over the chasing group, which by now included White.

As the record-breaking continued, Pat began his customary late charge and was soon closing in on Holmer. By the twenty-third mile, he was well clear in second, and the gap to Holmer had been reduced to eight hundred yards. As late as mile eighteen, not even the bookies had seen that coming from a man many had considered to be all washed up.

Holmer had little choice now but to run conservatively and, encouraged by Holmer's steadily diminishing lead, White now began to press hard, exciting punters and bookies alike. Fresh money changed hands. The result no longer seemed a foregone conclusion.

From the nineteenth mile onwards, both men were reportedly hitting intermediate times inside previous world records for those distances.[336] Pat, however, could not sustain the surge and eventually bowed to the inevitable. Holmer finished with a crowd-pleasing sprint to the line, setting a new world record of 2:33:21. White finished second in 2:36:45, a performance that, at that time, had been bettered only by Ljungstrom, Bouchard and Holmer.[337]

Pat was now the fastest Irishman ever over the London distance and the fourth-fastest of all time, an achievement for which he reportedly received no more than his £12 runner-up prize. Holmer, on the other hand, had not only carried off the £75 first prize but also, it was widely reported, approximately £1000 in winnings from the bookies.[338]

White's run in Edinburgh was all the more impressive for the courage, self-belief, and perseverance it had taken to get to the start line. After the humiliation of his American gamble, a lesser man might well have thrown in the towel. But White had never surrendered to self-pity or admitted defeat. Instead, he had got his head down, trained his way through the inevitable clouds of self-doubt, and fought his way back to the top. He could now, finally, put his American nightmare behind him.

It was a bittersweet redemption, for the prizemoney was even less than he had won in Castlerea. The steadily diminishing purses and the receding public interest in professional running served only to underscore the glory that might now have been his had he retained his amateur status.

The Olympic Games were to be held the following year in Sweden, and there was currently no one in the amateur ranks who had even come close to Pat's best times. The current amateur world record was four minutes slower than Pat's best; the Olympic record eighteen minutes slower.

Records, however, no longer held the significance they once did. It was Olympic champions who now claimed the glory. Records were transitory things, seemingly broken on an annual basis. The Olympic Roll of Honour, on the other hand, was a permanent record, there for all time.

In Stockholm one year hence, Olympic athletes would sign an entry form affirming that they had never competed for money or prizes, competed against a professional, coached in any branch of athletics for payment, or sold, pawned, hired out, or exhibited any prize for payment. And yet, at major amateur events all over the world, valuable gold watches and silver cups were being regularly presented as prizes and many British 'gentlemen amateurs' would arrive in Stockholm accompanied by their professional coaches in a form of master-servant relationship that would facilitate the turning of a selectively blind eye.[339] A host of professional soldiers and fencing masters, who were effectively full-time athletes, would also compete, and the American runners would be coached by Johnny Hayes. It wasn't fair, but there was nothing Pat could do about it now. He'd made his bed in 1905.

THE ROTUNDA
MARATHON

IN 1759, SIR Fielding Ould, Master of the Dublin Lying-In Hospital, commissioned the construction of a large auditorium on the hospital grounds. Variously called 'The Rotundo' or 'Round Room,' it was designed to facilitate year-round fundraising through the hosting of balls, concerts, organ recitals, and what would become popularly known as the 'Sunday Promenades.' By 1911, the 'Rotundo' was hosting picture shows, orchestral concerts, and political gatherings.[340] On several occasions, it had even functioned as a roller-skating rink.[341] The new building would later lend its name to the hospital itself, and to this day, the hospital is popularly known as 'The Rotunda'.

In February 1911, inspired by the success of the Gardiner vs. Pietri race at London's Albert Hall, someone proposed the hosting of an indoor marathon at The Rotundo on St. Patrick's Night. The dancefloor, it was estimated, could just about accommodate a circuit of 137 metres, 9m shorter than the track at the Drill Shed of the Sixty-Ninth Regiment Armoury, the tight bends of which had caused Pat's calf to cramp up in 1909. Invitations were sent out to the top runners in the kingdom, and with £30 going to the winner, few declined.

Among the 'big' names to confirm was C. W. Gardiner of Lewisham, the top English marathon runner and winner of the famous Albert Hall marathon. Also confirmed were Jack Price of Worcester, who had a best of 2:37, and local favourite Pat White, for whom it would be as close as he would ever come to taking a turn around that famous dancefloor. But this would be no mere exhibition event. It would be Ireland vs England, and as such, a fiercely nationalistic atmosphere was all but guaranteed. The Easter Rising was now just five years away.

The Round Room at the Rotunda.

On the night, with no fewer than ten athletes starting, the track was crowded during the early laps, which were led out by the English international, Billy Clarke of Sefton Harriers. Clarke had been an early leader in the 1908 Olympic marathon, in which he ultimately finished twelfth. In June of 1910, he had run 2:52:50 on a grass track in Salisbury, a respectable time, but not in the same class as White, Gardiner, or Price.

At fourteen miles, Clarke led by three laps from

White, who was being tracked by Gardiner, Fagan, Kitchener and Curtis. Two of the other Irish competitors, Mernagh and Lynch, had by that point dropped out. At mile fifteen, Pat began to ramp up the pace and, over the course of the next three miles, closed the gap on Clarke completely. By mile eighteen, he had lapped Clarke and settled in behind him, content, with his lap in hand, to let Clarke pace him for the remainder of the race.

Two laps from the finish, Clarke made a valiant effort to run away from White, but White would not be shaken off, and won by a full lap in a time of 2:37, just a minute slower than he had run in the world record race at Powderhall, but arguably a better performance given the poor air quality and the tightness of the course.[342] Those tight bends were probably worth a couple of minutes at least. Clarke got £10 for finishing second, and Kitchener covered his expenses with the £5 he received for finishing third, eleven laps behind Pat.

Pat's winnings for the year to date now amounted to £42,[343] a considerable sum for the time. And yet his family still lived in a thatched mud cabin. Pat, Bridget, and Peter were still unmarried, living with their parents, and helping to run the farm. If any of Pat's winnings had been diverted in the family's direction, then it was probably being used to lease more land (the lease had been extended to cover an extra two acres), rather than improve their living standards.

The family were still living pretty much as they had before Pat left for America, in conditions that appeared to belong to another century. John White, furthermore, was getting somewhat long in the tooth and at sixty-two was already showing signs of infirmity. But with two sons helping out part-time, the farm was still just about viable. John White had gained the status of a small farmer, but for all his back-breaking effort, he appears to have been no better off than he had been when labouring for the Harfords. He had, it seems, bought his way into a financial cul-de-sac.

The Rotunda race had scarcely finished when fresh challenges were thrown out. Fagan challenged Curtis to a head-to-head, and promoters from the North attempted to lure either White or Curtis to Portadown in May to face the new Ulster professional, Sam Lee.[344] Following the success of the Rotunda race, however, promoters were keen to match White against the top English runners again, not least because of the rising tide of Irish nationalism that would culminate just five years later in the Easter Rising. An Ireland versus England match-up would guarantee crowds, especially in Fingal and Meath, where White was still something of a folk hero and his brother, Peter, slowly becoming a prominent figure in republican circles.

A Whit Sunday match-up over twenty miles was subsequently arranged for the Agricultural Grounds in Navan between White, Clarke and Gardiner for £25 a side and winner takes all. Given White's form, it is doubtful that the English duo would have agreed to come over without a guaranteed fee or a percentage of the gate.

Then again, the prize was substantial enough in its own right, and they might just have thought it worth the gamble as the race would be six miles short of the point where White customarily came into his own. White, furthermore, had recently been contracted to compete in a full marathon as part of the Douglas Coronation Celebrations on 28 June. He might just have that in mind when the pressure came on.[345] And who knows, perhaps he had.

> The pace was moderate at first and White held his own until the fifteenth lap, when Clake took the lead and Gardner ran second. At the twenty-third lap Clarke had 250 yards lead over Gardner, who was 100 yards in front of White. Two laps later Clarke passed White, who was now plainly in distress, and fell out suffering from a pain in his side.[346]

THE CORONATION
MARATHON

WHEN EDWARD VII died on 6 May 1910, his eldest son became George V of Great Britain and Ireland. However, due to several bureaucratic delays, the coronation had been repeatedly postponed. It was now scheduled to take place on 22 June 1911.

As part of the coronation celebrations on the Isle of Man, it was decided to host a full marathon at Noble's Playing Fields in Douglas.[347] Sponsored by the *Daily Mail*, the race was to be called the 'Douglas Coronation and Jubilee Carnival World's Marathon Race'.[348] Travelling from Ireland to compete would be James Lynch of Dublin, Pat Conway of Wicklow and Pat White of Donabate. Also confirmed were the new world record holder, Hans Holmer, and the English runners Gardiner and Kitchener.

The weather on the day was positively Stygian, with high winds and gunmetal skies. Everyone knew it would be a slog, but that did not deter Miller, Gardiner, and Clarke from setting a fast early pace, with Gardiner doing most of the work. In the strong winds, the world record holder, Holmer, struggled to keep up and dropped out after eleven miles, removing the only man Pat truly feared and putting an end to the battle that most spectators had braved the inclement weather to see.

Pat had started steadily, as was his wont, and

it was not until mile fourteen that he moved to the front. Once there, he and Kitchener, running stride for stride, gradually pulled away from the field. The pair remained at the front until the final miles, when the clouds finally burst and turned the course into a quagmire, slowing and cooling the contestants considerably.

During the downpour, Pat, a self-proclaimed 'good mudder', managed to distance himself from Kitchener by almost half a mile and went on to win in a relatively slow time of 2:50:23. Kitchener came second, two minutes behind, with Price a further two minutes behind him in third.[349] Pat's finishing time was almost fifteen minutes slower than the times he had set in Edinburgh in January and Dublin in March,[350] but the conditions were poor, and a win was a win.

Following his victory, Pat was quickly challenged to a race over the full marathon distance by Frank Curtis.[351] He refused to bite, having been offered a rematch against Holmer over fifteen miles in Douglas on 30 August for a significantly larger purse put up by Frederick Arthur Lumley, owner of the Powderhall Grounds in Edinburgh. The distance was well short of Pat's best distance and very much in favour of Holmer. Pat, nevertheless, accepted the match, most likely on the understanding that it was effectively an exhibition run and a guaranteed payday.

That race, billed as a '15 Miles World's Championship', went pretty much as expected.[352] Pat took on the early pace and led by a few yards until mile five, when Holmer sped away from him, lapping the Irishman as he entered mile nine. Holmer, thereafter, took it easy, allowing Pat to catch up before speeding off again, ultimately

236

beating Pat by five hundred yards.

Holmer's winning time was 1:37:32; White's a minute and fifty-seven seconds slower.[353] Press reaction to the 'race' was largely predictable, and 'Pinex' – the athletics correspondent of the *Evening News* – had some sage advice for the Irishman.

> As anticipated, Holmer proved too speedy for White, and won easily. The Irishman would be well-advised to confine himself to the full Marathon distance in future, although his win on this occasion by no means makes Holmer out to be the best fifteen miles runner in the world.[354]

MAN-VERSUS-HORSE

HE WAS NOT the first to think of it. Back in 1907, Tom Longboat had raced a horse and buggy from Hagersville to Caledonia – a distance of 18 miles – and won.[355] Two years later, Alfie Shrubb had raced trotting horses in exhibition events in Canada in exchange for substantial purses and much-needed publicity.[356] Why then, thought White, shouldn't he do the same in Ireland?

Man-against-horse races were hardly novel. Back in 1818, at Feltham, Hertfordshire, a Mr J. Barnett had bet two hundred guineas that he could beat a fast horse in a 48-hour race. The horse had carried 168 pounds and won by 179 miles to 158, though it was believed the horse would not have survived had the race been extended much further.[357] In 1840, at Hyde Park in Sheffield, a certain Mr Cootes had challenged an old hunting horse, 'George IV', to a steeplechase over four-foot hurdles. On that occasion, the human won when the horse refused at the first.

By the mid-nineteenth century, it had been well established that horses could easily beat human runners over short distances. And so, to keep the betting public interested, promoters of these novelty races began to establish handicaps. In 1857, for example, in Rochester, New York, the runner Charles Curtis was pitted against the racehorse 'Frank Hayes'. The horse had to run three miles to Curtis' one. Curtis won that race by two seconds, to the delight of a raucous crowd. There had never, however, been a man-versus-horse race of any note in Ireland, and Pat was banking on the novelty attracting a crowd. What might be lost in the bet, he calculated, would be gained on the gate. Alas, it was to prove more than he could do to keep the idea to himself.

On 2 September 1911, just three days after his race in Douglas, White turned up in Clara, Co. Offaly, ostensibly to compete in a seventeen-mile handicap where a £10 first prize was on offer. White was due to run off scratch, with Pat Fagan running off three minutes. It was a big ask to race straight off the boat, and Fagan was never going to allow White time to settle. From the gun, Fagan set off at a strong pace and, after three miles, was so far ahead that Pat dropped out.[358]

The following morning, Pat dropped by the offices of Independent Newspapers on Middle Abbey Street to issue a novelty challenge, not to another athlete, but to Michael Horan's famous trotting mare, Katherine H. The challenge was for a ten-mile handicap race, with Pat running off a seventeen-minute head start. The following day, Horan made a counteroffer. His mare would race Pat over ten miles, but with Pat off sixteen minutes rather than seventeen, and for £10 or £20 a side.[359]

Before the match could be arranged, however, Pat Fagan beat White to the punch and, on 17 September, Fagan raced Horan's seventeen-year-old mare on the Jones' Road track in Dublin, starting off a handicap of eighteen minutes – a full minute more than Horan had offered to White. The horse won by three hundred yards.[360]

Having witnessed how Fagan had fared, Pat re-entered negotiations with Horan, and the pair eventually settled on a distance of ten miles and a handicap of nineteen minutes. The race was scheduled for 4 p.m. on Sunday, 15 October, on the same track.

Pat White and Michael Horan's pony, Kathleen H.

The month between the two events was significant. As an experienced cross-country runner, White had every reason to expect the season of drifting leaves and unmown grass to have softened the track. And while the sodden ground might slow *him* down, it would surely prove even more difficult for the mare, which had to pull the old man and his two-wheeled sulky behind her. Against that, there was always the risk of rain keeping the punters away. The purse was set at £20 and £10 a-side.[361]

The race took place as planned over thirty-five laps and 240 yards of the grass track at Jones

Road. The day was dry, and there was a large turnout. The heavy rains of the previous days had subsided, and the ground was declared to be 'soft, but holding.'

Pat started well and, during his nineteen-minute allowance, established a lead of twelve laps and eighty yards. The mare was trotted all out for the first eight miles, but as she completed the ninth, Horan eased her up and passed Pat three laps from the finish. The winning margin was thirty seconds. For what was effectively a solo run, Pat's time was fifty-six minutes.[362]

The following day, Pat was challenged to a ten-mile race for £10 a-side by Charlie Harris, one of the leading amateurs in the country. Harris had long been expected to turn professional, but nobody had expected it to be so soon.[363] As Harris' professional debut was bound to draw a crowd, the race was quickly agreed for a £20 purse and £5 a-side.

> Both men are training on the roads for the event. It should be a great contest. It will be Harris's first appearance as a professional, and to make a good start he must win. White, on the other hand, has a great reputation, and has come out on top in a number of very big events. It will not help his career to be overshadowed by Harris.[364]

That Pat, who had always been vulnerable over shorter distances, continued to accept such challenges is indicative of the priority he placed on pay days over reputation. He was not overly concerned with reputational damage. It mattered only that he got paid. At thirty-two years of age, he knew that he could no longer match the younger athletes in terms of speed. There is little evidence to suggest that he was employed in any other capacity during this time. It would appear that, in return for a share of the gate money, he was willing to endure any humiliation.

The match against Charlie Harris took place in torrential rain on Sunday, 12 November 1911, over thirty-two laps of the cycling track at Jones' Road. The admission prices were not steep – just sixpence and a shilling – but the wet weather kept many potential spectators away.[365] Both men did a little passing during the opening two miles on a cinder track made heavy by three days of rain, but, as the weather worsened, only one seemed up for the fight, and Harris quickly ran away to win by 545 yards in a time of 53:58.[366]

> White need not be despondent over yesterday's race. We don't think it was his distance, and he met a man in Harris who is no doubt the best of his class in the three countries at present. Harris's next engagement is with Mr. Michael Horan's trotting mare, Kathleen H., next Sunday at Jones' Road. He has an allowance of twenty minutes from the mare, and when the contests of Fagan, with an allowance of 18 minutes, and of White, at 19 minutes are considered, we have no doubt about the closeness of next Sunday's contest.[367]

Harris' race against Horan's mare took place on the bicycle track at Jones' Road rather than on the grass track. But, despite Harris' generous handicap, the mare passed him three hundred yards from home. Harris' finishing time was 52:30, more than three minutes faster than White had managed. The mare ran 31:57, a new Irish trotting record.

After the race, Pat's rematch with Harris was fixed for Christmas Day on the trotting course at the Lambeg Recreation Grounds in County Antrim.[368] By 16 December, however, the idea had been shelved by the organisers in favour of pony, horse, and whippet races.[369] More tolerated now than admired, Pat White no longer had drawing power, and the Irish public was fast losing interest in professional athletics.

POWDERHALL 1912

THE HANKERING AFTER a Powderhall victory had become something of a habit. Twice a runner-up, it was surely only a matter of time before the gods of victory favoured him with the laurels. But that favour would not be easily gained. The fourth running of the Powderhall Marathon would feature not only the largest, but also the strongest field in the event's history, at least in terms of reputation.

The previous year's race had been a record-breaking one, and the winner, Hans Holmer, had early been confirmed as an entrant for the 1912 race. Also confirmed were Tom Longboat, the Finn, Viljami 'William' Kolehmainen (who had beaten Holmer in America the previous year), Giovanni Vollato of Italy, Marcel Cahurel of France, and the English runners Gardiner, Price, and Kitchener.[370] There had not been such a prestigious line-up since the 'Grand Marathon Derby' in 1909, from which White had been excluded.

The starter's pistol was fired at ten o'clock sharp. Of the twenty-seven entries, just nineteen presented themselves at the starting line. A slight rain was falling, but there was no wind, and the track was in good condition. A crowd of 1,500 spectators saw them off, down significantly from previous years, although the numbers would increase

Pat White, Edinburgh, 1912.

substantially over the following hour.

Longboat took the lead from the start and was followed briefly by the Scottish athlete, Percy Smallwood of Littleburn, who, feeling the pace on just the second lap, promptly thought better of his decision and dropped back. That left the Nova Scotian, Fred Cameron, in second, thirty yards adrift of Longboat. At this stage, Holmer was lying in sixth, and Pat, as usual, was sitting well back in the pack.

Longboat went through the first mile in 4:55, considerably faster than Bouchard's split at the same point the previous year. This was too hot for Cameron, who fell back to keep pace with Holmer, three-quarters of a lap behind the leader. By mile five, Longboat's split was twenty seconds faster than Bouchard's. To those behind him, the pace seemed suicidal, and so it was to prove.

During mile eight, Longboat began to slow, much as Bouchard had done the previous year. As a matter of fact, their splits from eight to ten miles would be almost identical. Holmer and Cameron were at this stage running eighty yards behind Kitchener, who had moved into second, while Gardiner and Kolehmainen were trailing a further fifty yards back and about to be lapped by Longboat. White, by now, was a long way behind.

At mile fifteen, Longboat began to show signs of having injured his knee. He struggled on for a bit, but at mile seventeen he pulled up. Ignoring the pleas of his manager to carry on, he stepped off the track and abandoned the race. He would later explain that running clockwise (American tracks ran counterclockwise) had placed too much pressure on his left knee, which had given out.

Cameron now assumed the lead, followed closely by Kolehmainen, Holmer and Kitchener, and seemed secure in this position until mile seventeen, when Kitchener attempted to pass him. He fought off Kitchener and held on to his lead until the twenty-first mile, when he too began to pay for his early pace and was passed by Kolehmainen and Holmer.

There were now just nine athletes left standing, and White was coming with his customary late surge to join a trailing group of six that contained, amongst others, Cameron, Price, and Kitchener.

Kohelmainen breaks the tape, Holmar 10 yds behind.

Holmer, by now, was running so close to Kolehmainen that the latter protested that his heels were being clipped. The judges ignored his

247

claims. At the bell, there was nothing between them. Holmer began to surge down the back straight, but Kolehmainen refused to yield and, looking into his opponent's eyes, knew that he had him. Sprinting away to victory, he won by ten yards.[371]

Kohelmainen's winning time was 2:32:56. In the race for third, Cameron beat White by forty seconds. White's time of 2:38:00, nevertheless, proved that he was still a world-class performer over the full marathon distance, and he would finish the year in fourth place on the world ranking lists. His £4 prize, furthermore, ensured that he did not return home out of pocket.[372]

Little was heard of White for some time after that. If he did race, it was not reported on. Then again, following the sinking of the S.S. Titanic on April 14, the papers were interested in little else. Over 1,500 people had died in that disaster, more than a hundred of them Irish. The country was in mourning, and journalists had other priorities. Adding to White's troubles, professional Marathon records had begun to fall in rapid succession as new training methods, better shoes, and a younger and better-fed generation took control of the event. The sun was setting on his career.

White would later be listed amongst the entrants for a fifteen-mile race in Cardiff on 26 June,[373] at which the King was due to attend, but he either failed to appear or failed to finish, for his name did not feature in the results.[374] Three weeks later, in Stockholm, the Olympic Marathon was won by Ken McArthur of South Africa in 2:36, but on a course that was two kilometres short of the 'London Distance' and run during a heatwave. That title could so easily have been

Pat's.

Did he have regrets? How could he not? The rewards of professional running had proved fleeting, and he had little, if anything, to show for his career. He had sacrificed his youth on the altar of professionalism, and for what? He'd played the hands he'd been dealt with limited success, but in the end, the table always wins, and he was leaving it now, no better off than he had been when he started.

As for glory, whatever fleeting moments he had enjoyed had been paid for in spades. No matter how fast he had run, or who he had beaten, the simple truth of the matter was that there was, and never would be, a roll of honour in the professional game that could compete with the eternal title of Olympic medalist. The Olympic medal was now the gold standard of excellence. Compared to it, everything in the professional game was just so much tinsel.

On 18 August 1912, White was listed amongst the entrants for a six-mile road race from Inchicore to Saggart in County Dublin, a race organised as part of that summer's Saggart Bazaar.[375] Other entrants included Fagan, Curtis and Harris. Neither the result nor the purse was ever posted. In an Olympic year, not even the Irish newspapers were interested in minor professional events.

Having successfully organised two professional races in Douglas, promoters on the Isle of Man were eager, in 1912, to try their luck again at organising a 'World's Marathon'. And so a fifteen-mile track race was planned for August 22. Among the twenty entries accepted, the names of Siret, Holmer, and Kolehmainen stood out as pre-

249

race favourites.[376] The race distance would be eleven miles short of a full marathon, so nobody, perhaps not even Pat himself, expected him to be competitive. With six Irish competitors in the race, however, there was local interest, and special excursions were run from Dublin to Douglas by the Isle of Man Steam Packet Company at a cost of 9s 6d for saloon and 6s 6d for steerage.[377]

Before a crowd of 5,000 spectators and on a heavy track, twelve men started the race, the French runners Siret and Waltispurger having failed to show up.[378] Despite a late surge, shortly after mile ten, White was unable to make any inroads on the leaders, and Kolehmainen, Holmer and Kitchener took the first three places.[379] Among the Irish competitors, Charlie Harris, a specialist in ten-mile events, finished in fourth place.[380] White, who finished sixth, at least had the consolation of taking second prize in the sealed handicap.[381]

One month later, back at Jones' Road in Dublin, White would compete in a fifteen-mile handicap in which Charlie Harris would run off scratch, White off 500 yards and Fagan off 650. Fagan would win by 700 yards from Harris. Pat would finish third.[382] He would not race again that year.

POWDERHALL 1913

IF FURTHER PROOF were needed that professional athletics was rapidly becoming more show business than sport, it was evidenced in December 1912 when it was announced that, following the poor attendance of the previous year, the Powderhall 'marathon' would now be run over a distance of fifteen miles, rather than the 'London distance'.

> It may be recalled that after the race of January last had been decided, the leading men in the struggle, Kohlehmainen, the Finn; Holmar, the Anglo-American; and Longboat, the Canadian Indian, fought their battle over again with – the point is important – the difference that they departed from the regulation Marathon distance of 26 miles 385 yards, and dropped to 15 miles. At this distance Longboat beat the Finlander.
>
> The race was not decisive, very few people who saw it being convinced that it reflected the merits of the runners, but that is neither here nor there at present, the point is that the race set, as regards distance, the fashion for the year.
>
> Strictly speaking, a 15 miles contest is not a Marathon race. Popular fancy has it that it is, and when, convinced by experiences in South Wales and in the Isle of Man that 15 miles was a better distance for his purposes than 26 miles, Mr Lumley decided to take 11 miles off his distance, he simply came into line with popular opinion. The race remains the "Powderhall Marathon." [383]

251

Approaching his thirty-third birthday, Pat White was no longer a young man and had struggled to be competitive over the shorter distances for some years now. The annual trip to Edinburgh, however, was a hard habit to break, and he enjoyed a friendly relationship with the promoter, Frederick Arthur Lumley, proprietor of the Powderhall Grounds.

White would have known by now that he would stand little chance over the shorter distance, but there was a significant carrot that year. The 1913 race would feature a sealed handicap, with three prizes of £5, £3, and £2 on offer. These prizes, funded by the elimination of the sixth-place prize, were designed to reduce the number of retirees.

Amongst the absentees that year, the most prominent were Gardiner and Holmer, the latter of whom was carrying an injury. Holmer, nevertheless, still turned up to watch. The weather was perfect – windless, crisp, and dry – and of the twenty-seven entries, twenty-one started.

Local hero and novice professional, George McCrae of Banknock, led the field through the first two miles at a relatively slow pace, which suited White, a notoriously slow starter. During the third mile, the Londoner, Dinning, and the American, Queal, who held the American ten-mile record, surged to the front to join McCrae. By mile five, Pat had been lapped, although he was still closer to the leaders than the remainder of the field, which had dropped out of contention by this stage.

Local support was all for McCrae, who was still leading at the ten-mile mark. By mile twelve, McCrae had begun to suffer and dropped back.

With just three laps to go, Dinning jumped into the lead. Queal and Kitchener refused to let him go, and all three were still in a tight bunch at the bell.

Kitchener now found himself left for pace and, as Queal and Dinning sprinted down the home straight, Queal finally cracked and Dinning crossed the line twenty yards ahead of him. White finished in eighth place, in a disappointing 1:28:57, but still managed to pick up £3 for having come second in the sealed handicap, having received an allowance of six and a half minutes.[384] Three weeks later, White ran a fourteen-mile race at Musselburgh, five miles east of Edinburgh, which he allegedly won, but reports of which are lacking.[385]

It was unusual for White to remain in Scotland after the Powderhall, and his continued presence suggests that he was still trying to survive as a full-time athlete and did not have a job to return to. His ability to survive as a full-time professional, however, was waning; the twilight of his racing days descending.

DUBLIN TO BELFAST

WHITE'S CAREER THUS far, though marked by several world-class performances, had been haunted by the lack of a single memorable victory. His back-to-back wins in the *Herald* races were on their way to being forgotten, his victory over Svanberg stained with a question mark, and his win in the Coronation marathon blighted by a slow winning time. Showing more than a few grey streaks now, it was perhaps inevitable, as his career tapered to its inevitable conclusion, that he should seek to try something different, to encase his legend in concrete before the fabling of local schoolboys and garrulous old men stretched his half-remembered achievements beyond the borders of credibility.

Time was no longer on White's side, and full marathons were becoming fewer and further between. In need of an alternative income stream, he allowed his head to be turned towards ultra-distance running by a certain John O'Leary, an Irishman resident in Edinburgh. O'Leary was the current holder of the Dublin to Belfast record, which stood at twenty-two hours and fifteen minutes.

Having persuaded White to stay on in Edinburgh while the details were sorted out, O'Leary set about organising and promoting the event, the greatest interest in which would come from gamblers eager to make side-wagers on the result.[386] Finally, on 21 January 1913, in the sports

254

pages of the *Evening Herald*, White announced his intention make an assault on the Dublin to Belfast record – a distance of over one hundred miles.

PEDESTRIANISM, DUBLIN TO BELFAST
PAT WHITE TO MAKE THE ATTEMPT.

Pat White, an ex-winner of one of the "Herald" Marathons, will attempt to encompass the distance between the Dublin G.P.O. and the Belfast G.P.O. for a sporting wager next Monday. Should he cover the distance (roughly speaking about 100 miles) inside of 22¼ hours he will gain £50; inside 25 hours £25, and should he not succeed in this, expenses only. It is a big undertaking, considering the unsettled state of the weather, but the Donabate hero, who only returned to Dublin this morning from Edinburgh is sanguine of capturing the "big" money.

The attempt will be of a go-as-you-please nature, for White can run or walk as it suits him. He will start from the Dublin G.P.O. at 2.30 a.m. on Monday morning, being dispatched on his long journey by Mr. Rynd, "Evening Herald," and at various places en route, including Balbriggan, Drogheda, Dundalk, Newry, etc., his time of arrival and departure will be checked.

The contest is the outcome of a wager made by Mr. John O'Leary, who, himself, has already got the distance in the shortest time mentioned above. White, who has been located in Edinburgh since the New Year Marathon looks extremely fit, and if the going should prove anyway favourable he should succeed, for he has great staying powers.[387]

At 2 a.m. on Monday, 27 January 1913, a large crowd gathered outside the General Post Office on

Dublin's O'Connell Street, hoping to cheer on their sporting idol, Pat White, as he set out for Belfast. Among the crowd were Willie Maley, the legendary manager of Glasgow Celtic football club, and John O'Leary of Edinburgh, the current record holder and the man who had made the wager.[388] White had yet to arrive. A solitary reporter covered his departure. It was a far cry from his heyday.

> White, as unassuming as ever, put in an appearance about a quarter past the hour, accompanied by a number of friends. He did not seem to be in the least worried about the task he had undertaken, and to the writer he talked with much confidence as to his chance of success.
>
> "I never felt in better form," he said, "and the conditions are decidedly in my favour. I am out to lower the record, and if I don't succeed this time I shall try again. The hard, dry road will conduce to quick going, and when I get warmed up after a stiff walk to the outskirts of the city I shall break into a trot – the one you know so well – and probably here and there I shall cover an average of ten miles, with slow walking intervals."
>
> At 2.15 the atmosphere was beautifully mild; any wind there was, came from the south, and the moon shone nicely from a slightly clouded sky. While the preliminary matters were being arranged there were some amusing scenes. The first of these was when two bakers dashed across from Earl Street in their working regalia. In the distance they looked like ghosts, and there was much banter as they took up a position near the Nelson column.
>
> Then a car drove up, and two gentlemen who alighted from it commenced to bandy words as to

the merits of White. They got very aggressive as the minutes went on, and it took two constables to keep them asunder. However, the cry that White was ready brought peace, and all got to the pillars at the G.P.O., where White was standing under the clock for 2.30 to arrive. He did not change his attire – he intended to do so this morning after daylight – and all he had was some money to get refreshments on the way and a map of the road, which he did not know so well after he left Dundalk.

Just as the hand of the Post Office clock touched the half-hour, White, amid a great cheer, started at a brisk walking pace along the west side of O'Connell Street, followed for a considerable distance by those who had been waiting for the start. At the Parnell memorial, White waved his hand to his followers and then, quickening his pace, only the stalwarts were able to keep in touch with him. White expects to get to Belfast well before midnight.[389]

After that, no word was heard from White for quite some time. The weather had turned nasty. A rainstorm that had begun on Monday night and continued well into Tuesday morning had flooded much of County Louth. Several rivers had burst their banks, leaving many roads impassable and sections of the northern rail line under several feet of water.[390]

A telegram from a *Herald* correspondent in Drogheda would later claim that, despite exhaustive inquiries about the town, no news of White had been received by 2.30 that afternoon. He was due to be checked at Dundalk, Newry, and other places along the route, but by the early hours of the following morning, nothing had been heard from those checkpoints either. Late in the day, a telegram, signed 'M'Cabe,' was delivered to the offices of the *Evening Herald*. It read:

Wire from White; reached Belfast 1.10. Roads bad.

That night, at about 11.30 p.m., a telephone call was received at the *Herald* offices from someone claiming to be White. The caller stated that he had arrived in Belfast at ten minutes past one that morning. He had missed the record.[391] Tuesday evening saw the facts confirmed:

We are officially informed that Pat White arrived at the Belfast G.P.O. at 1.10 a.m. yesterday (Tuesday) morning. His task was to get the distance in 22¼ hours, but he failed to accomplish this, after having made a game effort under the most trying conditions, by 25 minutes.

It would appear that, on reaching Newry, rain began to fall heavily and, with this part of the country mostly under water, it being a low-lying district, his troubles began in earnest. In some places he had to wade through the mud, his limbs were black from exertion, while the muscles on his back were causing him great pain. He intends to have another "go" in March.[392]

Though he had missed the record by twenty-five minutes, Pat had still walked away from the attempt with a prize of £25 for having broken twenty-five hours. That was more than enough to tide him over for several months while he contemplated his next move.

Considering, perhaps, another man versus

horse extravaganza, he was spotted several weeks later training on the Grand National course at Aintree.[393] Upon his return to Dublin on 11 March, however, he made no mention of Aintree. Instead, he announced his intention to make a second attempt on the Dublin to Belfast record, but running in the opposite direction.

By reversing the course, White would have had greater support towards the end of the run, especially on the section between Drogheda and Swords, where he was still idolised. The attempt, however, never took place, presumably because he failed to raise the necessary financial backing. Instead, he accepted a challenge from Pat Fagan to reprise their old *Herald* rivalry on 25 May, in a race from Inchicore to Naas.

> Three o'clock is the hour fixed for the challenge race tomorrow between Pat Fagan (Dublin) and Pat White (Donabate – both winners of the "Herald" race in the past – over the Naas course. It will be a trying journey for the men should the weather prove to be sultry, but both are in capital condition for such a lengthy contest. Fagan had a 'trial' spin on Wednesday, and those who followed him are sanguine as to his chance. White is understood to have "readied" himself down Balbriggan way, and certainly the issue appears to be a very open affair.[394]

The race to Naas was not just a resumption of the rivalry between Fagan and White, but also a revival of the City vs. Country rivalry. A 'handsome purse' was secured by subscription, and both men were reported to have placed 'substantial' side bets.[395] Come the day, the pair put on a show, running stride for stride until they reached Naas Bridge, where Fagan put on a surge and ran away to win by 250 yards.[396] Unlike their epic battles of the past, the race barely merited a footnote in the papers.

Pat didn't race in June, most likely because the White family was consumed with preparations for the wedding of his sister, Bridget, to Thomas Nulty, a farm labourer from Bettyville, two miles north of Ballyboughal. They were married in Lusk, at St MacCullin's church, on June 15.

A week after Bridget's wedding, Charlie Harris challenged White and Fagan to race him over ten miles, with White and Fagan running five miles each for a £5 or £10 stake.[397] That race never took place, presumably because all three were subsequently invited to participate in a potentially lucrative ten-mile race in England.

Sponsored by the *Sporting Chronicle*, the 'Pedestrian Carnival of the Century' was scheduled to take place over the August bank holiday weekend at the grounds of Salford Football Club at Weaste. Holmer, Dinning, Kolehmainen, Kitchener, and Gardiner had all been invited.[398]

As a warm-up for Salford, Pat ran a three-mile race from Swords to Malahide against three unknowns and won easily.[399] Upon his arrival in Salford, however, he discovered that the ten-mile race had been changed to a one-hour race with a special prize offered to any athlete who could break Harry Watkins' record of 11 miles, 1286 yards.[400] No one did, and White dropped out at the halfway mark.[401] It was to prove his final race.

STRATHAVEN

AND THEN THE war came. There hadn't been a war since Crimea, but on the eve of the Douglas race, a Bosnian Serb by the name of Gavrilo Princip shot and killed Archduke Franz Ferdinand, heir to the throne of the Austro-Hungarian Empire. One month later, the Empire declared war on Serbia, marking the end of the Belle Époque and the beginning of the Great War.

On 4 August 1914, though initially reluctant to get involved in what it saw as a chiefly Balkan affair, Britain declared war on Germany. Three days later, the first British troops landed in France. Everyone believed it would be 'over by Christmas.' With modern guns and railways, and the best-organised army in the world, how could it not?

All dreams are finite, but not all are neatly resolved. Athletes who have dedicated their lives to any sport and have been the recipients of public adulation often find the end of their careers difficult to cope with. For some, it is as if a part of them has died, and the resulting sense of loss frequently leads to periods of grief, depression, and uncertainty.

At thirty-three years of age, it was Pat White's turn to float in that liminal space between racing and retirement, that murky twilight into which all sporting careers eventually taper. Stranded between realisation and acceptance, with the future revealing itself in glimpses rather than full-blown revelations, every attempt to recover his old fire was increasingly resembling the striking of flints on damp tinder. The heart was willing, but the flesh was weakening, a little more with every passing year.

He had been a runner for fifteen years. He had sacrificed his youth for that tenuous identity and, in return, it had gifted him a pedestal and a purpose, had taken him to places he might otherwise have never reached. It was still how he saw himself, and how the world saw him. What was he to be now, if not that?

In some respects, White was lucky. Running was not *all* that he had ever known. Officially classified as an 'agricultural labourer' – the result of a government scam to keep down the cost of agricultural production – he was, in truth, a highly skilled farmhand, a farmer without a farm. He had other means by which he could fill the empty days and an empty belly. In fact, since February 1914, he had been back working on Patrick Harford's farm at Baldurgan.[402]

The adrenaline rush of competition, however, and the luxury of being able to focus solely on the preparation for the next race, were highly addictive, and the path to sporting retirement littered with the illusory sense of unfinished business. Though back labouring for a living, he was simultaneously reported to be training for two upcoming marathons, the first at New Brighton, Merseyside, on Easter Monday, and the second, a 'World's Marathon' in Douglas on 29 June.[403]

In March, he accepted a challenge to race Thomas J. Allen from Inchicore to Naas on the first Sunday of May for £20 a-side, but nothing appears to have come of it.[404] In early May, he issued a challenge to race any man in Ireland over 20 miles for £10 or £30 a-side at either Croke Park or Shelbourne Park, but that offer, too, came to nothing. His offer to join a fifteen-mile match between Harris and Fagan was similarly rebuffed.[405]

Having scorned to share his good fortune when he was at his peak, no one was prepared to divide the gate with him now. He found himself now, ever so slowly, being nudged aside, and not just by the new generation, but by the old.

White had been the recipient of several other challenges over the early months of the year, but he was no longer interested in being a trial horse for younger athletes over the middle distances, and nobody was any longer accepting offers to race over twenty miles or more. The New Brighton race would never take place, and for some unknown reason, he declined the offer to run in Douglas.

There is nothing more humbling than the slow tumble from a pedestal, except, perhaps, a parallel slide into poverty. What Pat needed at this stage of his life was a means of stealing away from the spotlight and back to an everyday life, a logical progression by which his energies could be redirected into something meaningful, a new purpose that would still be respectful of his sporting achievements and self-identity.

Shortly after war was declared, Pat travelled to Edinburgh to discuss an offer to move into coaching. No longer receiving meaningful challenges, but unable to make a clean break from the sport, he accepted the post. Moving to

Scotland would allow him the space to detach from the sport and the seemingly endless questions about his plans. In the back of his mind, however, he had yet to abandon the hope that his form might yet return, and he continued to nurture ambitions of winning the Powderhall. Feeling somewhat diminished since returning to Richardstown, and tethered to a predictable and undesirable fate, he decided he would get himself to Scotland before he shrank any further. Red berries turned to black in his absence.

On 28 September 1914, Pat returned to Dublin from Edinburgh and announced his appointment as the new distance running coach at the Powderhall grounds, where he had for years been on friendly terms with the proprietor, Frederick Arthur Lumley. Several professional coaches worked out of the grounds, but it was far from sustainable employment. Those men had other jobs and only coached professional athletes on the side.

White was never going to be able to survive by coaching alone, or easily accommodate the sense of loss that follows the end of a sporting career. The offer, all the same, afforded him a dignified withdrawal, not just from the sport, but from the arenas of his youthful triumphs, which were all about him in Dublin, on every road and in every field he'd ever set foot upon. A bridge to the mundane, a stepping stone to anonymity, perhaps even a crutch to help him through the grieving process, the drift into coaching was all of that, and indicative of a tacit recognition that his racing days were, if not quite over, then coming to an end.

There may, however, have been another factor

informing his desire to get away. In documents filed as part of a pension application at a much later date, it would be stated that John White had been unable to work since 1914. The cause and nature of that disability were never stated, but his death certificate would later reveal it to be heart problems..

It is not known exactly when or why Pat White began to fall out with his family, or whether the fault lay in his relationship with his father or in his perceived viability of the farm under the terms of the current lease. Whatever the reason, he did not want to take over the running of it or to find himself working for his father. Peter could do so if he wished. But *he* was off to Scotland.

White's announcement of the Powderhall coaching appointment was to be the last that the Irish athletics community would ever see or hear of Pat White. His name would be listed amongst the entries for the following year's Powderhall Marathon – the habit was hard to break – but he would not appear on the starting line.[406]

As was perhaps to be expected following the outbreak of war, the coaching appointment did not work out. With so many young men having volunteered, there were no longer enough athletes left to coach. And so, not long after his return to Edinburgh, Pat finally admitted defeat, put aside the tattered remnants of his sporting career, and set out for Lanarkshire in search of employment as an agricultural labourer, the only other trade he had ever known. There, where he had never raced, he would be unknown. He could start again, return to the life that Fate had originally mapped out for him, the proverbial slate wiped clean, his sleeves free of even the slightest trace of chalk dust.

Following the rush to volunteer in the early days of the war, Lanarkshire had been left with an acute shortage of farmhands and skilled ploughmen. Scarcely a day passed that the *Hamilton Advertiser* did not carry job offers from local farmers. And so, sometime in early 1915, White fetched up in Strathaven, a market town seventeen miles south of Glasgow, where he found employment on a local farm.

Strathaven was a pleasant little hamlet of narrow streets and historic buildings, its mediaeval origins still visible around its Common Green – the market square about which the town was laid out. Its greatest charm, however, lay in its ordinariness. Like many an Irish country village, it was quiet, functional, and unpretentious, as good a place as any to reflect on what had been lost, which for most retiring athletes is usually far more than just the sport itself.

Strathaven, early 1900s.

White's arrival in Strathaven should have marked a return to the simplicity, tranquillity and anonymity of life before running, to structured routines and seasonal rhythms that offered the troubled soul far more than mere nostalgia. In his head, it probably looked like the ideal place to recover himself, but that was not how the world was turning at the time.

When he arrived, the talk was not about weather and crops, but the progress of the war; about which house had been the latest to receive the dreaded postman's knock or place a black-bordered card in the parlour window. Before the war, he would have fit right in, but in the current climate, his civilian clothes stood out like a wasp in a window.

Back in Dublin, Pat's brother Peter had, until recently, been parading about as a captain in John Redmond's National Volunteers, a nationalist paramilitary force created to resist the Ulster Volunteer Force, then hell-bent on opposing Irish Home Rule.[407] But when Redmond encouraged his volunteers to sign up and fight for Britain in what he believed would be a short war, Peter, along with many other militant nationalists, had left in disgust.

Pat White's idea of patriotism differed greatly from that of the average Scot. But while Irish nationalism was easily asserted in Dublin, it was not so easily, or wisely, done in Strathaven. Indeed, it took nerve to stroll about the town in civvies when so many local men had volunteered to fight. It would become especially provocative in the aftermath of Gallipoli.

Pat quickly found lodgings at 53 Castle Street, a rudimentary weaver's cottage in the oldest part of the town. A short walk from the Claverhouse Inn and close to the ruins of Strathaven Castle, this sloping thoroughfare was terraced on both sides with a mix of single and two-storied dwellings. Very much a working-class enclave, it was populated primarily by labourers, council workers, coal miners and factory hands, a significant number of whom were either Irish or of Irish extraction. Settling in was made easier by the sense of familiarity.

Castle Street from the junction with North Street.
The old weavers' cottages can be seen on the right.

Next door to White, at number 51, there lived a twenty-two-year-old mother of two. Her name was Maggie McArthur. The house he was moving into had, until very recently, been her sister's. She knew it like her own. Maggie wore a wedding ring – he would have noticed that immediately – and, despite her youth, a black mourning dress. Under

268

normal circumstances, they might have shared little more than daily pleasantries as they passed. But these were not normal circumstances ... for either of them.

MAGGIE

BACK IN 1911, Gilbert McKinnon McArthur, a twenty-four-year-old former soldier, had come to Strathaven to take up civilian employment as a ploughboy on the farm where Maggie McNair was employed as a servant. A native of Bowmore on the Isle of Islay, he was three years Maggie's senior. The attraction was instant, and in January 1912, Maggie discovered she was pregnant. Dismissed from their jobs, they moved in with Maggie's widowed mother, Elizabeth, who ran a six-room boarding house at 54-56 Castle Street.[408]

Five months later, on 14 June 1912, Maggie and Gilbert were married at St Patrick's Catholic Church in Strathaven. Shortly afterwards, Gilbert found regular employment with a local building contractor, and the couple moved out of Elizabeth's and into a house on 4 North Street. It was here, on 25 October 1912, that Gilbert Junior was born. Eighteen months later, on 2 May 1914, the couple welcomed his sister, Lizzie, whom they had named after Maggie's mother.

Shortly after Lizzie's birth, the couple moved back to Castle Street and leased a two-room cottage at no. 51, directly across the street from Elizabeth's boarding house, and next door to the house that Maggie's sister, Catherine, had recently vacated following her marriage and move to Tulliallen.[409] Upon Britain's entry into the war, in August 1914, Gilbert re-enlisted in his old regiment and was straight away deployed to the Western Front.[410] For Gilbert's regiment, there was to be no Angel of Mons, and no lucky escape. A report in the *Hamilton Advertiser* recorded his fate:

> We regret to have to record the death of Pte. Gilbert McKinnon McArthur, 1st Btn Cameron Highlanders whose home address is in Castle Street. Pte. McKinnon rejoined the Cameronians on mobilisation and was almost immediately sent to the front. Until three weeks ago he was unscathed and then he was wounded in the head and neck by a shell.
>
> Removed to a London hospital he was twice operated on and was supposed to be doing well. On Thursday, however, his wife received a summons by telegram to go and see him and shortly after her arrival he died... The deceased soldier was in the employment of Mr. R. W. Hamilton, Contractor, Waterside Street. He leaves a widow and two young children.[411]

Following Gilbert's burial in London's Brompton Cemetery, Maggie returned to Strathaven.[412] Her whole life lay ahead of her, but the one she had wanted was gone. Clueless as to how she should cope with her grief or navigate life as a war widow, she found herself left to raise two-year-old Gilbert and six-month-old Lizzie with precious little money on which to support herself. But at least there had been a funeral – few other military widows had been so fortunate – and across the road, she still had her mother. She was not, therefore, entirely alone.

Maggie's predicament was far from unusual.

But what had made it so galling was that Gilbert's sacrifice had been unnecessary. He had only just found steady employment and, as a married man, was not at the time legally obliged to re-enlist. But, hearing the bugle call, he had become seized with a thirst for adventure and had raced to answer it. 'It'll be over by Christmas,' was what everyone was saying. 'You've got to get out soon, otherwise you won't see anything.' Well, Gilbert McArthur was one of the first to get out. He saw action, but not Christmas.

Maggie could only grin and bear it now, and continue her life as if nothing had happened, expected, like every other war widow, to become a living memorial to the glorious dead. Her survival was now dependent on the 'separation allowance', which continued to be paid for twenty-six weeks after her husband's death, and on the war widow's pension, both of which she received from the Soldiers' and Sailors' Families Association (SSFA).

Founded by Sligo-born Sir James Gildea in 1885, the SSFA charity provided philanthropic assistance to the families of serving British soldiers and sailors, who often faced inadequate wages or insufficient state support. Such payments, however, were frequently late or non-existent. They also came at a price.

In the early years of the Great War, wives receiving separation allowances were the subject of a 'moral panic.' Without the guiding hand of their husbands, and with money of their own to spend, they were feared to be at moral risk and frequently subjected to home visits by 'almoners' from the SSFA, who would inspect the home to ensure that the recipient was still a 'deserving' case.

Less than a year after Maggie buried her husband, and her sister Catherine had moved out of number 53, a thirty-six-year-old, blue-eyed labourer moved into the cottage that, until recently, she had been able to treat as an extension of her own. The new tenant was a quietly spoken Irishman. He had travelled, and had seen America. He was also, like her, a Catholic, someone with whom to share the Sunday walk to or from St. Patrick's, and a coal fire of a winter's evening. It had been only a year since Gilbert died, and Maggie was still attempting to navigate the grief and trauma of that loss. A friendly ear was especially welcome on the lonely winter evenings when the children were sleeping.

Almost old enough to have been her father, her new neighbour possessed the kind of maturity and self-confidence that her late husband had lacked. He was short of stature, and no Owen Moore, but he was handsome in his own way. His prospects, no more than her own, seemed poor, but he came across as honest and reliable. And maybe that was what drew her to him; that, and a faint sense of panic as she confronted each day the chilling prospect of facing life as a single mother.

Maggie McArthur would have been among the first of the young military widows in Strathaven to wear the black mourning dress that traditionally declared the altered social status of the widow and marked her chastity and piety. A long-observed tradition, it would fall into disuse as the death toll rose, and the sight of so many mourning dresses became injurious to public

Castle Street c. 1910.
The arched gateway is the entrance to the cemetery.

morale.

In 1915, however, the tradition was very much alive, and Maggie, who had been born and bred in Strathaven, would have been instantly recognisable as a widow and subject to all the social pressures and expectations that came with the black dress.[413] And yet, of all Pat's Scottish neighbours, Maggie McArthur was perhaps the least likely to pass judgement on a man reluctant to volunteer, let alone in the service of a King and country he did not recognise as his own.

It most likely began with odd jobs, neighbourly tasks for which a strong pair of hands might be required, such as the carrying of coal or the chopping of wood, in return for which a friendly cup of tea might be offered and a story or two exchanged at the kitchen table. It soon became a chain: one favour exchanged for another until the other's stories became an integral part of their own. In no time at all, Pat was crossing the backyard of an evening to share a convivial table, the warmth of a lambent hearth and, ultimately, her bed.

Providential it may have been, but their relationship was far from idyllic and had, of necessity, to be conducted discreetly. During the Boer War, most war widows had been left to fend for themselves, largely because the rank-and-file had been recruited from the lower classes and, as such, were considered of little consequence. From the start of the current war, however, when it became clear that millions, rather than tens of thousands, of soldiers would be needed, the government had been forced to cast a wider net. The inclusion of the middle classes had forced a change in the manner in which widows were viewed, not least because middle-class recruits would not stand for their wives and children being treated in such a manner.[414]

Old prejudices, alas, died hard and the attitude of the Victorian upper and middle classes towards the wives of rank-and-file soldiers continued much as it had during the Crimean War, when they were looked upon as 'drunken slatterns' or, at best, as being on a par with servants and therefore 'in need of watching'.[415]

To receive her pension, therefore, a soldier's widow was expected to honour her husband's sacrifice by living up to Victorian norms of respectability and the moral dictates of the Soldiers and Sailors Families Association, the charity charged with dispensing relief to servicemen's families. A war widow who did not live up to these ideals, or who became the subject of public gossip, risked not just public scorn, but the loss of her pension: a regular income often envied by women whose incomes were less secure, and by those who had belatedly come to regret not having married their boyfriends before they were killed.[416]

And so, between the envy of other women and middle-class notions of patriotism and duty, a societal expectation was placed squarely upon the shoulders of the war widow that she would not sully her husband's memory by engaging in disreputable behaviour, such as cohabitation or extra-marital sex. As a war widow, Maggie McArthur would have been only too well aware of the fact that she was being watched.

But even that was not the full extent of it. Widows who had been granted a pension were also required to regularly present their children to a volunteer 'almoner' to prove that they were still living. During such interviews, mothers would be questioned on their morals and, in some cases, be required to provide documentary proof of church attendance.

As 'evidence' of falling standards could include unsubstantiated neighbourhood gossip, and the decision as to whether the recipient was truly 'deserving' depended on the unregulated personal judgement of the almoner, it was not unusual for pensions to be revoked.[417] There was, furthermore, no right of appeal.[418] Until their relationship became permanent, Pat and Maggie had little choice but to be discreet.

On the face of it, the pair were grossly mismatched, not least because of the fourteen-year age difference. But they had met at a time when the needs of each happened to intersect in an empathetic and practical conjunction, and so they had slipped quickly and easily into a comfortable and fulfilling relationship, though not so comfortable that Maggie could afford to risk losing her pension. For the time being, discretion was the better part of romance.

WHITE FEATHERS

As AN OUTSIDER in the town, Pat White had thus far remained untouched by the war. But, as the recruitment campaigns gathered momentum, it became almost a badge of shame for a man to be seen out of uniform. The volunteer soldier had become the contemporary ideal of masculinity – a man willing to make the 'supreme sacrifice' for community and country – and the public respect for him was frequently manifested in the large crowds that gathered to cheer him and his comrades off to war.

Conversely, the man who chose to remain on the home front was seen as a lesser creature, his courage marked with an unspoken question mark, his masculinity openly questioned. New words entered the popular lexicon to describe him. 'Shirker' came into use as early as August 1914, and 'slacker' by September of the same year.[419]

With attitudes rapidly hardening, an Admiral Charles Fitzgerald began to organise a group of thirty women, including the authors Emma Orczy and Mary Augusta Ward, to hand out white feathers to men in civilian attire, in the belief that the fear of being white-feathered by women was the most effective way of shaming the shirkers into enlisting. This movement – the White Feather Brigade – spread quickly throughout the kingdom and forced the government to issue lapel badges to public servants, honourably discharged soldiers, and men in reserved occupations, to prevent them from being accosted in the street.

The White Feather: A Sketch of English Recruiting

And yet, despite the orgy of volunteering and the practice of white-feathering, remaining a civilian was far from a minority experience, with almost three-quarters of all men between the ages of fifteen and forty-nine declining to volunteer. There was, however, only so long that Pat could hold out against the tide of condemnation if he wished to continue his relationship with Maggie McArthur, especially following the arrival in town of five families of Belgian refugees for whom there was such universal sympathy that a great community effort went into housing and feeding them.[420]

The arrival of the Belgians; the constant call for donations to the War Relief Fund; the numerous flag days and patriotic pageants; the fundraising concerts at the Public Hall; the sharing of letters

279

from the front and, most potently of all, reports in the *Hamilton Advertiser* of local men who had died in the trenches, suffered injuries or amputations, been made prisoners of war, or awarded medals for gallantry, all served to focus the public mind on the 'shirkers'.

On 29 June 1915, eleven months into the war, parliament passed the National Registration Act, obliging all persons between the ages of fifteen and sixty-five, who were not members of the armed forces, to register for National Identity Cards. The information thus supplied enabled the authorities to determine who should be called up for military service and who, in the national interest, should be retained in civil employment. Labour exchanges were now asked to mark or 'star' the papers of men employed in essential industries such as munitions manufacturing and farming.

On Friday, 20 August 1915, an open-air recruitment meeting was held on The Green in Strathaven to shame the local shirkers. Pat would have had to be deaf, dumb and blind not to see what was coming next and, in January 1916, when the National Registration Act followed by the Military Service Act, more commonly referred to as the Conscription Act, all single men between the ages of eighteen and forty-one were now deemed eligible for compulsory military service. The act still allowed for exceptions – namely, widowers with children, ministers of religion, and men engaged in a reserved or protected occupation, such as farming. But it was only a matter of time before they, too, were revoked.

Due to the political situation in Ireland, conscription was never applied there, and all Pat

TO STARRED OR BADGED SINGLE MEN OR SINGLE MEN IN RESERVED OCCUPATIONS.

Have you attested under the Group System?

If not, you are urged to do so. You should inform the Recruiting Officer when attesting of your special position. You will not be called up as long as your "Starring," &c. holds good.

IF YOU DO NOT ATTEST, you will come under the provisions of the Military Service Act on March 2nd, 1916 and will require a certificate of exemption.

BADGED MEN. If on March 1st, 1916, you hold a Badge Certificate issued to you in connection with a War Service Badge granted by the Ministry of Munitions, the Admiralty or the War Office, your Badge Certificate will be a Certificate of Exemption under the Act, so long as you continue rightfully to hold it.

STARRED MEN. If you are a starred man or in a reserved occupation, you will have to apply (no previous application will be taken into account) to the Local Tribunal for an individual Certificate if you wish to be exempted from the Military Service Act.

Any application for such a certificate by a starred man, or a man in a reserved occupation, must be made BEFORE March 2nd.

It is important that any man starred or badged or in a reserved occupation who has attested under the Group System and happens to be called up on Army Form W 3195 should AT ONCE notify the Recruiting Officer that he is starred or badged, or in a reserved occupation.

NOTE.—The starred and reserved occupations are now known as certified occupations. A list of these may be seen at the offices of the Local Tribunal or of the Recruiting Officer.

ATTEST NOW

would have had to do to avoid being called up was to go home. But he didn't. For the first time in his life, he was sharing his life with another, and in the grip of that addictive sense of rejuvenation that comes hand in glove with an intergenerational romance. It was early days, and he and Maggie were still dancing to a tune of uncertain rhythm, but, ever so hopeful, Pat was reluctant to leave her.

And so, rather than hop on a boat to Dublin, Belfast or Derry, Pat chose instead to enlist in the Volunteer Training Corps (VTC) of the Argyll and Southern Highlanders, a self-organised corps of infantry reserves, drawn almost exclusively from men who were overage or engaged in reserved occupations. Established in 1914, the VTC was a voluntary home defence force roughly equivalent to the Home Guard of World War II. It provided a means by which men who couldn't join the main army could contribute to the war effort.

Maggie must have wondered at the beginning what strange aversion had brought him to Scotland, where he had no roots, no family, and few friends. Was it the shame or embarrassment of having fallen on hard times? Had he fallen out with his family? Or was it simply a matter of pride, of wanting to be remembered at home as his better self, the local hero, the humble farm boy who took on the best in the world and made his country proud? Whatever he may have been running from then, there was little doubt about what was keeping him in Strathaven now. There was nothing mysterious or abstruse about it. It was her.

Pat was now a 'starred' or 'badged' man whose occupation or trade was deemed so essential to the war effort that he was allowed to remain in his civilian job. As a VTC reservist, furthermore, he was also entitled to wear a uniform, which provided much-needed protection from the insults, the stigma of being labelled a coward, and the prospect of being 'white feathered.' It would not have gone unnoticed by him, however, that back in Dublin, the VTC had been deployed during the Easter Rising in a combat role against a citizen army that may well have included his brother.

Barely a month had passed since the fires of the Easter Rising had been doused when, on 25 May 1916, an amendment to the Military Service Act was passed which narrowed, with Whitehall's customary impersonal elegance, the categories of work deemed to be of national importance. A call-up of reservists was creeping ever closer, which on its own was enough to tighten a man's intestines. But then Maggie dropped a bombshell of her own. She was pregnant.

AN IRREGULAR
MARRIAGE

WHY THEY DID not marry straight away is anybody's guess. They may have been waiting on permission – enlisted soldiers could not typically marry without it. The most likely reason, however, is money, or rather the fact that Maggie would lose her service widow's pension if she remarried. However, as the pregnancy progressed and became increasingly difficult to conceal, they knew that, sooner rather than later, they would have to marry. That was the why. The when was decided elsewhere.

When the Conscription Act was first debated in the House of Commons, the Government had given assurances that it would not be applied to migrant workers from Ireland, upon whom many Scottish farms depended during the harvest. But resentment had been steadily growing over the Irish exemptions of late, and, over a period of four days, in August 1916, Scottish police began to raid huts, lodging houses and workplaces in the Mossend district of Glasgow, rounding up Irish workers, even from the munitions factories.

Hauled through the streets in handcuffs, over fifty Irish labourers were brought before an unsympathetic Sheriff's Court that refused to entertain their protests. Transported to Hamilton Barracks, the only concession allowed them was the option of joining an Irish regiment.[421] At this time, Pat was attached to the VTC of a Scottish

284

regiment and was safe from the round-ups. But not from deployment.

On 1 September 1916, the infantry reserve was reorganised. Prior to this, most infantry regiments contained reserve battalions to which recruits were posted for basic training before being posted to an active service unit. With the introduction of conscription, however, the regimental system was unable to cope with the numbers and a new structure had to be implemented – the Training Reserve.

The local nature of recruitment for infantry regiments was thus abandoned, and the entire system was centralised. Reserve units of all regiments were redesignated as battalions of the Training Reserve and organised into new brigades. From these battalions, recruits could be deployed at any time and to just about anywhere.

Three weeks after the formation of the Training Reserve, Pat's reserved occupation status was cancelled and, sometime around 22 September 1916, he received his call-up papers. He was given two weeks to report to Hamilton Barracks.[422] He knew at once he would have to go.

With no guarantee that Pat would ever return, Maggie had little choice now but to accept that she might once again be left on her own and plan accordingly. In the widespread climate of impending bereavement, when working-class wives not only dreaded the death of a military husband but half-expected it, there was little point in seeking reassurance. So she and Pat decided to marry, and to do so immediately. It would be better that way, for both her *and* the baby.

With no time to organise the banns, let alone a church wedding, they had little choice but to procure a civil marriage and, on the following Thursday, 28 September 1916, Maggie put away for good her widow's weeds, Pat donned his military uniform, and the pair took the morning train to Glasgow. Here, at John Higgins' photographic studio on Wellington Street, close to Glasgow Central Station, they contracted a marriage by declaration.[423]

Maggie McArthur was pregnant by a man who was not her husband. Were he to be killed, or her illegitimate pregnancy to become common knowledge, she would lose all of her allowances for having broken the moral contract of the war widow. If they were to be married before he left, Maggie would still be entitled to a pension should the worst come to pass. By doing so at a photographer's studio, she and the child would have a face to remember him by.

The law in Scotland had for centuries held that any single man and woman who publicly acknowledged themselves to be married became, *ipso facto,* husband and wife. This form of union, known as an 'irregular marriage by sheriff's warrant,' required the presence of neither a minister nor a priest, and as such was frowned upon by the churches. Though legal, such marriages had been relatively rare during the nineteenth century. By 1914, however, they accounted for approximately twelve per cent of all marriages registered in Scotland.

All that was legally required to contract such a marriage was a declaration, signed before two witnesses, that the couple would subsequently present to a sheriff or magistrate. The couple would then be 'convicted' as parties to an irregular marriage. That done, the sheriff or magistrate would officially notify the registrar and the marriage would be registered and certified. The witnesses, in Pat and Maggie's case, were the photographer, John Higgins, and a machinist, Mary Laughlin.[424]

On the day the clocks went backwards for the first time, the newly-minted Mrs Maggie White surrendered her cottage at no. 51 Castle Street and moved herself and her children in with her new husband at no. 53. One week later, on 6 October 1916, Pat reported to Hamilton Barracks and was assigned to the 3rd (Reserve) Battalion of the Royal Irish Fusiliers. He was promptly dispatched to County Donegal, where infantry reserves were being trained for active deployment.

Pat and Maggie may have procured some Catholic ceremony or blessing on the morning of his departure, but no record of it can be found, apart from declarations made many years later by Maggie on two of her children's birth certificates that the date of her marriage was 6 October 1916.[425] The official marriage certificate, however, still records the date as 28 September.

For the second time in the space of three years, and no better prepared for the loneliness and anxiety than she had been on the previous occasion, Maggie White bid farewell to her husband and settled down to raise her children on her own. Having remarried, she was no longer entitled to her widow's pension. She would receive a lump sum equivalent to one year's pension, but after that, she would be reliant on the 19s 6d separation allowance that was paid to the wives of active soldiers, approximately a third of which would go on rent and insurance. She was still reasonably comfortable and no worse off than any other infantryman's wife. Life, however, was about to take a turn for the worse for the new Mrs White.

DESERTER

JUST SIX MONTHS had passed since the 3ʳᵈ Battalion of the Royal Irish Fusiliers helped to put down the Easter Rising in Dublin. During that time, they had been stationed in Dublin's Portobello Barracks, but following the collapse of the Rising, they had been removed to County Donegal, where the battalion was now charged with the training of recruits for deployment to active frontline regiments.

Upon the outbreak of war in 1914, the British Army had established a training camp in the Straid area of Clonmany, a quiet village near established military forts at Leenan and Dunree, and with a train station that provided easy access to Derry. Comprised of rows of galvanised huts mounted on concrete blocks, the camp was short on home comforts and completely lacking in privacy.

The residents of Clonmany village, which had been a hotbed of subversive activity in recent years, did not exactly welcome their new neighbours. With up to 5,000 soldiers billeted in close proximity to the village, local girls were promptly forbidden from walking around the parish unescorted. An especially cold shoulder was reserved for soldiers who spoke with Irish accents. That hostility had, if anything, intensified following the execution of the leaders of the 1916 uprising.

This was never going to end well for Pat White. For almost all his working and sporting life, he had spent the greater part of his day in his own company. Solitary or quiet individuals, furthermore, did not always have an easy time of it in the army, where a certain esprit de corps was not only encouraged, but expected.

Clonmany, early 1900s.

Adding fuel to the emotional combustion was the fact that White had returned to Ireland in a uniform that, even among his own family would most likely, in the current climate, have been perceived as a betrayal of both his class and his race, not least because his brother was currently an active member of Sinn Féin and soon to be a captain in the Fingal Brigade of the Irish Volunteers.[426]

Peter, it was true had worn the King's uniform

once, but that was before the unpleasant business at Kilmainham. But Peter had deserted twice and been dishonourably discharged, so his army career, brief as it was, could hardly be held against him. The 1916 executions had changed everything, and the drape of the King's uniform on an Irishman's shoulders hung more heavily now than it ever had before.

The Easter Rising may have ended in failure, but the War of Independence was far from over, and though Pat's decision to wear a British Army uniform had been largely a matter of expediency, it begged the rather obvious question: would he be prepared to fight in it, perhaps even against his own brother? The scenario was far from impossible.

Pat was still stationed at Clonmany when, at 3 a.m. on 15 February 1917, Maggie gave birth to a son. In her husband's absence, she named the child John McNair White (a combination of her maiden and married surnames).[427] Twenty-three days later, before the scent of carbolic acid had fully disappeared from the house, the child died of pneumonia.[428] To lose a child at any time was hard. To lose one while nursing was unbearable. Maggie was bereft.

The reasons are unclear. Perhaps Pat had been refused, or failed to return from, compassionate leave; perhaps he had gotten word of a call-up to permanent service and decided to put himself beyond the reach of German lead; perhaps he had succumbed to pressure from his staunchly republican family; perhaps it was all of that, and more. The upshot of it all, however, was that shortly after the death of his son, Pat White deserted.[429]

He would have known there would be consequences for Maggie as much as himself, but then again, perhaps she was a party to it, more willing to accept the loss of income than to suffer the death of another loved one. We have no way of knowing.

Pat's movements over the next two years are difficult to determine. Living on the run in wartime, and in what was effectively a military state, could not have been easy. He had strong republican connections in Dublin, if he could reach them safely, but even that was problematical. He had effectively cut his ties with his family in 1914, and the republican movement did not trust British Army deserters, whom it tended to view as spies. It is possible, perhaps even probable, that he adopted an alias and sought employment as an agricultural labourer in some remote part of Ireland where he was not known – he would have needed to earn a living somehow – but nothing is known for certain.

As desertion in times of war carried the death penalty, many commanding officers would bend over backwards to find a means of applying the lesser charge of 'Absent Without Leave,' a charge that assumed an intention on the part of the missing soldier to return to duty eventually. But a C.O. could only do this if the soldier left him enough wriggle room to do so. Only in the most clear-cut cases was the charge of desertion generally applied.

Pat was not the first soldier to have deserted from Clonmany. Back in January, a Private John James Wishard of the 4th (Extra Reserve) Battalion of the Royal Inniskilling Fusiliers was court-martialled on a charge of desertion and sentenced to eighty-four days' detention. Sent to the front upon his release, his subsequent attempts to get home to a sick daughter saw him shot at dawn by a regimental firing squad.[430]

Wishard's second desertion, however, had taken place in the theatre of war. Desertions on the home front did not generally carry the same weight as desertions in battle. A deserter on the home front – and there would be more than 130,000 of them during the war – was more likely to be sent before a district court-martial, where the maximum punishment was two years imprisonment.

The vast majority of home front deserters were sentenced, therefore, not to execution, but to some form of penal servitude. Sent to prisons and military detention centres, they would forfeit their pay for every day they had been missing and for every day of their incarceration.

Weeks and then months flew by, and still White did not return. His commanding officer, therefore, was left with no alternative but to apply the more serious charge. In August 1917, a tribunal was convened, sworn evidence was introduced, and Pat White was found guilty. The following month, his name was publicly listed as a deserter in the *Police Gazette*.[431]

Feelings on the subject of deserters and conscientious objectors in general were running so high in Strathaven at this time that, between 10 and 31 August 1918, following services to mark the fourth anniversary of the declaration of war, several heated letters on the subject were exchanged in the pages of the *Hamilton Advertiser*.[432]

The cost of desertion, therefore, was not borne

by the soldier alone. His wife also suffered, becoming a social pariah in her parish and losing her separation allowance. Attempting to starve or shame the wife into submission was considered a valid tactic in encouraging her to give up a deserter's location. Still, it is unlikely that she knew for sure where Pat was. He could not easily write to her for fear of a postmark betraying his whereabouts, and she would have been unable to join *him*, as the aiding or harbouring of a deserter was a criminal offence, punishable by up to six months' hard labour. She had the children to think about.

Approximately sixty per cent of War Office service records were destroyed in a bombing raid in 1940, so we may never know precisely what happened to Pat White between 1917 and 1920. All that can be said with any degree of exactitude is that, between 1914 and 1920, over 82,000 courts martial were held in the British Army and Dominion forces to deal with charges of desertion and unauthorised absences, and Pat White's name cannot be found in any of the surviving records.

THE RETURN

NOVEMBER 1918. KAISER Bill abdicates. The war in Europe is won. There are still some 350 soldiers held in penal servitude and another 1,600 in prison. Later that same month, the Prime Minister, David Lloyd George, declares his intention to make Britain 'a fit country for heroes to live in' and introduces the Out-of-Work Donation scheme, a precursor of unemployment benefit. It is not, however, available to deserters, and it is still unsafe for Pat to come home.

By January 1920 the number of deserters remaining in prison has been reduced through suspensions and commutations to approximately two hundred.[433] Government priorities are changing. No formal amnesty is declared or enacted for deserters, nor will it ever be. Nevertheless, the anxiety to avoid any political controversy that might be used to mobilise or radicalise the working class, such as that which led to the Bolshevik Revolution in 1917, sees the evolution of a discretionary practice under which a trial can be dispensed with in favour of a dishonourable discharge, but only if a deserter turns himself in and signs a formal confession.[434]

And so, on 27 May 1920, under Section 392 XI of the King's Regulations (misconduct), Pat White turns himself in and, like his brother before him, is dishonourably discharged from the army.[435] To be demobbed in such a fashion means the forfeiture of all military benefits, including pensions and medals. On the other hand, it means that he is no longer a fugitive from justice.[436] He can go home.

A dishonourable discharge was hardly a ringing endorsement of his character. Still, it meant that it was now safe for employers to hire him, if they were so inclined, without running the risk of being charged with sheltering a deserter. Returning to Strathaven, however, in the early days of June, he found the town a lesser haven for a returning deserter than it was for a returning hero. Finding work was going to be difficult, readjusting to family life, perhaps even more so.

It was only natural to feel a little strange among them at first. Lizzie and Gilbert had been just two and four when Pat was conscripted. They could have only the haziest recollection of him. When he'd left, they had been toddlers riding on their mother's hip. He was a stranger to them now, and they to him: scampering, chatty little personalities whose memories he had never been a part of, except, perhaps, for a flying visit following the death of baby John.

That said, Gilbert and Lizzie would also have had little or no recollection of their biological father, beyond whatever idealised version Maggie had deemed appropriate to share with them. Pat would never be able to compete with that. The glorious dead were untouchable in their perfection.

As an army deserter returning home to parent the children of a war hero, Pat was also stepping into a social and emotional minefield. The slightest hint of happiness on his part could so easily prove a provocation to those from whom the war had taken far more than a reputation. The children, as of yet, were too young to be judgmental or to notice the occasional evasive eye, but it was only a matter of time before even they, or their peers, began to question their stepfather's contribution to the war.

And then there was Maggie, who for four long years had been building her psychological defences against a second widowhood. She, too, had changed. Less girlish and more authoritative, she had grown to womanly maturity in his absence; had borne and buried a child, become accustomed to her independence. They were locked in a legal and emotional embrace, but they were different people now. The war had changed everything.

Maggie White was no longer a girl of twenty-two. She was a grown woman who no longer needed a protector. The relationship would have to be rebuilt and connections reestablished, only this time without the preamble of a courtship or the excitement of subterfuge. That said, the weight of the last four years would not be lightly discarded.

The world had changed so much during the years that separated Pat White's wedding day from his reunion with his wife that the fourteen-year age gap had become a generational chasm. Hemlines had risen, corsets had been discarded, and women of all classes had bobbed their hair and cast aside forever the chains of Victorian modesty and subservience. By 1918, women over thirty who met certain property requirements had even won the right to vote. The world was teetering on the precipice of the Jazz Age – a fast-changing and modern world in which old traditions were everywhere being set aside in favour of the new. The balance of power in the marriage had shifted.

Today, only about 8% of couples have an age gap of ten years or more, and studies have shown that such couples become dissatisfied more quickly and are more likely to divorce than couples who are closer in age. For Pat and Maggie, those risks were accentuated by the fact that, four years after their wedding, they had still to enjoy a prolonged period of family life together and were effectively starting afresh.

The cottage at no. 53 had been leased in Maggie's name during her husband's absence, but the first renewal following his return saw the lease returned to Pat. Every year after that, however, it would be in Maggie's name. The reasons are unclear, but it is possible that Pat's struggles to find regular employment meant that he was frequently working away from home, most recently as a labourer on William Meikle's farm at Whitehill, two miles outside Strathaven, close to the village of Glassford.[437]

During the war, Maggie had taken over the lease on the cottage and made the place her own. She had grown accustomed to ruling the roost and doing things *her* way. It had been *she* who had paid the rent and *she* who had decided what was to be bought and how much was to be spent. She had presided over her household with complete and unquestioned authority, and had done so in the face of a host of financial hardships that had been imposed upon her, not through any act or fault of her own, but on account of the actions of her husband.

During this challenging period, Maggie had, of necessity, come to rely on the support of both her mother and her sister, Susie. Susie would never marry, and her mother, a widow who ran the boarding house opposite No. 53, would never remarry. The three had survived without men during the war and had enjoyed a degree of independence that was unlikely to be surrendered lightly.

Like many a demobbed soldier, Pat White came home after the war to find himself an unfamiliar, and at times an unnecessary, appendage to an efficiently functioning household. But the children were not the children he'd left, and neither was the wife. The homecoming was not as he had envisioned, but the love was still there. They could build something new upon that.

In the immediate aftermath of the war, married life may have been challenging for the Whites, but when all was said and done, they had been fortunate. Almost one in every six men recruited or conscripted from Strathaven during the war had died in action or during the Spanish Flu pandemic of 1918. Following the return of the generation that would never again take birdsong for granted, and for whom the war would never be fully over until they could once again laugh and dance guilt-free, employers felt obliged to offer what work was available in the first instance to the returning heroes.

The Whites were in no position to complain and, as the world slipped like a landslide into the Roaring Twenties, they could do little but count their blessings, hope for better times, and settle for the first time into the rhythms and compromises of everyday family life. And settle they did. Within months of her husband's return, Maggie White was pregnant.

THE KILLING OF
SERGEANT KIRWAN

IN APRIL 1916, Irish republicans launched an armed uprising against British rule and proclaimed an Irish Republic. Though the rebellion failed, the execution of its leaders created nationalist martyrs and provoked such a wave of public sympathy that it galvanised rather than destroyed public support for Irish independence.

Two years later, in December 1918, the republican party, Sinn Féin, won a landslide victory in Ireland and, on 21 January 1919, proceeded to form a breakaway government called 'Dáil Éireann'. That same day, two Royal Irish Constabulary officers were assassinated in an ambush at Soloheadbeg in Co. Tipperary by republican volunteers acting on their own initiative. Further acts of subversion followed in short order, most of which involved the capture of weaponry and the freeing of prisoners.

As the Dáil set about building an independent Irish state, Pat's oldest sister, Teresa, was finally settled. A forty-two-year-old spinster, she was still working at the time as a domestic servant at Baldurgan. Her new husband, Peter Brennan, was a fifty-eight-year-old recently widowed farm labourer from New Haggard, near Lusk.[438] Such marriages were always tinged with a mixture of poignancy and relief. Shortly after Teresa's wedding, on 16 November 1919, her sister, Sarah, married John Maher, a labourer from

Athy, Co. Kildare and went away to live with his people.[439] Not one of the family had married up, or married early, and of all the siblings, only Peter, by now the heir presumptive, remained at home, that is, when he was not away on 'missions' with local subversives.

Shortly after Teresa's wedding, in September 1919, the British government outlawed the Dáil. Republican paramilitaries responded by ambushing Royal Irish Constabulary and British Army patrols, forcing isolated barracks to be abandoned. The British response was to bolster the Royal Irish Constabulary with recruits from Britain – the notorious Black and Tans – whose ill-discipline and reprisal attacks on civilians served only to escalate the violence. By late 1920, the death toll had risen to about three hundred.

On 21 November 1920, a day forever inscribed in the annals of Irish history as the first 'Bloody Sunday', fourteen British intelligence operatives were assassinated, provoking a reprisal attack by the Royal Irish Constabulary, who fired into a crowd attending a Gaelic football match at Croke Park in Dublin. Fourteen civilians were killed that day, and sixty-five were wounded. One week later, seventeen British Army auxiliaries were killed in an ambush outside the village of Kilmichael in County Cork. By December, much of Ireland was under martial law.

Throughout this period, Peter White was far from an impartial observer. On 2 February 1921, for example, when R.I.C. Constable Samuel Green was assassinated by a lone gunman in Kathleen Fagan's public house in Balbriggan, Peter, an active member of the Irish Volunteers, was reported to have been involved in the shooting.[440]

302

Two months later, on 12 April, Peter was also reported to have participated in the attempted murder of R.I.C. Sergeant Kielty in the same town and to have taken part in several raids in which guns and ammunition had been stolen.[441] The engagement that was to cost him his life, however, would take place much closer to home, in the village of Ballyboughal, two kilometres from his parents' cottage, and close enough for them to have heard the gunfire.

Early in the evening of 18 April 1921, a car load of Royal Irish Constabulary from Balbriggan arrived in Ballyboughal where, entirely by chance, an armed party of Irish Volunteers happened to have gathered at O'Connor's pub following an aborted ambush earlier in the day. The reason for the car's stop at O'Connor's remains mired in speculation.

The armed group consisted of Paddy 'Lucky' Donnelly, Jack Hagan, James 'Red' Wilson, Jack Shiels and Peter White, the latter of whom was a Captain in the Fingal Brigade of the Irish Volunteers and probably the only one with formal military training. Wilson was outside the pub chatting with his girlfriend, Bridget Delaney. She had cooked breakfast for the 'boys' earlier in the day. Hearing a car approaching from the direction of the Naul, Wilson, correctly assuming it could only be the R.I.C. or the Black and Tans, sent Bridget home and went to warn his comrades.

As the police car pulled up opposite the pub, the senior officer of the party, Sergeant Stephen Kirwan, ordered his three constables and their Black-and-Tan driver to wait in the vehicle while he made his way to the pub's back door, the entrance to the private living quarters. The paramilitaries immediately left the pub by the front exit and exchanged some banter with the waiting R.I.C. men. Seeing young Eddie O'Connor, the son of the pub landlord, and another youth guiding some cattle towards the back of the pub, the men went to help open the haggard gate and drive in the cattle. Out of sight of the waiting R.I.C. car, they proceeded to lie in wait for Kirwan.

In the ensuing encounter, Kirwan was shot once in the temple and once over the heart, and Peter White took a bullet to his upper abdomen. As Kirwan fell to the ground, White took his revolver and made his escape in the direction of Ballyboughal Post Office, where he collapsed in the street. Knowing that his wound would most likely prove fatal, he insisted that his parents not be sent for, or told how badly wounded he was.

Carried by local people out of the street and into the post office, he was given the last rites by local Catholic priest Father Delaney and attended by Doctors Bradley and May from Swords, as well as a Doctor Cooney from Lusk. They helped to sustain him through the night.

The following morning, Peter was taken prisoner by the R.I.C. and brought by ambulance, still breathing and still fighting to hang on, to King George V Military Hospital in Dublin, the same hospital to which Kirwan had been taken the previous evening. Though both men were conscious upon arrival, both would die later that day from blood loss.[442] Peter was the first to go, at 7:30 p.m. Kirwan died three hours later.

The following day, Peter's body was released to the family and a small wake was held at the family home. All work ceased in Richardstown

304

that day. The men donned their Sunday best, the women their best shawls, and together they proceeded to the wakehouse to sit until morning with a mother who had lost her youngest son to a bullet, and her eldest to emigration.

Fearful of reprisals, attendance at Peter's funeral was strictly controlled by crown forces and restricted to family and close associates. He was laid to rest in the family plot at the old graveyard in Ballyboughal.[443] Whether Pat was there that day to witness his mother empty her heart for her favourite son is unclear. But it seems unlikely. Just four years later, his mother would be claiming to have no knowledge of his whereabouts. She had an inkling he was still in Scotland, but he had by then vanished from all their lives.

After the funeral, Pat's sister, Bridget, and her husband, Thomas Nulty, moved in with her parents, the farm being too much for John White to manage. John was suffering from Bright's Disease – a kidney complaint frequently accompanied by high blood pressure and heart disease – he had not been able to work for the past seven years and had been relying on Peter to keep the farm going.

Prior to his death, Peter had settled down somewhat and had been working locally as a labourer, earning twenty-five shillings per week, of which he contributed twenty to his father's upkeep. His death left his parents in dire financial straits. To tide them over, following the death of the breadwinner, the family received a £25 charitable donation from the Irish White Cross, a recently formed organisation whose task was to distribute funds raised by the American

Committee for Relief in Ireland.[444]

Under normal circumstances, it should have been Pat, as the eldest son, who moved back home to help his father run the farm, but these were not normal circumstances. The family had not just been devastated by Peter's death; they had been marked as sympathisers. Given that a policeman had died, a reprisal attack was not out of the question. Pat, furthermore, had only just got his life back on track, having reunited with his family after four years on the run.

There may even have been some residual tension between Pat and the family, Pat having emigrated to Scotland rather than help his ailing father to farm his seven-acre smallholding. All that is known for certain, however, is that on 9 May 1921, just three weeks after his brother had been laid to rest, Pat White celebrated the birth of his second son and named him Peter, in honour of his late brother.[445]

The birth of Peter marked a marriage reborn, and a little over a year later, on 22 August 1922, baby Peter was followed by his sister, Mary. If there had ever been even the remotest possibility of Pat White returning to Richardstown, it had been well and truly scuppered now. A farm that could barely support a family of three was never going to sustain eight. He would never set foot in Ireland again. All letters to him would go unanswered.

THE GREAT DEPRESSION

TIMES WERE TOUGH for a while after the births of Peter and Mary, but there was always work beneath the dignity of heroes: filthy work around slurry, afterbirth, and manure, in winter ditches and back-breaking furrows, irregular and inconstant. He'd been there before, as a roving and carefree youth, and survived well enough.

But it was different now, with a family to provide for. He could not simply get on his bike and ride, could not simply return to the cabin of his birth, and unburden himself of his troubles or reach for a helping hand. He had set down roots, had allowed himself to be tied down. He had responsibilities.

December 1922 saw the Anglo-Irish Treaty ratified and the establishment of the Irish Free State. If ever White had needed a political justification for his wartime behaviour, he had it now. He was Irish, not British. It was not, had never been, his war.

Did Irish independence soften attitudes in Scotland? Who can tell? It did, however, just happen to coincide with an improvement in Pat's financial circumstances and the securing of full-time employment. He could even afford to start putting a little something away for a rainy day. The horizon was slowly brightening.

With the birth of two babies in two years, Maggie now had her hands full. But as they lived just across the road from Maggie's mother, Elizabeth, help had always been on hand. In April 1924, all that changed. Elizabeth suffered a stroke that left her paralysed down one side of her body. The roles of mother and daughter were instantly reversed.

The babies were two and three by then, and ten-year-old Lizzie and twelve-year-old Gilbert were old enough to start helping out around the house. Nevertheless, the cottage on Castle Street had become dreadfully cramped and between caring for a crippled mother and two demanding toddlers, Maggie was soon in need of a break. That summer, Pat broke into their savings and treated the family to a much-needed holiday.

On 8 August 1924, Pat White bundled his family onto a train to Glasgow, and from there onto another bound for Arbroath, a fishing village and popular seaside resort on the east coast of Scotland. They based themselves at a lodging house on Church Street, a ten-minute walk from the harbour rockpools, and a thirty-minute walk from the beach.[446]

Located just off High Street, the guest house was no less cramped than the cottage on Castle Street, but for one glorious week, arm in arm along the strand, they could leave the war behind them and be a family like any other, watching the children swim and play, and cooling their feet in the cold North Sea.

Nine months later, on 5 May 1925, Maggie was delivered of a son. They called him Patrick, after his father.[447] By that time, they had outgrown the cottage on Castle Street and moved to 56 Waterside Street, a residential house on a shopping thoroughfare that would be demolished four years later to make way for the office building that now houses the local Co-op Funeral Care. Maggie was still only thirty-two, but Patrick was to be her last.

Waterside Street

It was just then, when they appeared to be at their happiest and most optimistic, that the hardest years began. Just six weeks after Patrick's birth, Pat's father died of heart failure brought on by chronic 'Bright's Disease', an archaic medical term encompassing a vast range of renal ailments.[448] His passing was followed, on 9 September, by that of Maggie's mother, who had failed to recover from the stroke that had paralysed her the previous year.[449]

Exactly when, or even if, Pat received news of his father's passing is unknown. The family knew that he had married, so they were obviously in touch in 1918, and possibly again after Peter died, but they had lost touch with him since then. At the time of John White's death, they did not even have a current address for Pat.[450]

Prior to his passing, John White had been attempting to claim a £30 pension gratuity under the Army Pensions Act in respect of his son, Peter, who had been killed in action 'whilst performing his duties as a member of the Irish Volunteers'. Following John's death, his widow had since taken up the claim. In a letter to the Army Finance Officer, in October 1925, she claimed that she had no knowledge of Pat's current whereabouts and, more importantly, was not receiving any income from him.

For a son to completely cut off contact with his mother would seem to suggest that Pat's rift with his father was not a trivial matter. For him to cut off contact with his entire family, suggests a sharp and deep-rooted bitterness. He had obviously wanted to disappear for some time, but had been unable to cut the final thread. As for why, and why now, we are again in the realms of speculation, but Peter's death appears to have emboldened him in some way to burn the last of his bridges. Perhaps it had been Peter, after all, who had been the thread, a thread that existed now only in the person of the son he had named for him.

On 12 June 1927, in her eightieth year, Pat's mother died of the same disease that had taken her husband.[451] She had survived a famine, a revolution, and a civil war, and had lived to see the removal of the imperial statues, the greening of the post boxes, and the creation of the Irish Free State, for which her youngest son had given his life. Her death was notified to the coroner by Thomas Nulty, Bridget's husband, who by then had taken over the running of the farm.

That it would be Bridget who took over the

lease upon its renewal in 1928, however, and not her husband, suggests that, even then, there may have been some nebulous expectation that Pat could return and be about his father's business.[452] We know that John White left a will and that he had initially intended to leave the farm to Peter.

It would also appear, from a legal document signed by his wife on 5 September 1925, that following Peter's death, Pat's name, which had been excluded from the original document, had now been substituted for his.[453] Pat's whereabouts at the time, however, were still unknown to the Whites.

Pat would never return to Richardstown. He was content to remain in Scotland, where his wife and children had deep roots and maternal relatives. The land his father had been leasing from the Harfords, furthermore, had been recently sold to a new landlord, Richard Knox. There was no way of knowing what might happen when the lease came up for renewal. How much, if anything, Pat White knew of that, however, is unclear.

By choosing to remain in Lanarkshire, Pat and Maggie would never have a permanent home of their own. They would always be renting, always on the move. Pat's employment would always be low-paid and insecure, and as soon as the children had completed their primary education, they would be sent out into the world to work, establish their independence, and reduce the financial burden on their parents. As it was in the beginning...

Following the Armistice of 11 November 1918, public opinion had slowly come around to accepting that men who had fought for their country and survived the war should be entitled to retire to a smallholding on British land, which would provide them with a livelihood. In line with this sentiment, Scottish County Councils had been granted compulsory purchase powers in 1925 to requisition land. This land was intended to be let in smallholdings to ex-servicemen, who would be allowed to purchase it with a council loan.

If anyone was equipped to make a success of an agricultural smallholding, it was Pat White. But no council was ever going to hand over land to a deserter. So Pat remained trapped in a cycle of irregular and low-paid employment, barely able to support his growing family, and reliant on an early form of unemployment benefit when the work dried up. His failure to take up the offer of a smallholding, however, would have been noted by all who knew him, or of him, and conclusions drawn as to the reason.

In such a small town, there was no escaping the past, or indeed questions about the circumstances that had seen his family left behind, when the families of other ex-servicemen were being offered a helping hand. That would have been a difficult enough cross to bear, even without the spectre of Gilbert McArthur, Maggie's first husband, whose medals, awarded posthumously, Maggie had by now received.

Every year, on Armistice Day, the town of Strathaven would remember its glorious dead by hosting memorial services and solemn marches to the War Memorial on Kirkhill. Here, as wreaths of Flanders poppies were laid, the patriotism, virtue, and courage of men like Gilbert McArthur would be extolled and remembered. His widow and children were almost honour-bound to attend, the

312

vividly imagined memory of him hovering over them like a halo, setting his children apart from their half-siblings, and a husband from his wife. On such days, when old loves were resurrected with bugle blast, and a lost youth mourned in silence, the past, for two whole minutes, became as real as the present. *They* had not grown old. Age had not wearied *them*.

That Memorial Obelisk on Kirkhill, on which the names of Gilbert McArthur and the other Strathaven boys who had made the 'supreme sacrifice' were indelibly inscribed, would forever loom over Pat White like a finger raised in permanent rebuke. It is not hard to imagine the emotional toll that this would have taken on his blended family.[454] In a cramped and crowded household, where two were the children of a war hero and three the children of a deserter; where teenage flare-ups were inevitable, and the children's sense of nationality differed starkly from that of their father or stepfather, shame was a scabbarded sword that could be drawn at any moment, and by any of the children.

Not that Maggie was without a sword of her own. She hadn't exactly fallen on hard times with Pat – her father had been a labourer and her mother had run a boarding house for working men – but no woman in her situation could have resisted speculating on the life she might have lived had her first husband not rushed to volunteer. She had not fallen out of love with Gilbert McArthur; he had been taken from her. In any second marriage, that would have been significant.

Pat White was a proud, hard-bitten, and resilient man; he had proven that repeatedly, both as an

313

athlete and as a tireless provider. But no man is invulnerable. He had been somebody once, had been widely liked and admired. On Armistice Day, however, he became no more than a rock in a river, passed by, and passed over, in a flood of solemn remembrance. But at least it only came once a year. Other challenges were more or less permanent.

Before the war, marriages with significant age differences had been common. In its aftermath, they had become far less so, as young women were increasingly forced to seek partners of similar age or younger. For single women in their twenties, getting married during the war had been largely impossible, or undesirable, and most of them were still single when the war ended.

The available dating pool had been significantly reduced by a war in which approximately eleven per cent of the male population of the UK had been killed, seventy-one per cent of whom were between the ages of sixteen and twenty-nine. In the post-war period, single women in their early to mid-twenties faced a deficit of men of their own age, and a significant percentage of them were drawn into relationships with men who had been too young to be conscripted during the war. The implication for Pat and Maggie was that their marriage, with its significant age gap, stood out even more in Strathaven after the war than it ever had before. Maggie's peers were of a generation with whom Pat White no longer had much in common. He and she were still together, and still surviving. But only just.

Sometime around 1929, having successfully navigated the turbulent seas of the Roaring Twenties, the Whites left Strathaven and moved to Glassford, where they took a house at 35 Millar Street. The village was close to the farm where Pat was currently working and where his stepdaughter, Lizzie, now fifteen, had found employment as a domestic servant. As he would soon find work as a ploughboy, young Peter was most likely also helping out about the farm. It was common at the time for children to work from the age of five in the evenings, on Saturdays, and during school holidays. With seven mouths to feed, every penny counted.

Millar Street, Glassford.

But then, in the autumn of 1929, tragedy struck. Lizzie contracted meningitis. Taken to the Infectious Diseases Centre at Udston Hospital in Hamilton, she died at 2:20 a.m. on the morning of 18 October.[455] For the second time in her young life, Maggie White was obliged to follow the coffin of one of her children.

Maggie was destroyed. The death of baby John

had been a hard enough cross to bear, and she had known him for just twenty-three days. Her memories of Lizzie, however, were more plentiful and more complex, tied to another life, another death, and to a multi-faceted wound that was bleeding still in the unvanished past.

If someone had asked the Whites how they were feeling at the time, it would have been only too easy for Pat and Maggie to complain that the family had shouldered more than its fair share of misfortune. But nobody was going to ask, and, with the war still fresh in the memory, and Armistice Day only weeks away, they were neither alone in their sorrows nor uniquely deserving of sympathy.

When Baby John died, the country had been at war, and Pat had been stationed in faraway Clonmany. He had not been there to support his wife in the awful moment, had not experienced the horror firsthand. With Lizzie, it was different, or, at the very least, no different than it was for every other couple who had lost a child in such fashion. It was one thing to hear of a death, quite another to be in the room, to be holding and comforting a child during their final breath.

The consequences of such trauma are notoriously complex and perilous for a marriage. Living and grieving in the same space, it is not unusual for each parent to deal with their anguish in different ways. Once the standard obsequies have been observed and the cumbersome consolations have been put behind them, grief can lead a couple down separate paths that never fully reconnect. They may struggle on for a while, but all too frequently it is at the cost of a growing resentment of the other's emotional unavailability.

For Pat and Maggie, the emotional distance was possibly complicated by the fact that Lizzie was not Pat's child. She had been a part of his life since she was a toddler, but she had never been adopted, and had never taken his surname. She was the child of a trench hero, gone now to meet her heroic father in the peaceful hereafter. He may have loved her and helped to raise her, but she had never been less than a constant reminder that his wife had once loved and lain with another man. He could never mourn Lizzie in quite the same way as her mother, for whom the memories were entangled with the life and love she had shared with her first husband.

And then, one by one, the scattering began. The house felt bigger and noticeably quieter. Gilbert was the first to leave, moving in 1930 to Bothwell Haugh to find work in a local coal mine.[456] Some years later, Peter took up live-in employment as a ploughboy on the farm of William Cochrane at Sandford, a small village two miles outside Strathaven.[457] With only Mary and young Patrick remaining at home, family finances improved, but the glue that had held the family together was weakening, and with Gilbert gone, Maggie had lost the only remaining person with whom she could still talk of her life with his father. A vital part of her had become unshareable.

In 1932, Patrick and Mary made their confirmations at St. Patrick's, with Pat and Maggie standing as sponsors.[458] It was to be their last big celebration as a family, for the Great Depression hit Scotland shortly afterwards. Prices for arable products plummeted and as livestock required far less labour than tillage, struggling farmers began to transition from arable crops to 'dog and stick' farming. The family, as a result, slipped rapidly into hard times.

As small farms were slowly absorbed by larger ones, job losses in the sector began to rocket. The farm at Glassford was sold, and Pat's full-time employment came to an end. Returning to Strathaven, unemployed and penniless, the family settled on North Street, a dilapidated area that would be demolished just twenty years later.[459]

North Street, Strathaven.

It was here that Maggie had begun her married life with Gilbert McArthur, and it was here that her married life with Pat White was to end. It was not exactly a full-circle moment. She had not been this poor when she and Gilbert had lived here, nor had her prospects ever appeared so bleak. There was never enough money, and the chores were more wearing in the absence of the older boys.

Now in his late fifties, Pat struggled to find regular employment. Farming was all he knew, but it was not all that he was fit for. He had also, in the course of his labouring, acquired some woodworking skills, good enough at any rate for him to have made a table for one of his neighbours back in Richardstown.[460]

With the general unemployment rate in Scotland now at twenty-seven per cent, and the Dominions shutting their doors to immigrants, finding work became increasingly difficult. With no shortage of younger and fitter men seeking agricultural employment, competition for work was cutthroat. It was the same everywhere. There was little point in emigrating.[461]

With a wife and two children to feed, Pat was soon reduced to claiming unemployment benefits and scraping by with casual work as an agricultural drainer – a backbreaking winter activity that involved a lot of ditch digging. He may have found occasional work during the lambing, calving, harvest, and ploughing seasons, but such opportunities would have been few and far between, and shrivelling with every passing year for a man of his advancing age.

At fifty-seven, Pat was slowing down and resting more frequently on his shovel than had once been his habit. As he thawed his aching limbs before a blazing fire of a winter's evening, he would have known that his days of outdoor labouring were numbered. Sooner or later, something was bound to give, if not within him, then about him.

It was during this transition period that Pat found himself in the news for the first and only time since he retired from competitive running. The incident occurred in January 1937 while he was renovating and unclogging a ditch at Overfield House on the Glassford Road.

In the course of his work, Pat unearthed a canister, inside of which he found a gold watch, a pin, a pendant, and several other expensive items. Back in August 1933, these had been stolen from Roselyn House on the Glasgow Road by a notorious housebreaker with a string of criminal convictions. His name was Alexander Brown. A native of Strathaven, Brown had secreted them in a ditch, intending to retrieve them later.

Despite the stolen items having never been found, Brown had been convicted of breaking and entering and sentenced to six months in prison.[462] During his incarceration, Brown had forgotten the canister's exact location and, following his release, had struggled to locate it.

How or why Brown happened to be walking along Glassford Road that day would never be explained, but recognising the canister that Pat had placed on the lip of the drain he was clearing, he snatched it up and legged it. Unlike Tom Longboat, who once chased a shoplifter down 31st Street, White decided to let the man go and to report the theft later to the police. He could hardly walk into a station in his draining clothes. The stolen items were subsequently recovered from Brown's house.

The case against Brown was heard at Hamilton

Sheriff's Court on Monday, 27 January 1937, and Pat was called as a witness. Brown protested that double jeopardy applied, as he had already served time in prison for the theft of the items recovered. The deputy fiscal, however, proceeded on the basis that the current charge related to his theft of the items from White, and Brown was sentenced to a further thirty days in prison.[463] Throughout all of this, Pat and Maggie continued to reside on North Street. But storm clouds were gathering over the Sudetenland. Everything, everywhere, was about to change.

PEACE FOR OUR TIME!

Wᴴᴇɴ ɴᴇᴠɪʟʟᴇ ᴄʜᴀᴍʙᴇʀʟᴀɪɴ returned from Germany on 30 September 1938 and declared to the world that he had secured 'Peace for our time', not everyone was convinced. That same day, 15,000 people protested against the Munich Agreement in Trafalgar Square; three times more than had welcomed him at 10 Downing Street. The prospect of another war was now being openly and widely discussed. For those who had lived through the last one, there was a sense of living on borrowed time.

That same year, Michael Sweetman, a seventy-year-old bachelor farmer from Ballyboughal, told a local National School student researching a school essay on local heroes that Pat White was alive and well, and living, not in Strathaven, but in Glasgow.[464] His wife, however, was still living in Strathaven, as indeed were his two youngest children.

The reason for Pat's move to Glasgow is unclear. He had, of late, been increasingly obliged to travel in search of work, agricultural jobs having grown scarce due to rising unemployment and changing farming practices. There were, however, still unskilled industrial jobs to be had in Glasgow. The shipbuilding industry was thriving, and there were thousands of jobs going in the construction of the Empire Exhibition. As these jobs were likely better paid than ditch digging, it is quite possible that Pat was there, and not in Strathaven, when, on 3 September 1939, Britain declared war on Germany.

This time, nobody was saying it would be over by Christmas. Having just turned sixty, Pat was exempt from military service. As a working ploughman, his son Peter would fall under the category of a reserved occupation and would likewise be exempt. To return to Strathaven, however, would be to risk the excavation of old resentments.

None of that, however, explains why, after so much time, he and Maggie separated. The reasons are likely complex, and the exact timing impossible to establish, but whatever the whys and wherefores, the upshot of it all was that, sometime in 1939, Maggie White and her two youngest children, Mary and Patrick, moved into a three-bedroom council house at 9 Station Road, a move suggestive, though hardly proof, of desertion.[465] Mary, at that time, was apprenticed to a hairdresser, and Patrick to a woodcutter. Though living with their mother, they were slowly approaching legal and financial independence.

We can speculate till the cows come home as to the cause, but all that can reasonably be surmised from the few records that remain is that *something* happened between Pat and Maggie in 1939, perhaps even between Pat and the entire family. Whatever that was, it remains a mystery. Life had been unkind to them both. They had shared a life of unrelenting hardship for almost twenty-three years.

Twenty-three! There was that milestone again. His firstborn, John, had lived for twenty-three days. Mile twenty-three, the point at which Siret broke him in London. Twenty-three, the age at which he decided to commit himself to running. Now here it was again.

In the marathon, as in life, once you start down a particular road, you either stop or you finish. You cannot un-run the miles you have already run. So why now, so late in the day, after all those miles and with so many memories piled up in store, would one or the other call time on the marriage?

The house at 9 Station Road, Strathaven.

There are so many potential pitfalls that come hand-in-glove with a life of prolonged hardship: alcoholism, resentment, exhaustion, depression, guilt, humiliation, cowardice. Any one of these on its own could prove fatal to a relationship. Without knowing the circumstances, it would be

324

foolhardy to apportion blame. Even the strongest bough will fall from the tree if subjected to enough stress; even the strongest legs will buckle when their fuel runs out.

For Pat's stepson, Gilbert, the war allowed him the opportunity to relinquish the inherited shame of his stepfather's politics and dishonourable discharge. Raised on the facts and fables of his 'heroic' father, he did not wait for conscription to be introduced but enlisted straightaway in the Cameronians (Scottish Rifles), his father's old regiment. The sight of that uniform must have reawakened a host of old anxieties and difficult memories for his mother.

Like his father before him, Gilbert was deployed straight to France as part of the ill-fated British Expeditionary Force, from where he was rescued in May 1940 as part of the Dunkirk evacuation. He would go on to have a distinguished military career, serving in Palestine, France, and Italy. Wounded twice in action, he would receive the Military Medal for bravery in battle.[466]

Not long after the conscription of women began in February 1942, Mary, a hairdresser at the time, enlisted as a private in the Auxiliary Territorial Service. Posted to Glasgow, she met and fell in love with Yorkshireman Denis Siddall, an infantry lieutenant in the Duke of Wellington's Regiment. The pair married three years later, on 14 July 1945, at the Methodist Church on Glasgow's Claremont Street.[467]

It is not known if Mary had any contact with her parents while in Glasgow, but in 1945, attitudes towards interreligious marriages were largely negative and even discriminatory, especially amongst Catholics. Her parents, furthermore, and despite the civil nature of their marriage, had continued to identify as Catholic. Back in 1932, when she and Peter had made their confirmation, Pat had stood as sponsor for Peter, and Maggie had stood for Mary.[468] It would not have been unusual, therefore, for her parents to have refused to attend a Methodist service.

As for Maggie, having to live again in the shadow of war was a torturous experience, and one endured with little or no emotional support. Living from day to day in the constant fear of losing yet another child, she had also to deal with the double shame of being the wife of an absent husband, and the mother of a daughter who had married outside of her faith.

The stress of it all took a heavy toll on Maggie and, on Saturday, 28 July 1945, just two weeks after Mary's wedding, it all came to a head. Maggie fell prey to a perforated ulcer and began to vomit blood. As the bleeding was internal, there was nothing that could be done for her. She was just fifty-seven.[469]

Following Maggie's death, the house on Station Road returned to the council, and the Cringan family, formerly of Stonehouse Road, moved in. For the next three generations, the Cringans would carry with them the belief that the house was haunted by a ghostly presence, most commonly felt in the downstairs bedroom, just off the kitchen, where Maggie White had collapsed.[470]

After the war, the remaining family members scattered to the four winds. Mary headed to Yorkshire to start a new life with her husband, and Gilbert, who by now had risen to the rank of warrant officer, was posted to Hamburg, where in

1953 he met and married twenty-eight-year-old Edith Korngiebel.[471] A son, Michael Edward, was born the following year and baptised at Hostert in Luxembourg. When Edith died in February 2007, she was still living in Germany. It is at least possible, then, that Gilbert had settled abroad.[472]

It is not known what became of Peter, who was still working as a ploughman in Sandford in 1940, but Patrick remained in Scotland, found employment in Glasgow as a council roadman, and settled in the Stonehouse area of the city. On 13 November 1946, he married twenty-four-year-old Margaret Ferguson Burns at the Blythswood Registry Office. On his marriage certificate, he declared that both his mother *and* father were dead. His father, however, was very much alive, though whether Patrick was aware of this at the time is unclear.

In 1948, Patrick and his new wife, Margaret, celebrated the birth of a daughter. She was christened Margaret McNair White, after her paternal grandmother. One of Margaret's earliest childhood memories would be that of her Irish grandfather, Pat, calling to the house sometime in the early 1950s and knocking meekly on the window.

Now in his seventies, Pat appeared anxious to reconcile with his youngest son and to meet his granddaughter, but the words that could have ended the estrangement cost too much to say, and Patrick Junior, holding fast to his anger, sent his father packing, though not before Pat could press a shiny half-crown into his granddaughter's hand.[473] In the years to come, that impulsive gift would be all that Margaret would remember of her grandfather. She never saw him again.

327

Pat White's life had unravelled like an old sweater during the Second World War. But exactly when that unravelling began is impossible to ascertain, as are the various misfortunes that beset him in its aftermath. We know from reports of his court appearance in 1937 that he was still living with his family on North Street in January of that year, and that sometime between then and 1938, he moved to Glasgow, possibly in search of work.

Exactly when and why Pat decided not to return to Strathaven, if he ever consciously made such a decision, is a matter of speculation. All that can be said for certain is that he was not in Strathaven when his wife died and that his final years were haunted and lonely.

With no savings to fall back on or family to support him in his old age, Pat slipped into an isolated and largely welfare-dependent existence.[474] Moving from job to job and from one cheap boarding house to another, he eventually ended up at the Trades Hotel in Burbank, Glasgow, an early form of homeless hostel for single men.

Known locally as 'The Model,' and run for many decades by Irishman Joseph Doyle and his son, Henry, it was pleasant enough as such places went, but it lacked the privacy of a bedsit and was a far cry from independent living. Here, for his daily sixpence, a man could get a clean bed and, for a few pence extra, a bowl of broth.

Built by subscription in 1907, this three-storey building was considered a model of social housing in its day. Conveniently situated, with a tram stop outside, it was surrounded by green recreational space and park benches, and was just a thirty-minute walk from the countryside. It had a large

The Trades Hotel, Burnbank.

entrance hall and an even larger dining hall, where residents would be allowed the use of cooking utensils and expected to prepare their own meals on the dining hall's four-foot-square grill plate, an implement most commonly used for frying bacon.

The dormitories on the first and second floors consisted of 260 wooden cubicles, each with a single bed. They were small and cramped, but most residents had few possessions with which to clutter up the place. There was a small shop and a recreation room, but in pleasant weather many of the men preferred to lounge outside on the entrance steps or sit on the outside wall. Washing and toilet facilities were communal.

Not everyone who lived at the Trades Hotel did so out of necessity. Some did so by choice, for the hostel provided a sense of community that could not be found in a cheap bedsit. Some even had employment during the day. In practice, the majority relied on poor relief or begging to pay for their bed.

In the early 1960s, Pat, now in his eighties, was admitted to Hairmyres Hospital for tests. Yellowing like an old newspaper left too long in the sun, he was diagnosed with stomach cancer – a disease long associated with deprivation and a high salt diet, and one in which the symptoms did not commonly present until the cancer was far advanced. Pat's cancer had already spread to his liver. Treatment options were limited.

THE FINISH LINE

AT 10.40 A.M. on 16 July 1963, after a slow and painful withering, Pat White died of liver failure at Hairmyres Hospital in East Kilbride.[475] He was eighty-four. His death was notified to the registrar, not by any member of his family, but by a Mr G. W. Forrest.

Hairmyres Hospital.

Tall, stout, and broad-shouldered, Forrest lived in a thatched house on a small farm off the Meikle Earnock Road in Hamilton. Prior to his retirement, he had been a successful ironmonger. How Pat White came to be taken up as a friend by a man like Forrest is anybody's guess, but it was most likely through farming. As an agricultural drainer, Pat could have come to know him through his

331

shop on Quarry Street or even his farm. We may never know.

On Pat's death certificate, Forrest would describe himself as simply 'a friend.' [476] But he must have been a particularly good friend for, following his funeral, Pat's body was laid to its eternal rest, not in Glasgow, but in Strathaven, and in the cemetery at the northern end of Castle Street, close to where he and Maggie had begun their lives together. This was the last landscape in which Pat White had truly felt at home, where his firstborn son, John, and perhaps even his wife had been buried. Was his wish to be buried here an act of contrition or nostalgia? A belated acknowledgement, possibly, of regret? Or was it simply one last desperate plea to be found, to be remembered?

It says much that Strathaven was where Pat chose to be buried, but it says even more that both the plot and the headstone were paid for by Forrest, and not by his children. [477] In retrospect, the 'Loving Memory' inscription appears ironic. The headstone mentions only his name, the date of his death, and an estimate of his age (inaccurate by two years). That the death certificate does not include the Christian names of his parents would also suggest very little, if any, family involvement. I could find no record of where Maggie and Lizzie were buried.

Pat White's demise passed largely unlamented for a man who had been one of Ireland's greatest athletes. There were no eulogies, no sharing of stories, no final toasts to his memory. He came and he went and the world kept walking. Even in Dublin, his death passed unnoticed and unremarked.

Pat White's Headstone, Strathaven Cemetery.

Twice in his life, in 1908 and 1911, Pat White had ranked second on the world ranking list for the marathon, and his time of 2:36:45 for the 'London Distance', set in 1911, would not be bettered by another Irish athlete until Hugh McEleny's 2:33:19 in Dublin on 28 June 1958, forty-seven years later.

McEleny's Irish record, however, is hardly comparable with Pat's 1911 time, which had been run on a heavy 440-yard cinder track in the middle of a Scottish winter. Such tracks were estimated to be one to two seconds slower per lap than modern synthetic tracks, with tighter curves and a surface that would deteriorate as the race progressed. The constant bends would also have had an adverse effect on White's time.

Realistically, it would not be until Noel McGowan's 2:29:23 on 27 July 1958 that an Irishman would post an equivalent performance, and even then, this would have been at a time when footwear, nutrition, and training methods had evolved immeasurably from the leather shoes, basic diets, and long walks of the early 1900s. Back then, runners were more born than made, and their training programs were light, even by the standards of today's recreational runners.

For almost half a century, Pat White had been Ireland's greatest marathon runner, an inspirational figure whose performances had, for a short while, allowed even the poorest Irish labourer, competing on local fields and village greens, to dream of one day headlining at Madison Square Garden. On account of having been, not just a professional athlete, but perhaps the most unashamedly mercenary athlete the country had ever seen, he was effectively erased from both official and popular sporting histories. This process appears to have been underway as early as 1946, when William Dooley published his *Champions of the Athletic Arena*. In Dooley's book, the Irish marathon record is credited to William 'Billy' Morton, at 2:47:28 (eleven minutes slower than Pat's best).

The omission of White's name, if indeed it was deliberately omitted and not already forgotten, may well have been because the author was concerned only with amateur records. In the same book, however, an account of Tom Hynes' career, including some of his professional wins, marathons included, covered no less than three pages without once mentioning the name of his great rival, Pat White.[478]

White's achievements at the marathon, it seemed, were destined to become no more noteworthy than the furrows he once ploughed in the wheatfields of Fingal. And while his great rival, Tom Hynes, who had enjoyed a stellar amateur career before turning professional, has had a road named after him in Galway, in his native Fingal, there is currently not a single memorial to White.

Towards the end of what had been an exceptionally harsh and challenging life, as much could probably be said against Pat White as could be said in extenuation, but in the decade that preceded the Easter Rising, White had been an authentic Irish hero, a beacon of hope and much exalted source of national pride. Those years should never have been taken from him. One can only hope that this imperfect account of White's imperfect life will go some small way towards restoring them to him, and in some small way become the epitaph he never had.

A decade after Pat's death, the International Track Association would organise a world tour of professional athletes, attracting such sports giants as Kip Keino and Jim Ryun. It would fold just three years later. Amateurism in athletics, however, would not be abandoned entirely until the 1990s.

The demonisation of professional athletes as mercenary, ignoble, or even immoral is thankfully far behind us now. Perhaps it is time, then, that the stories of men like Pat White of Donabate were resurrected and added to the official history of Irish Athletics, even if their performances have to be suffixed with an asterisk: time, perhaps, that their stories were allowed to run again, to become more than a note in the margins of a crowded page. Far from obscure figures during their lifetimes, their stories deserve more than sporting oblivion.

ACKNOWLEDGEMENTS

The writing of this book has been a largely solitary obsession. Still, it could not have been completed without the particular support of the Nulty family of Richardstown, direct descendants of Pat White's sister Bridget and her husband, Thomas Nulty. Especial thanks go to Martin Nulty, who provided me with several leads that helped me to uncover the details of Pat's life in Scotland. My gratitude is also due to Aidan and Bernard Arnold, who tracked down the Nultys for me. Aidan also brought 'Paddy White's Field' on Liam Cooney's farm to my attention, as well as some photographs I had missed.

I am similarly grateful to Gillian Scott, who generously provided the photograph of the house at 9 Station Road and the story of the ghost in the downstairs bedroom, and likewise to Eddie Rynn, whose late wife, Margaret, was Pat's granddaughter. Eddie graciously provided me with personal information regarding Pat's relationship with his youngest son, Patrick, and additional family lore regarding Pat's stepson, Gilbert.

I am likewise grateful to Padraig Ashe for permission to use his photograph of his great-uncle Thomas Ashe dressed in his piping uniform; to Adam Schofield for the photograph of Pat's headstone; to Charlie Verrall for the postcard of Ballymaclinton and to Mark Monie for several photos and links to resources on the history of Strathaven and Glassford.

A number of institutions were also helpful in providing images for this book, and I would particularly like to thank Terre Heydari at the DeGolyer Library, Southern Methodist University, for photographs of the Mauretania, and Carla Reczek at the Detroit Public Library for permission to use the images of Pat at Clifton Racetrack.

As ever, my greatest thanks are reserved for my wife, Cliona, and my daughter, Eleanor, who have tolerated my obsessions and shared their home with all manner of loose sheets, death and birth certificates, sundry books, and yellowing newspapers for quite some time. I could not have completed this project without their patience and understanding.

ILLUSTRATIONS BY CHAPTER

RICHARDSTOWN

Two-windowed cottage of the type the Whites lived in 1911. Courtesy of Library of Congress, Rep LC-USZ62-93720.

INTO THE WEST

Farm Boy at Kanturk Market 1903. Public Domain. Courtesy of Library of Congress. Reproduction Number: LC-DIG-stereo-1s27745 (digital file from original) LC-USZ62-59328 (b&w film copy neg. of right half stereo). Underwood & Underwood Publishers.

INTERNATIONAL ATHLETE

Two Digitally enhanced photographs of Pat White at Hamilton Palace 1903. Public Domain. From same photograph.
http://www.scottishdistancerunninghistory.scot/1903-international-cross-country-championships/

THE 1905 HERALD RACE

The Winner's Cup. *Irish Independent*, 17 June 1905, p.7.

DEFENDING THE TITLE

Pat White, *Sunday Independent*, 11 October 1908, p.7

THREE IN A ROW

Herald Cup 1907, *Evening Herald*, 8 June 1907, p.7.

TROUBLE ON THE HILLS

Vesuvius raining mud and ashes, By Banks, Charles Eugene, 1852-1932. via Wikimedia Commons. No restrictions. https://commons.wikimedia.org/w/index.php?curid=43716156

White City , from "Fourth Olympiad 1908 London Official Report" published by the British Olympic Association in 1909.

'The Champion Chaired', *Evening Herald*, 22 June 1908, p.2.

THOMAS ASHE AND THE BLACK RAVENS

Thomas Ashe in full piping regalia. Photo courtesy of Padraig Ashe from family-held historical items.

THE OLYMPIC MARATHON OF 1908

Pietri falls on the stadium track. Illustrated London News, 1 August 1908.

Pietri being assisted across the line via Wikimedia Commons. https://en.m.wikipedia.org/wiki/File:Dorando_Pietri_1908.jpg. Sullivan, James Edward. *Marathon Running.* New York, American sports publishing company, 1909. Retrieved from the Library of Congress, <www.loc.gov/item/09015974/>.

THE £100 MARATHON

E.P. Weston in New York 1913, courtesy of Library of Congress, Bain News Service photograph collection, Call Number: LC-B2- 2703-9 [P&P].

Princess Victoria with the starting pistol, *La Vie au grand air*, Paris, 17 October 1908, p.8. Personal Copy.

White passing through Ruislip, *Illustrated Sporting and Dramatic News*, 17 October 1908.

Siret, passing through Ruislip, *Daily Mirror*, 12 October 1908.

White at London Marathon, *La Vie au grand air*, Paris, 17 October 1908, p.8. Personal Copy.

Siret enters the stadium, *La Vie au grand air*, Paris, 17 October 1908, p.8. Personal Copy.

LOCAL HERO

Ballymaclinton, 1908. Courtesy of Charlie Verrall Collection, https://www.flickr.com/photos/31514768@N05/4370625651/in/photostream/

TREADING THE BOARDS

Empire Palace Advert, *Irish Independent*, 20 October 1908, p.4.

THE POWDERHALL MARATHON

Map of the Route. *Edinburgh Evening News,* 12 December 1908.

Henri St. Yves, *New York Daily Tribune*, 17 March 1909.

THE MAURETANIA

The Mauretania. Courtesy of John Oxley Library, State Library of Queensland.

Second Cabin State Room. Photo from *R.M.S. Mauretania*, Bedford, Lemere & Co., London, 1907. Courtesy of De Golyer Library, SMU, Dallas, Texas.

BROOKLYN

Still from "The Skyscrapers of New York," Smith, James Blair, camera; Thomas A. Edison, Inc., New York, 20 May 1903. Courtesy of Library of Congress. https://hdl.loc.gov/loc.mbrsmi/ntscrm.00045654

The Lusitania at the end of a record voyage. Pier 54 Waterfront, 1907. Image courtesy of Library of Congress, Reproduction Number: LC-DIG-ds-07216.

THE RINGER

Patrick T. Powers. Reach, A.J., The Reach Official American League Baseball Guide 1904-1905, Philadelphia, 1904. p.110.

Johnny Hayes, Courtesy of Library of Congress LC-B2- 2420-7 [P&P].

Start of Brooklyn Marathon 1909, Courtesy of Library of Congress, Call Number: LOT 11146-15 <item> [P&P].

Matt Maloney and Handler. Sullivan, James E. *Marathon Running*. New York, American sports publishing company, 1909. Library of Congress, <www.loc.gov/item/09015974/>.

MARATHON MANIA

The Marathon Mania, Illustration in *Puck*, v. 64, no. 1664 (1909 January 20), centrefold. Courtesy of Library of Congress.
'Effect of the Marathon Craze' by Charles Dana Gibson. *Collier's Weekly*, 6 February 1909. Image courtesy of Library of Congress, Call Number: CAI - Gibson, no. 51 (D size) [P&P]

NEW BEGINNINGS

Pat White. Publicity photograph. *Brooklyn Daily Eagle* 13 February 1901, p.1.

Frank Curtis & Pat Fagan, *Evening Herald*, 10 March 1909.

Madison Square Garden, 6-day cycle race, 1908, courtesy of Library of Congress, Reproduction No: LC-DIG-ggbain-01532.

Svanberg, Sweden, 1906 Intercalated Games, Athens 1906. From Sullivan, James Edward. *Marathon Running*, New York, American Sports Publishing Company, New York, 1909, p.96.

SNUBBED!

Start of Shrubb-Dorando Marathon Derby, 3 April 1909. Courtesy of Library of Congress, Call Number: LC-B2- 676-13 [P&P].

Dineen, White and Orphée, *Boston Globe*, 7 April 1909, p.4.

Louis Orphée, James Gallivan starter, Pat Dineen, Pat White at start of Huntingdon Avenue race. *Boston Daily Globe*, Sun, Apr 11, 1909 ·Page 8

DECLINE AND FALL

Pat White and an unidentified man at Clifton Stadium. Image courtesy of National Automotive History Collection, Detroit Public Library, Resource ID: na018156. Spooner & Wells, April 1909, Lazarnick Collection.

Pat White at Clifton Stadium. Courtesy of National Automotive History Collection, Detroit Public Library, Resource ID: na018154. Spooner & Wells, April 1909, Lazarnick Collection.

Polo Grounds Marathon, *New York Tribune*, 9 May 1909, p.10.

Pat White, *San Antonio Light and Gazette*, 28 May 1909, p.9.

Lowell Marathon, *Boston Daily Globe*, 10 September 1909, p.4.

White and Maloney publicity photos for the Wakefield Park Marathon. *The Evening Journal* (Wilmington), 8 November 1909.
Indoor Marathon, Albert Hall, *Illustrated London News*, 25 December 1909.

Pat White in his pre-race attire. Image courtesy of National Automotive History Collection, Detroit Public Library, Resource ID: na018152. Spooner & Wells, April 1909, Lazarnick Collection.

C.K. Hamilton, 2 July 1910, via Wikimedia Commons.
https://commons.wikimedia.org/wiki/File:First_Public_Flight_in_Co nnecticut_%26_New_England,_July_2,_1910,_Charles_K._Hamilton, _Walnut_Hill_Park,_New_Britain,_CT_- _New_Britain_Industrial_Museum_-_DSC09827.JPG

THE WORLD RECORD RACE

Hans Holmer. Public domain, via Gallica.
http://catalogue.bnf.fr/ark:/12148/cb40492897.

THE ROTUNDA MARATHON

Jerome Robbins Dance Division, The New York Public Library. "Grand Masonic ball at the Rotundo [sic], Dublin, in honour of the marriage of the Prince of Wales" The New York Public Library Digital Collections. 1863-05-09.

MAN vs HORSE

Pat White and Mr Michael Horan's trotting pony, Kathleen H. *Irish Independent*, 17 October 1911.

1912 POWDERHALL

Pat White, *Edinburgh Evening News*, 21 December 1912.

Kohelmainen Breaks the tape, Holmar 10 yds behind, *Edinburgh Evening News*, 2 January 1912.

STRATHAVEN

Bridge Street, Strathaven, c.1925. Valentine's Postcard. Public Domain.
Castle Street from the junction with North Street, c 1900. Photo by Dr. Alan Watt.

MAGGIE

Castle Street, c.1900, photo by Dr. Alan Watt.

"The White Feather: A Sketch of English Recruiting", Arnold Bennett, 1914, Public Domain.

WW1 Poster, courtesy of Library of Congress, Reproduction Number: LC-USZC4-10957.

DESERTER

Clonmany, Co. Donegal, early 1900s. Public Domain, Photographer unknown.

THE GREAT DEPRESSION

Waterside Street, from multi-view postcard by Archibald Sellers, dated 1909.

Millar Street, Glassford. Photo by John Melvin circa 1905.

North Street, early 20th century. Photo by Dr. Alan Watt, c. 1905.

PEACE FOR OUR TIME

The house at 9 Station Road, Strathaven © Gillian Scott.

The Trades Hotel, Burnbank. Photo courtesy of Paul Veverka at www.blantyreproject.com.

THE FINISH LINE

Hairmyres Hospital. Photo by Elliot Simpson via Wikimedia Commons. CC BY-SA 2.0.

Pat White's Headstone, Strathaven Cemetery, © Adam Schofield.

ENDNOTES

1   Stone, Duncan. "Deconstructing the Gentleman Amateur" in *Cultural and Social History*, vol. 18, issue no.3, 2019, pp. 315-336.

2   Adams, James Ring. "The Jim Thorpe Backlash: The Olympic Medals Debacle And the Demise of Carlisle", in *American Indian*, vol.13, no. 2, Summer 2012.

3   *Sporting Life*, 16 July 1902, p.3; Ibid, 16 July 1902, p.3; *Scottish Referee*, 18 July 1902, pp.3-4.

4   Chambers, Robert. *The Book of Days*, London, 1869, p.98.

5   Pronounced *Straven*.

6   Census (Ireland) 1911, Dublin, Lusk, Richardstown, House No.4.

7   Registry of Births, Balrothery, Lusk, 20 August 1877, No.362.

8   Registry of Births, Balrothery, Balbriggan, 8 March 1879, No. 222.

9   Registry of Births, Balrothery, Lusk, 26 July 1881, No.241.

10 Registry of Births, Balrothery, Lusk, 4 November 1883, No. 216.

11 Registry of Births, Balrothery, Lusk, 14 April 1887, No. 40.

12 Breen, Richard. "Farm Servanthood in Ireland, 1900-40," in *The Economic History Review*, vol. 36, no. 1, 1983, pp. 87–102.

13 *Midland Tribune*, 1 July 1899, p.2; Ibid., 22 July 1899, p.2; *Dublin Daily Nation*, 22 March 1900, p.7.

14 Hadgraft, Rob. *The Little Wonder*, Desert Island eBooks, 2012, p.14.

15 O'Donoghue, Tony. *Irish Championship Athletics 1873-1914*, 2005, p.67.

16 *Freeman's Journal*, 30 January 1899, p.7.

17 *Dublin Daily Nation*, 27 March 1899, p.7.

18 Listed on their birth certificates as Mary A. Harford.

19 Census 1911, Dublin, Lusk, Richardstown.

20 *Drogheda Independent*, 13 November 1897, p.5

21 *Dublin Sporting News*, 1 September 1891, p.3.

22 *Drogheda Conservative*, 5 June 1897, p.5.

23 *Dublin Sporting News*, 6 December 1901, p.3.

24 *Sunday Independent*, 30 January 1910, p.10.

25 My thanks to Aidan Arnold and Liam Cooney for this obscure piece of local history.

26 Registry of Deeds, 1902, Book 1, No. 1, Harford to White.

27 *Kildare Observer*, 10 May 1902, p.8.

28 *Freeman's Journal*, 17 May 1902, p.6; Ibid, 26 May 1902, p.8.

29 *Sport* (Dublin), 4 January 1902, p.7; *Cork Examiner*, 9 February 1903, p.7.

30 O'Donoghue, Tony. *Irish Championship Athletics 1873-1914*, 2005, pp.129,140.

31 *Lancashire Evening Post*, 13 March 1903, p.5.

32 http://www.scottishdistancerunninghistory.scot/1903-international-cross-country-championships/. Retrieved 19 June 2025.

33 *Irish Daily Independent*, 25 May 1903, p.5.

34 Ibid.

35 *Kerry News*, 27 May 1903, p.3; *Galway Observer*, 30 May 1903, p.2.

36 *Tuam Herald*, 30 May 1903, p.2.

37 *Leinster Leader*, 30 May 1903, p.8.

38 House of Commons Debate, Volume 29, 31 July 1911, Agricultural Workers, retrieved on 2 July 2024 from https://hansard.parliament.uk/debates/GetDebateAsText/7e73e71f-ba33-4e64-9e52-196e24ae6f61

39 *Sporting Life*, 12 October 1908, p.7; *Boxing World and Mirror of Life*, 17 October 1908, p.11.

40 *Ulster Echo*, 5 April 1904, p.2.

41 *Sport* (Dublin), 12 November 1904, p.2.

42 *Irish Independent*, 13 March 1905, p.3.

43 *Irish Independent*, 13 March 1905, p.3

44 *Freeman's Journal*, 6 March 1905, p.7.

45 *Morning Mail* (Dublin), 27 December 1904, p.4.

46 *Glasgow Herald*, 27 March 1905, p.12; *Connaught Tribune*, 21 May 1966, p.16.

47 Royal Hospital Chelsea, Pensioner Service Records, 1760-1925, Job No. 16-030, Ref. No. WO.97, Army Forms B217 & B200 , No. 8511, Peter Whyte.

48 *Irish Independent*, 17 June 1905, p.7.

49 *Evening News* (Waterford), 26 June 1905, p.4.

50 *Irish Independent*, 26 June 1905, p.5.

51 *Drogheda Independent*, 1 July 1905, p.4.

52 Ibid.

53 *Evening News* (Waterford), 26 June 1905, p.4.

54 *Buffalo Evening News*, 1 June 1905, p.12

55 *Royal Horse Artillery* (R.H.A.).

56 *Evening News* (Waterford), 26 June 1905, p.4.

57 *Irish Independent*, 26 June 1905, p.4.

58 *Enniscorthy Echo and South Leinster Advertiser*, 28 July 1905, p.2.

59 Hadgraft, Rob. *The Little Wonder: The Untold Story of Alfie Shrubb*, Desert Island eBooks, 2012, p.71.

60 *Ottawa Free Press*, 28 July 1905, p.5.

61 *Kilkenny People*, 16 October 1805, p.7.

62 Royal Hospital Chelsea, Pensioner Service Records, 1760-1925, Job No. 16-030, Ref. No. WO.97, Army Forms B217 & B200, No. 8511, Peter Whyte.

63 *Drogheda Independent*, 21 October 1905, p.4.

64 Crowley, Clare & Lennon, Ian. *The Heritage of Naul, Co. Dublin*, Naul Community Council, October 2021, p.49.

65 *Drogheda Independent*, 12 January 1901, p.2.

66 *Drogheda Independent*, 1 July, 1905, p.4.
67 National Archives, Property Losses (Ireland) Committee, PLIC/1/4335, Patrick Halford, Baldurgan, Donabate.
68 Royal Hospital Chelsea, Pensioner Service Records, 1760-1925, Job No. 16-030, Ref. No. WO.97, Army Forms B217 & B200 , No. 8511, Peter Whyte.
69 *Kildare Observer and Eastern Counties Advertiser*, 26 May 1906, p.7.
70 Ibid.
71 Ibid.
72 *Kildare Observer and Eastern Counties Advertiser*, 26 May 1906, p.7.
73 *Drogheda Independent*, 11 August 1962, p.8.
74 *Kildare Observer and Eastern Counties Advertiser*, 26 May 1906, p.7.
75 *Drogheda Independent*, 26 May 1906, p.5.
76 *Drogheda Independent*, 16 June 1906, p.4.
77 *Irish Independent*, 14 June 1906, p.3.
78 *Drogheda Independent*, 2 July 1906, p.4.
79 Kenneth Arly Rynd, Sports reporter with the *Irish Independent* and *Evening Herald*.
80 *Evening Herald*, 16 July 1906, p.6.
81 Ibid.
82 *Drogheda Independent*, 11 August 1906, p.8.
83 Royal Hospital Chelsea, Pensioner Service Records, 1760-1925, Job No. 16-030, Ref. No. WO.97, Army Forms B217 & B200 , No. 8511, Peter Whyte.
84 UK National Archives, WO 35/159B/36, Peter White, 19 April 1921.
85 *Dublin Evening Telegraph*, 18 August 1906, p.5; *Drogheda Independent,* 1 September 1906, p.4.
86 'Patterns' or 'Patrons' were festivals celebrating local saints.
87 *Drogheda Independent*, 1 September 1906, p.4
88 *Drogheda Independent*, 20 October 1906, p.4.
89 *Newcastle Daily Chronicle*, 15 October 1906, p.10; Ibid., 9 November 1906, p.10.
90 *Weekly Irish Times*, 29 December 1906, p.7.
91 Petty Sessions Order Books, CSPS1/9026, Dublin, No. 105, 15 December 1906; *Weekly Irish Times*, 29 December 1906, p.7.
92 Irish Prison Registers 1790-1924, Kilmainham Prison, General Register of Prisoners 1907, Reference, 1258.06.
93 UK National Archives, WO 35/159B/36, Peter White, 19 April 1921.
94 My thanks to Martin Nulty for this piece of family lore.
95 Petty Sessions Dog Licence Registers, CSPS 2/0914, Registry No. 204.
96 *Evening Herald*, 8 February 1907, p.3.
97 *Irish Independent*, 17 June 1907, p.5.
98 Ibid.
99 *Kildare Observer and Eastern Counties Advertiser*, 22 June 1907, p.4.
100 *Irish Independent*, 17 June 1907, p.5.
101 Ibid.
102 *Kildare Observer and Eastern Counties Advertiser*, 22 June 1907, p.4.
103 Ibid.

[104] Ibid.
[105] Ibid.
[106] Ibid.
[107] *Irish Independent*, 27 August 1907, p.3.
[108] *Drogheda Independent*, 31 August 1907, p.7.
[109] *Irish Independent*, 5 September 1907, p.6.
[110] *Drogheda Independent*, 27 July 1907, p.6.
[111] *Evening Herald*, 26 September 1907, p.3.
[112] *Galway Express*, 12 October 1907, p.4.
[113] *Drogheda Independent*, 19 October 1907, p.4.
[114] *Evening Herald*, 19 October 1907, p.7
[115] *Evening Herald*, 17 October 1907, p.3.
[116] *Evening Herald*, 19 October 1907, p.7.
[117] *Sunday Independent*, 6 October 1907, p.10.
[118] Garry, James. "Townland Survey of County Louth: Moneymore (Continued),"in the *Journal of the County Louth Archaeological and Historical Society*, vol. 24, no. 2, 1998, p.220.
[119] *Evening Herald*, 11 November 1907, p.3.
[120] Ibid.
[121] *Evening Herald*, 26 November 1907, p.5; *Galway Express*, 30 November 1907, p.4.
[122] *Tuam Herald*, 7 December 1907, p.4.
[123] *Irish Times*, 25 January 1908, p.4; *Dublin Daily Express*, 18 January 1908, p.8.
[124] *Sport* (Dublin), 5 August 1911, p.3.
[125] *Tuam Herald*, 4 January 1908, p.4.
[126] *Evening Herald*, 22 June 1908, p.2.
[127] *Irish Independent*, 9 June 1908, p.6; Ibid., 10 June 1908, p.2.
[128] Ibid.
[129] *Evening Herald*, 22 June 1908, p.2.
[130] *Irish Independent*, 22 June 1908, pp.5-6.
[131] *Irish Independent*, 10 August 1908, p.6; *Boxing World and Mirror of Life*, 17 October 1908, p.11.
[132] *Drogheda Argus and Leinster Journal*, 19 September 1908, p.6.
[133] An Roinn Cosanta, Bureau of Military History, Statement by Witness, W.S. 645, Nora Aghas, File No. S.1757.
[134] National Folklore Collection, UCD, The Schools' Collection, Volume 0786, Page 183.
[135] Herodotus actually identifies Pheidippides as the runner who carried news of the Persian invasion to Sparta, covering 150 miles in 48 hours, and surviving the ordeal.
[136] Kieran, John and Daley, Arthur. *The Story of the Olympic Games: 776 B.C. to 1960 A.D.*, Lippincot, 1961, p.35.
[137] Cook, Theodore Andrea. "Chapter IV. The Olympic Games of 1908. Athletics. XI. – The marathon race." in *The Fourth Olympiad. Official Reports of Olympics.* Vol IV. British Olympic Association, London, 1909, pp. 68-84.
[138] *New York Times*, 21 December 1907, p.8.

[139] *History Ireland*, Reviews, Vol. 20, Issue 4, July/August 2012.
[140] Cooper, Pamela. *The American Marathon*, Syracuse University Press, Syracuse N.Y.,1999, p.35; Lucas, John A., *The Modern Olympic Games*, A.S. Barnes & Co., London, 1980, pp.58-62.
[141] Lucas, John A., *The Modern Olympic Games*, A.S. Barnes & Co., London, 1980, p.62.
[142] Greaves, John. "Doped Professionals and Clean Amateurs: Amateurism's Influence on the Modern Philosophy of Anti-Doping", in *Journal of Sport History*, vol. 38, no. 2, 2011, p.244.
[143] Brown, William. *Remembering Tom Longboat: A Story of Competing Narratives*, Master of Arts Thesis (History), Concordia University, Montreal, January 2009, pp.2-3
[144] 'Dorando', Words and Music by Irving Berlin, Ted Snyder & Co., 1908; See also https://youtu.be/rdph5rEp8AI
[145] *History Ireland*, Issue no. 4, Vol.20, July/August 2012.
[146] *Evening News* (London), 17 August 1908, p.1.
[147] *Evening News* (London), 24 August 1908, p.1.
[148] *Westmeath Independent*, 26 August 1908, p.6.
[149] Heggie, Vanessa. "Sports Doping, Victorian Style" in *The Guardian*, 19-June-2012.
[150] Ibid.; Karch, Stephen B. *A Brief History of Cocaine*, 2nd ed., CRC Press, Florida, 2017, pp. 18-19; *Lancet*, 18 March 1876, p.447.
[151] George, Walter G., *Training for Athletics and Kindred Sports,* Universal Press Agency, London, 1902.
[152] *Middlesex Gazette,* 29 August 1908, p.2.
[153] *Bayswater Chronicle*, 17 October 1908, p.3.
[154] *Evening News* (London), 10 October 1908, p.3.
[155] *Southwark and Bermondsey Recorder*, 5 September 1913, p.5; *South London Press*, 22 August 1913, p.12.
[156] *The People*, 11 October 1908, p.8; *Sunday Independent*, 11 October 1908, p.7; *Fermanagh Herald*, 17 October 1908, p.2.
[157] *The Referee*, 11 October 1908, p.9.
[158] *Lloyd's Weekly Newspaper*, 11 October 1908, p.25
[159] *The Referee,* 11 October 1908, p.9.
[160] *Sporting Life*, 12 October 1908, p.7; *Boxing World and Mirror of Life*, 17 October 1908, p.11.
[161] *Sporting Life*, 12 October 1908, p.7.
[162] *Irish Independent*, 13 October 1908, p.5.
[163] *Newry Reporter*, 17 October 1908, p.8; *Irish Independent*, 13 October 1908, p.5.
[164] *Galway Observer*, 17 October 1908, p.2
[165] *Drogheda Argus and Leinster Journal*, 17 October 1908, p.4.
[166] *Newry Reporter*, 17 October 1908, p.5.
[167] *Irish Independent*, 26 October 1908, p.6; *Sunday Independent*, 1 November 1908, p.1.
[168] *Track Newsletter*, Vol 5, no.2, Track and Field News, Los Altos California, 19 August 1958, p.1.
[169] *Freeman's Journal*, 20 October 1908, p. 10.

170 *Irish Independent*, 20 October 1908, p.6.
171 *Freeman's Journal*, 20 October 1908, p. 10.
172 *Irish Independent*, 14 October 1908, p.6.
173 Ibid.
174 *New Ross Standard*, 23 October 1908, p.2; *Wexford People*, 24 October 1908, p.2.
175 *Irish Independent*, 19 October 1908, p.6.
176 *Freeman's Journal*, 21 October 1908, p.10.
177 *Irish Independent*, 27 November 1908, p.5; *The Washington Post*, 26 November 1908.
178 *Dublin Evening Telegraph*, 17 December 1908, p.2.
179 *Wicklow News-Letter and County Advertiser*, 26 December 1908, p.5.
180 *Ulster Herald*, 12 December 1908, p.8; *Donegal News*, 12 December 1908, p.1.
181 Jamieson, David A. *Powderhall and Pedestrianism*, W & A K Johnston, Edinburgh, 1943, p.13.
182 *Newry Reporter*, 29 December 1908, p.5; *Irish Independent*, 4 January 1909, p.3.
183 Batten, Jack. *The Man Who Ran Faster than Everyone*, Tundra Books, Toronto, pp.1-2.
184 *Edinburgh Evening News*, 1 January 1909, p.3; Ibid., 2 January 1909, p.2.
185 *Falkirk Herald*, 2 January 1909, p.5.
186 *Free Press* (Wexford), 9 January 1909, p.11; *Edinburgh Evening News*, 2 January 1909, p.2.
187 *Irish Independent*, 4 January 1909, p.3.
188 *Falkirk Herald*, 2 January 1909, p.5.
189 *Free Press* (Wexford), 9 January 1909, p.11.
190 *Irish Independent*, 4 January 1909, p.3.
191 *Edinburgh Evening News*, 1 January 1909, p.3
192 *Newry Reporter*, 5 January 1909, p.6.
193 *Daily Record*, 2 January 1909, p,6.
194 *The Evening World* (N.Y.), 3 March 1909, p.12
195 *Irish Independent*, 4 January 1909, p.3
196 *Dundee Courier*, 2 January 1909, p.6.
197 *Free Press* (Wexford), 9 January 1909, p.11.
198 *Irish Independent*, 9 January 1909, p.8
199 *Edinburgh Evening News*, 2 January 1909, p.2.
200 *Edinburgh Evening News*, 4 January 1909, p.3.
201 Jamieson, David A. *Powderhall and Pedestrianism*, W&AK Johnston, Edinburgh, 1943, p.147.
202 *Dundee Courier*, 28 January 1909, p.6.
203 *Sporting Life*, 22 January 1909, p.4; *Dublin Daily Express*, 25 January 1909, p.8; *Weekly Irish Times*, 30 January 1909, p.23; *Sport* (Dublin), 30 January 1909, p.2.
204 *New York Tribune*, 8 March 1909, p.8.
205 *Scottish Referee*, 29 January 1909, p.3; *Dundee Courier*, 28 January 1909, p.6.

206 *Irish independent*, 27 January 1909, p.3.
207 Ellis Island Passenger Records, 29 January 1909, Passenger id: 101512110051; Ibid., passenger id:101512100281.
208 New York City Passenger Lists 1909, NARA publication number M237 & T715, Ship name: Mauretania, Arrival place: New York, Departure Port Liverpool, Arrival Port Relation: John Lally (friend).
209 List or Manifest of Alien Passengers for the U.S. Immigration Officer at Port of Arrival, S.S. Etruria, Arrival Date: 5 May 1901, Port of Departure: Queenstown, Passenger ID: 605281010145.
210 *Brooklyn Daily Eagle*, 30 January 1909, pp.1,2.
211 Ellis Island Passenger Records, 29 January 1909, Passenger id: 101512110051, frame 396, line number 6.
212 List or Manifest of Alien Passengers for the U.S. Immigration Officer at Port of Arrival, S.S. Baltic, 28 January 1905, Nois 927628/9. In the census of June 1905, Josie gives her age as 16, rather than the 17 stated on the ship's manifest. They had married on 7 January 1905 in Ballygar, where John worked in a draper's shop and had sailed from Queenstown twelve days later. The parents of neither party witnessed the marriage.
213 Register of Marriages, Mountbellew, Killeroran, Ballygar, No. 178, 17 January 1905, Group Registration Id: 1932673.
214 *Irish News and Belfast Morning News*, 31 July 1905, p.7.
215 *Freeman's Journal*, 30 August 1907, p.9.
216 Batten, Jack. *The Man Who Ran Faster than Everyone*, Tundra Books, Toronto, pp.1-2.
217 Llewellyn, Matthew P. "Viva l'Italia! Viva l'Italia! Dorando Pietri and the Norh American Professional Marathon Craze 1908-1910" in *North American Society for Sport History. Proceedings and Newsletter*, 2008, pp.63-64.
218 *The Buffalo Courier*, 2 December 1908, p.10
219 *Washington Times*, 6 February 1909, p.10.
220 *Augusta Herald*, 25 February 1909, p.3.
221 *Duluth Evening Herald*, 1 February 1909, p.9.
222 *New York Times*, 27 December 1908, p.1.
223 *Irish Runner*, vol.4, no.3, April 1984, pp.38-39.
224 *Sporting Life*, 30 January 1909, p.6.
225 *Evening Herald*, 5 February 1909, p.3.
226 *Irish Independent*, 6 February 1909, p.5.
227 *Buffalo Courier*, 10 February 1909, p.10
228 *Brooklyn Daily Eagle*, 13 February 1909, p.1.
229 *Augusta Herald*, 25 February 1909, p.10
230 *The Washington Post*, 10 May 1909.
231 *The Washington Post*, 29 December 1908.
232 *The Marathon Craze*, Vitagraph Company of America, released 1 May 1909 as a split reel with *The Sculptor's Love*.
233 *Evening Star*, 9 May 1909.
234 Hjertberg, Ernst W. Athletics in Theory and Practice, G.P. Putnam's Sons, New York, 1914, pp.139-141

[235] *The Evening World*, 8 March 1909, p.12.
[236] *The Coaticook Observer*, 2 September 1927, p.7.
[237] *The Evening World* (N.Y.), 5 March 1909, p.4.
[238] *The Evening World*, 6 March 1909, p.7; *Billings Gazette*, 12 March 1909, p.8.
[239] *Washington Times*, 22 February 1909, p.10; *The New York Evening Call*, 3 March 1909, p.3.
[240] *New York Times*, 22 February 1909, p.7.
[241] *The Brooklyn Daily Eagle*, Sports Supplement, 4 March 1909, p.4.
[242] Welch, Richard F. "Big Tim Sullivan – King of the Bowery", in *New York Irish History Roundtable*, vol. 20, New York, 2006, pp.5-15; *Desseret Evening News*, 5 March 1909, p.9; *Evening Star* (Washington D.C.), 5 March 1909, p.19.
[243] *Ottowa Free Press*, 6 March 1909, p.15.
[244] *Victoria Daily Times*, 6 March 1909, p.1.
[245] *The Evening World* (NY), 6 March 1909, p.7; *Irish Runner*, vol. 4, no. 3, April 1984, pp.38-39; *Belfast Newsletter*, 8 March 1909, p.3; *Freeman's Journal*, 8 March 1909, p.10.
[246] *The Topeka Daily State Journal*, 6 March 1909, p.2.
[247] *Boston Daily Globe*, 6 March 1909, p.9.
[248] *The Age-Herald* (Birmingham, Alabama) 15 March 1909, p.8.
[249] Martin, David E., and Gynn, Roger W., *The Marathon Footrace*, Charles C. Thomas, Springfield Illinois, 1979, p.32.
[250] *New-York Tribune*, 8 March 1909, p.8.
[251] *The New York Evening Call*, 13 March 1909, p.3.
[252] *New York Daily Tribune*, 12 March 1909, p.8.
[253] *The Evening World* (N.Y.), 13 March 1909, p.6.
[254] *New York Daily Tribune*, 13 March 1909, p.5.
[255] *New York Daily Tribune*, 14 March 1909, p.10.
[256] Ibid.
[257] *Freeman's Journal*, 15 March 1909, p.8; *Evening Herald*, 15 March 1909, p.4; *Irish Independent*, 15 March 1909, p.3; The Ohio State Journal, Sporting Section, 14 March 1909, p.1.
[258] *Irish Independent*, 15 March 1909, p.3.
[259] *Irish Examiner*, 12 March 1909, p.3; *Irish Independent*, 13 March 1909, p.3; *Sunday Independent*, 14 March 1909, p.19.
[260] *New York Daily Tribune*, 29 March 1909, p.8.
[261] *Evening Star* (Washington D.C.), 5 April 1909, p.15; *Daily Kennebec Journal*, 8 April 1909, p.12.
[262] *New York Daily Tribune*, 14 April 1909, p.8.
[263] *Daily Kennebec Journal* (Augusta, Me.), 8 April 1909, p.12.
[264] *Boston Daily Globe*, 10 April 1909, p.5.
[265] *Norwich Bulletin* (Norwich, Conn.), 9 April 1909, p.3.
[266] *Brooklyn Daily Eagle*, 11 April 1909, p.17.
[267] *Boston Daily Globe*, 11 April 1909, p.8.
[268] *Washington Herald*, 11 April 1909, p.2; *The Sun* (N.Y.), 11 April 1909, p.10.
[269] *San Antonio Light* (Tex.), 11 April 1909, p.6.
[270] *The Johnstown Daily Republican*, 12 April 1909, p.3.

271 *Sport* (Dublin), 10 April 1909, p.2.
272 *The Gazette Times* (Pittsburgh), 9 March 1909, p.9.
273 *New Castle News* (PA.), 26 Aug 1916, p.1
274 A form of hopscotch played with tin cans that had been flattened by placing them on trolley tracks.
275 *The Brooklyn Citizen*, 17 August 1911, p.6
276 *The Meriden Daily Journal,* 18 December 1911, p.8.
277 *New York Daily Tribune*, 14 April 1909, p.8.
278 *Perth Amboy Evening News* (N.J.), 17 April 1909, p.9.
279 *Free Press* (Wexford), 10 April 1909, p.11.
280 *The New York Evening Call*, 14 April 1909, p.4.
281 *Newark Star and Newark Advertiser* (N.J.), 17 April 1909, p.6.
282 *New York Tribune*, 19 April 1909, p.8.
283 *The New York Evening Call*, 19 April 1909, p.4.
284 *Boston Globe*, 28 April, 1909, p.4.
285 *Desseret Evening News*, 27 April 1909, p.11.
286 *The Utica Observer*, 8 May 1909, p.2.
287 Ibid.
288 *Warsaw Daily Times*, 8 May 1909, p.3; *New York Herald* 1 May 1909, p.13.
289 *New York Tribune*, 9 May 1909, p.1
290 *New York Tribune*, 9 May 1909, p.10.
291 Ibid.
292 *San Francisco Call*, 1 June 1909, p.11; *The Sun* (N.Y.), 1 June 1909, p.5; Boston Globe, 1 June 1909, p.1.
293 *The Sun* (N.Y.), 1 June 1909, p.5.
294 *Los Angeles Herald*, 1 June 1909, p.6.
295 *The Philadelphia Record*, 3 June 1909, p.7.
296 *The Philadelphia Record*, 6 June 1909, p.2.
297 *The Philadelphia Record*, 19 June 1909, p.12.
298 St. *Joseph News Press*, 25 June 1909, p.13.
299 *The Philadelphia Record*, 6 July 1909, p.13.
300 *Irish Independent*, 10 July 1909, p.7; The race was won by Thomas O'Flynn of Ballinamult, Co. Waterford.
301 *San Antonio Light and Gazette*, 18 July 1909, p.1; *Perth Amboy Evening News* (N.J.), 19 July 1909, p.9.
302 *The Sun* (N.Y.), 26 July 1909, p.6.
303 *Sport* (Dublin), 7 August 1909, p.4.
304 *The Sun* (N.Y.), 7 September 1909, p.9.
305 *The Sun* (St. John, N.B.), 10 September 1909, p.7; *Boston Daily Globe*, 10 September 1909, p.4.
306 *Perth Amboy Evening News*, 30 November 1909, p.9.
307 *Boston Evening Transcript*, 15 November 1909, p.8.
308 *New York Times*, 5 December 1909, p.2.
309 *New York Daily Tribune*, 5 December 1909, p.12.
310 *The Brooklyn Daily Eagle*, 14 December 1909, p.8.
311 *Sporting Life*, 17 December 1909, p.1; Ibid., 3 January 1910, p.2;

357

312 *Richmond Virginian*, 5 February 1910, p.3; *East Oregonian*, 12 February 1910, p.1.

313 *New York Daily Tribune*, 13 February 1910, p.9.

314 *Newark Evening Star* (N.J.), 8 February 1910, p.10.

315 *Cairo Bulletin* (Il.), 15 February 1910, p.1; *The Sun* (N.Y.), 15 February 1910, p.8.

316 *The Brooklyn Daily Eagle*, Sports Supplement, 13 February 1910, p.7.

317 Ibid., p.8.

318 *New York Daily Tribune*, 23 February 1910, p.8.

319 *New Haven Union*, 6 March 1910, p.7; *The Daily Gate City*, 6 March 1910, p.7.

320 *New Haven Union*, 20 March 1910, p.9.

321 *The Sportsman*, 17 March 1910, p.6.

322 *New Haven Union*, 8 April 1910, p.12; *Norwich Bulletin* (Conn.), 11 April 1910, p.3; *The Sun* (N.Y.), 11 April 1910, p.5.

323 *New Haven Union*, 11 April 1910, p.6.

324 *The Referee* (Sydney, N.S.W), 27 April 1910, p.9, from an article in the Vancouver *Daily Province*, of 18 March 1910.

325 *New York Tribune*, 15 May 1910, p.16.

326 UK National Archives, Board of Trade: Commercial and Statistical Department and Successors: Inwards Passenger Lists; Class: Bt26; Piece: 430; Item: 2, Queenstown, May 1910.

327 *Carlow Nationalist*, 28 May 1910, p.2.

328 *Irish Independent*, 23 May 1910, p.2.

329 *Irish Independent*, 25 May 1910, p.3; Ibid., 26 May, p.7.

330 Census (Ireland) 1911, Dublin, Lusk, Richardstown, House No.4.

331 *Westmeath Guardian and Longford News-Letter*, 19 August 1910, p.4;

332 *Drogheda Independent,* 10 September 1910, p.8.

333 *Irish Independent*, 23 September 1910, p.4.

334 *Aberdeen Daily Journal*, 4 January 1911, p.7; *The Scotsman*, 11 January 1911, p.10.

335 *Sporting Life*, 4 January 1911, p.7.

336 *Evening Herald*, 3 January 1911, p.3; *Lancashire Evening Post*, 3 January 1911, p.2; *Weekly Freeman's Journal*, 7 January 1911, p.1.

337 *Dundee Courier*, 4 January 1911, p.3.

338 *Evening Despatch*, 4 January 1911, p.8.

339 Day, Dave. "Massaging the Amateur Ethos: British Professional Trainers at the 1912 Olympic Games", in *Sport in History*. Issue 32, 2012, pp 1-26.

340 *Irish Independent*, 1 January 1911, p.4.

341 *Freeman's Journal*, 17 March 1911, p.11.

342 *Skibbereen Eagle*, 18 March 1911, p.12.

343 *New Ross Standard,* 24 March 1911, p.2.

344 *Portadown News*, 25 March 1911, p.5.

345 *Drogheda Independent,* 27 May 1911, pp.1,4

346 *Skibbereen Eagle*, 10 June 1911, p.1.

347 *Free Press* (Wexford), 17 June 1911, p.2.

[348] *The Douglas Coronation and Jubilee Carnival World's Marathon Race (Distance 26 miles, 386 yards) on the new track at Noble's Playing Fields on Thursday June 29, 1911*: programme, 1911.
[349] *Evening Herald*, 30 June 1911, p.5.
[350] *Morning Leader*, 30 June 1911, p.5.
[351] *Evening Herald*, 13 July 1911, p.5.
[352] *Cheshire Observer*, 2 September 1911, p.6.
[353] *Irish Independent*, 31 August 1911, p.8.
[354] *Evening News* (London), 2 September 1911, p.5.
[355] Batten, Jack. *The Man Who Ran Faster than Everyone*, Tundra Books, Toronto, pp.1-2.
[356] Hadgraft, Rob. *The Little Wonder*, Desert Island eBooks, 2012, p.17.
[357] *Bath Chronicle*, 12 November 1818, p.4.
[358] *Evening Herald*, 5 September 1911, p.3.
[359] Ibid.
[360] *Free Press* (Wexford), 23 September 1911, p.10; *Dublin Evening Telegraph*, 14 September 1911, p.4.
[361] *Freeman's Journal*, 13 October 1911, p.12; *Dublin Evening Telegraph*, 12 October 1911, p.4.
[362] *Dublin Evening Telegraph*, 16 October 1911, p.4.
[363] *Freeman's Journal*, 17 October 1911, p.11; *Sport* (Dublin), 21 October 1911, p.2.
[364] *Dublin Evening Telegraph*, 1 November 1911, p.5.
[365] *Dublin Evening Telegraph*, 8 November 1911, p.4; Ibid., 9 November 1911, p.4.
[366] *Freeman's Journal*, 13 November 1911, p.11.
[367] Ibid.
[368] *Irish Independent*, 28 November 1911, p.8.
[369] *Belfast Telegraph*, 16 December 1911, p.7.
[370] *The Sportsman*, 20 December 1911, p.3; *Sporting Life*, 27 December 1911, p.3.
[371] *Edinburgh Evening News*, 2 January 1912, p.4.
[372] *Free Press* (Wexford), 06 January 1912, p.3; *Sporting Life*, 3 January 1912, p.2.
[373] *Western Mail*, 15 June 1912, p.6.
[374] *Sporting Life*, 27 June 1912, p.6; *South Wales Echo*, 27 June 1912, p.4.
[375] *Evening Herald*, 17 August 1912, p.4.
[376] *Edinburgh Evening News*, 8 August 1912, p.3.
[377] *Irish independent*, 13 August 1912, p.6.
[378] *Scottish Referee*, 19 August 1912, p.2.
[379] *Edinburgh Evening News*, 16 August 1912, p.2.
[380] *Northern Daily Telegraph*, 16 August 1912, p.3; *Sporting Life*, 16 August 1912, p.8.
[381] *Sport* (Dublin), 17 August 1912, p.2.
[382] *Irish Independent*, 17 September 1912, p.8.
[383] *Edinburgh Evening News*, 21 December 1912, p.8.
[384] *Dublin Daily Express*, 3 January 1913, p.9.

[385] *Freeman's Journal*, 22 January 1913, p11.

[386] *Evening Herald*, 21 January 1913, p.3.

[387] Ibid.

[388] *Freeman's Journal*, 22 January 1913, p11; Dublin Evening Telegraph, 21 January 1913, p.4.

[389] *Evening Herald*, 27 January 1913, p.2.

[390] *Drogheda Independent*, 1 February 1913, p.4.

[391] *Irish Independent*, 28 January 1913, p.8; Ibid., 29 January 1913, p.6; *Evening Herald*, 28 January 1913, p.3.

[392] *Evening Herald*, 29 January 1913, p.4; *Irish Independent*, 30 January 1913, p.7.

[393] *Evening Herald*, 11 March 1913, p.3.

[394] *Evening Herald*, 24 May 1913, p.3.

[395] *Evening Herald,* 20 May 1913, p.2.

[396] Ibid.; Ibid., 26 May 1913, p.2.

[397] *Evening Herald*, 23 June 1913, p.3.

[398] *Evening Herald,* 17 July 1913, p.3.

[399] *Evening Herald*, 26 July 1913, p.3.

[400] *The Sportsman*, 4 August 1913, p.3.

[401] *Sporting Life*, 4 August 1913, p.1.

[402] *Evening Herald*, 24 February 1914, p.3.

[403] Ibid.

[404] *Dublin Evening Telegraph*, 7 March 1914, p7; Ibid., 17 March 1914, p.5; *Freeman's Journal*, 17 March 1914, p.10.

[405] *Dublin Evening Telegraph*, 8 May 1914, p.6.

[406] *Edinburgh Evening News*, 19 December 1914, p.8.

[407] *Weekly Freeman's Journal*, 10 April 1915, p.5.

[408] Census 1911, 621/14/8, Avondale, Strathaven, p.8.

[409] Ibid., pp.8,10.

[410] UK, WWI, British Army Medal Roll Index Cards, 1914-1920, McArthur, Gilbert, Gordon Highlanders, Regiment No. 13349, 193367; 1921 Census, Scotland, 621/14/13, Avondale/Strathaven, No.97, p.13, White, Patrick.

[411] *Hamilton Advertiser*, 28 November 1914, p.6.

[412] Commonwealth War Graves Commission, Brompton Cemetery, McArthur, No. 172725, service no. 8487.

[413] Whitmore, Lucie. "A Matter of Individual Opinion and Feeling": The Changing Culture of Mourning Dress in the First World War" in *Women's History Review*, Vol. 27, No. 4, 2017, pp. 579-594.

[414] Kenney, Rowland. "Soldiers' Dependents" in *The English Review*, Vol. 19, 1914, pp.112-118.

[415] Macnicol, John. *The Movement for Family Allowances*, Heinemann, London, 1980, p.18.

[416] Barry, Iris. "We enjoyed the war" in *Scribners*, vol. 96, 1934, pp.280-283.

[417] Lomas, Jonas. "'Delicate Duties' – Issues of class and respectability in government policy towards the wives and

widows of British Soldiers in the era of the Great War" in *Women's History Review*, Vol. 9, Issue no. 1, 2000, pp.125-147.

[418] Smith, Stuart W.R. *The Official and Unofficial Treatment of War Widows and Disabled Ex-Service Personnel in Britain, Ireland and Northern Ireland 1900-2000*, M.Phil. dissertation, Kingston University, School of Art, September 2020, p.30.

[419] Gregory, Adrian. *The Last Great War: British Society and the First World War*, Cambridge University Press, 2008, p.90; Pattinson, Juliette. "'Shirkers', 'Scrimjacks' and 'Scrimshanks': British Civilian Masculinity and Reserved Occupations, 1914-15," in *Gender & History*, Vol. 28, No. 3, November 2016, pp.709-710.

[420] *Hamilton Advertiser*, 23 January 1915, pp.4-6.

[421] *Bellshill Speaker*,18 August 1916, p.3; *Motherwell Times*, 11 August 1916, p.8;

[422] Index Record for White, P., Service No. 27839, *Police Gazette*, Vol. XXXIII, September 1917.

[423] Statutory Registers, Scotland, Marriages, 644/10, Blythswood, Glasgow, 1916 p.1098, No. 2196.

[424] Statutory Registers, Marriages, 644/10 2196, Blythswood, Glasgow, 1916, p.1098, No. 2196.

[425] Register of Births, Scotland, Entry ID: 6535593, Birth Index ID: 7218513, White, Patrick, 1925, Avondale, Lanark, Entry: 47, Ref 621/.

[426] Military Archives, Defence Forces Ireland, Ireland Military Pensions and Medals 1916-1922, File Refs. MD42889, 1D450, F534; Peter was a captain in E Company, 3 Battalion, Fingal Brigade.

[427] Statutory Registers, Scotland, Births, 621/13, Parish of Avondale, County of Lanark, 1917, No. 13, p.5.

[428] Register of Deaths (Scotland), Avondale, Lanark, 1917, p.6, No.18, White, John McNair.

[429] UK WW1 Pension Ledgers & Index Cards, 1914-1923, 121/0584/MCA-MAC, McArthur, Gilbert (8487).

[430] National Archives U.K., WO71/563.

[431] Index Record for White, P., Service No. 27839, *Police Gazette*, Vol. XXXIII, September 1917; *Police Gazette*, 18 September 1917, p.4.

[432] *Hamilton Advertiser*, 10, 17, 24 & 31 August 1918.

[433] "Military Notes" in Journal of the Royal United Services Institute, January 1920.

[434] Under the provisions of Section 73 of the Army Act.

[435] UK, WWI, Pension Ledgers and Index Cards, 1914-1923, Ref. No. 241/0901/WHI-WHI, Regimental No. 27839/3988, White, Patrick.

[436] Anthony, Richard. "The Scottish Agricultural Labour Market, 1900-1939: A Case of Institutional Intervention" in *The Economic History Review*, vol. 46, no. 3, 1993, p.565.

[437] Census (Scotland), 1921. White, Patrick (621/14/13), Avondale, Strathaven, p.13, no.97.

[438] Civil Register, Balrothery, p. 396, no.26, 2 August 1919, Group Registration id: 1678977

439 Civil Register, Athy, Group Registration ID: 1689111, 16 November 1919, No.65.
440 Abbot, Richard. *Police Casualties in Ireland 1919-1922*, Mercier Press, Cork, 2000, p.192; Ibid. 2019 ed., p.244; O'Halpin, Eunan and Ó Corráin, Daithí. *The Dead of the Revolution*, Yale University Press, New Haven and London, 2020, p.291.
441 Statement of V. W. Scully, Military Court of Inquiry (Peter White), 7 May 1921, (TNA, PRO, WO 35/159B).
442 UK National Archives, WO 35/159B/36, Death of Peter White, 19 April 1921; *Evening Echo*, 21 April 1921, p.4; *Irish Independent*, 26 April 1921, p.7.
443 Boland, Cathal. *Who Shot Sergeant Kirwan? – A Commemorative Film*, Creative Ireland, 2021.
444 Irish Military Archives, P.B. 1/D/450, Peter White.
445 Statutory Registers, Scotland, Births, 621/52, Parish of Avondale, County of Lanark, 1921, No. 52, p.18.
446 *The Arbroath Guide*, 9 & 14 August 1924, p.6.
447 Statutory Registers, Scotland, Births, 621/47, Parish of Avondale, County of Lanark, 1925, No. 47, p.5, Patrick White.
448 Civil Registry, Deaths, Balrothery, Lusk, 1925, No.167, John White.
449 Statutory Registers, Deaths, 621/36, Avondale, Lanark, 1925, p.12, no. 36.
450 Military Archives, Defence Forces Ireland, Ireland Military Pensions and Medals 1916-1922, File Refs. MD42889, 1D450, F534; Peter was a captain in E Company, 3 Battalion, Fingal Brigade.
451 Civil Registry, Deaths, Balrothery, Lusk, 1927, No.265, Margaret White.
452 Civil Registry, Deaths, Balrothery, Lusk, 1927, No.265, Margaret White; Registry of Deeds, v. 11-13, 1928, no. 294.
453 Military Archives, Defence Forces Ireland, Ireland Military Pensions and Medals 1916-1922, File Refs. F534, Form of Declaration prescribed under Section 8 of the Act 5051 Vict. Cap 67.
454 Gregory, Adrian. "The complicated History of Remembrance", in *History and Policy*, 7 November 2023.
455 Statutory Registers (Scotland), Deaths, 647/434, Lanark, Hamilton, 1929, p.145, no. 434, Elizabeth McArthur.
456 Valuation Rolls, VR010700496-/71, Lanark County, 1930, p.71.
457 Valuation Rolls, VR010700676-/446, Lanark County, 1940, p.446.
458 Scottish Catholic Archives, Record set Scotland Roman Catholic Parish Congregational Records, Confirmations, 7 May 1932, MP/532/1/3/1, p.20.
459 Strathaven Conservation Area Appraisal, South Lanarkshire Council, 2017, paragraphs 3.83 and 4.9.
460 My thanks to Liam Cooney for this piece of family lore.
461 Anthony, Richard. "The Scottish Agricultural Labour Market, 1900-1939: A Case of Institutional Intervention" in *The Economic History Review*, vol. 46, no. 3, 1993, p.558.
462 *Dundee Evening Telegraph*, 3 August 1933, p.4.

463 *Daily Record and Mail*, 28 January 1937, p.3.
464 National Folklore Collection, UCD, The Schools' Collection, Vol. 0787, p.350.
465 Valuation Rolls, VR010700677, Lanark County, 1940, p.54.
466 U.K. National Archives, WO100/503; Supplement to *Military Gazette*, 29 June 1944, p.3071.
467 Register of Marriages (Scotland), 644/9 252, Kelvingrove, Glasgow, 1945, p.126, no. 252, Denis Siddall & Mary White.
468 Scottish Catholic Archives, Record set Scotland Roman Catholic Parish Congregational Records, Confirmations, 7 May 1932, MP/532/1/3/1, p.20.
469 Statutory Registers, Scotland, Deaths, 621/44, Avondale & Glassford, Lanark, 1945, No. 44, p.15.
470 I'd like to thank Gillian Scott, granddaughter of Una Scott (neé Cringan), whose family moved into 9 Station Road between 1945 and 1946, for this family lore. The ghost was never seen, just felt. Unaware of the story of the previous occupants, they assumed it to be male.
471 My thanks to Eddie Rynn for this piece of family lore; See also trauer-in-nrw.de/traueranzeige/edithmac-arthur/anzeigen
472 England & Wales Marriages 1837-2005, vol.14, p.1146.
473 Margaret McNair White died in 2000. I am grateful to her husband, Eddie Rynn, for this information concerning her father and grandfather.
474 Rutherford, Tom. *Historical Rates of Social Security Benefits*, Standard Note SN/SG 6762, House of Commons Library, 22 November 2013.
475 Statutory Registers Scotland, Deaths, East Kilbride, Lanark, 643/370, p.124, White, Patrick.
476 My thanks to Terry Murphy of Hamilton, for biographical information on G.W. Forrest.
477 My thanks to Eddie Rynn for this information.
478 Dooley, William. *Champions of the Athletic Arena*, The Powell Press, Dublin, 1946 pp.59-61.

INDEX

368